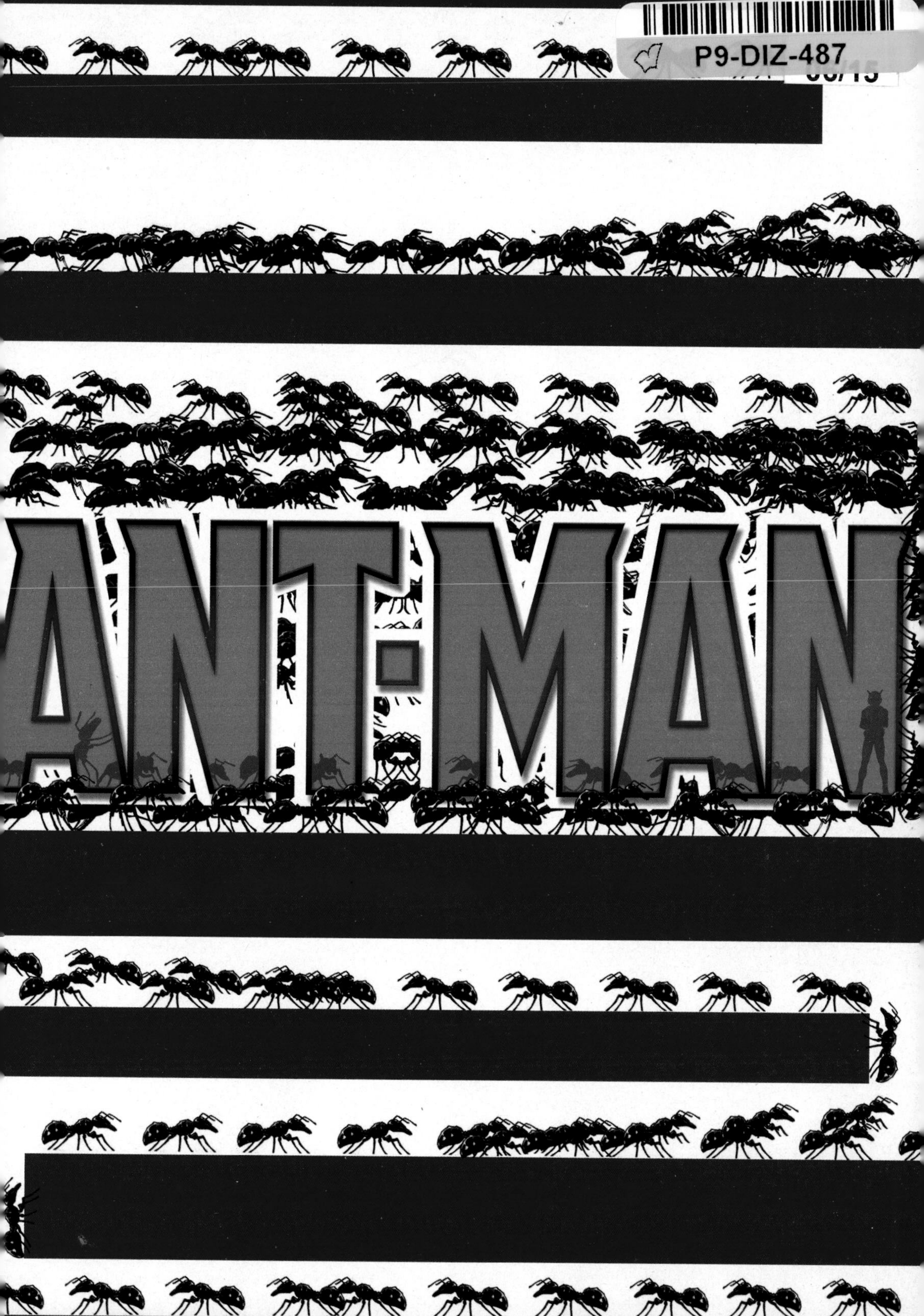
ANT-MAN

N VOL. 1: SECOND-CHANCE MAN. Contains material originally published in magazine form as ANT-MAN #1-5. First printing 2015. ISBN# 978-0-7851-9387-6. Published by MAR-LDWIDE, INC., a subsidiary of MARVEL ENTERTAINMENT, LLC. OFFICE OF PUBLICATION: 135 West 50th Street, New York, NY 10020. **Printed in Canada.** ALAN FINE, President, Marvel Entertainment; DAN BUCKLEY, President, TV, Publishing and Brand Management; JOE QUESADA, Chief Creative Officer; TOM T, SVP of Publishing; DAVID BOGART, SVP of Operations & Procurement, Publishing; C.B. CEBULSKI, VP of International Development & Brand Management; DAVID GABRIEL, SVP Print, Marketing; JIM O'KEEFE, VP of Operations & Logistics; DAN CARR, Executive Director of Publishing Technology; SUSAN CRESPI, Editorial Operations Manager; ALEX MORALES, Publishing s Manager; STAN LEE, Chairman Emeritus. For information regarding advertising in Marvel Comics or on Marvel.com, please contact Jonathan Rheingold, VP of Custom Solutions & Ad jrheingold@marvel.com. For Marvel subscription inquiries, please call 800-217-9158. **Manufactured between 4/17/2015 and 5/25/2015 by SOLISCO PRINTERS, SCOTT, QC, CANADA.**

ANT-MAN

SECOND-CHANCE MAN

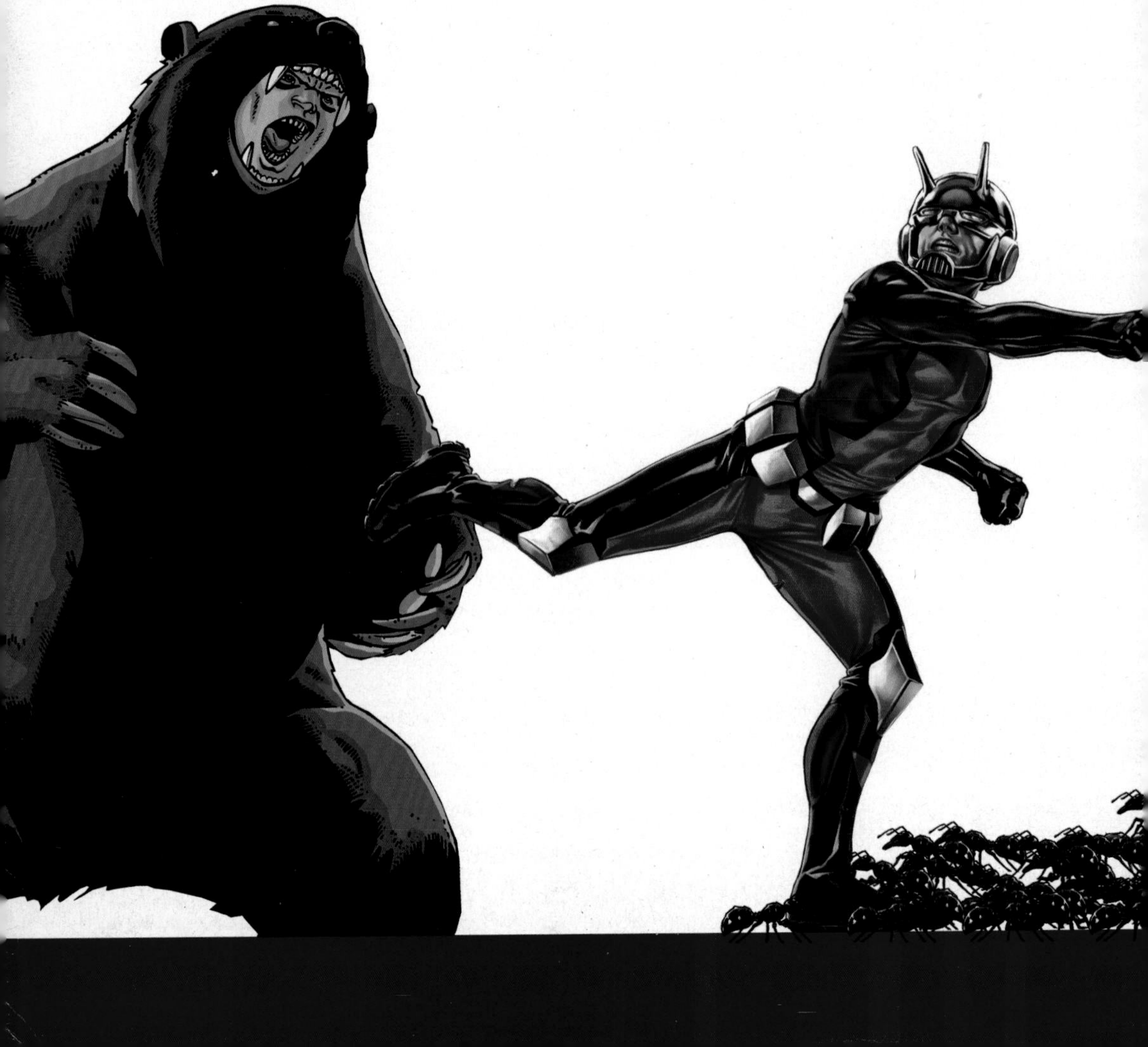

Writer: Nick Spencer
Artist: Ramon Rosanas

Colorist: Jordan Boyd
Letterer: VC's Travis Lanham
Cover Art: Mark Brooks

Assistant Editor: Jon Moisan
Editor: Wil Moss

Collection Editor: Sarah Brunstad
Associate Managing Editor: Alex Starbuck
Editors, Special Projects: Jennifer Grünwald & Mark D. Beazley
Senior Editor, Special Projects: Jeff Youngquist
VP Print, Sales & Marketing: David Gabriel

Editor in Chief: Axel Alonso
Chief Creative Officer: Joe Quesada
Publisher: Dan Buckley
Executive Producer: Alan Fine

Ant-Man created by Stan Lee, Larry Lieber & Jack Kirby

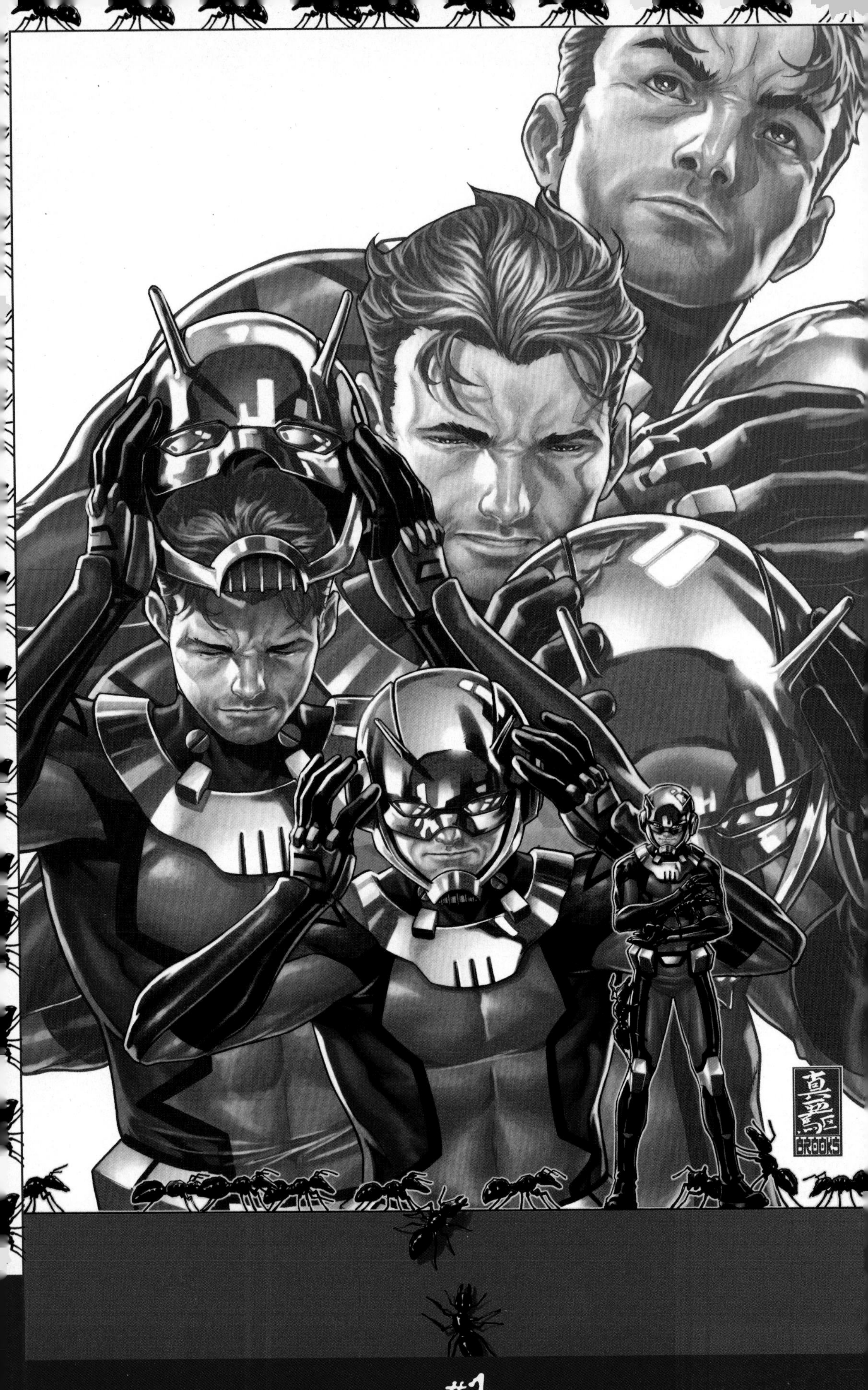
BROOKS

#1

ANT-MAN

When HANK PYM, the original ANT-MAN, retired from the job, another man rose to the occasion (Err, stole the costume) — none other than SCOTT LANG! His somewhat sordid past behind him, Scott took on the size-changing, ant-communicating abilities of ANT-MAN!

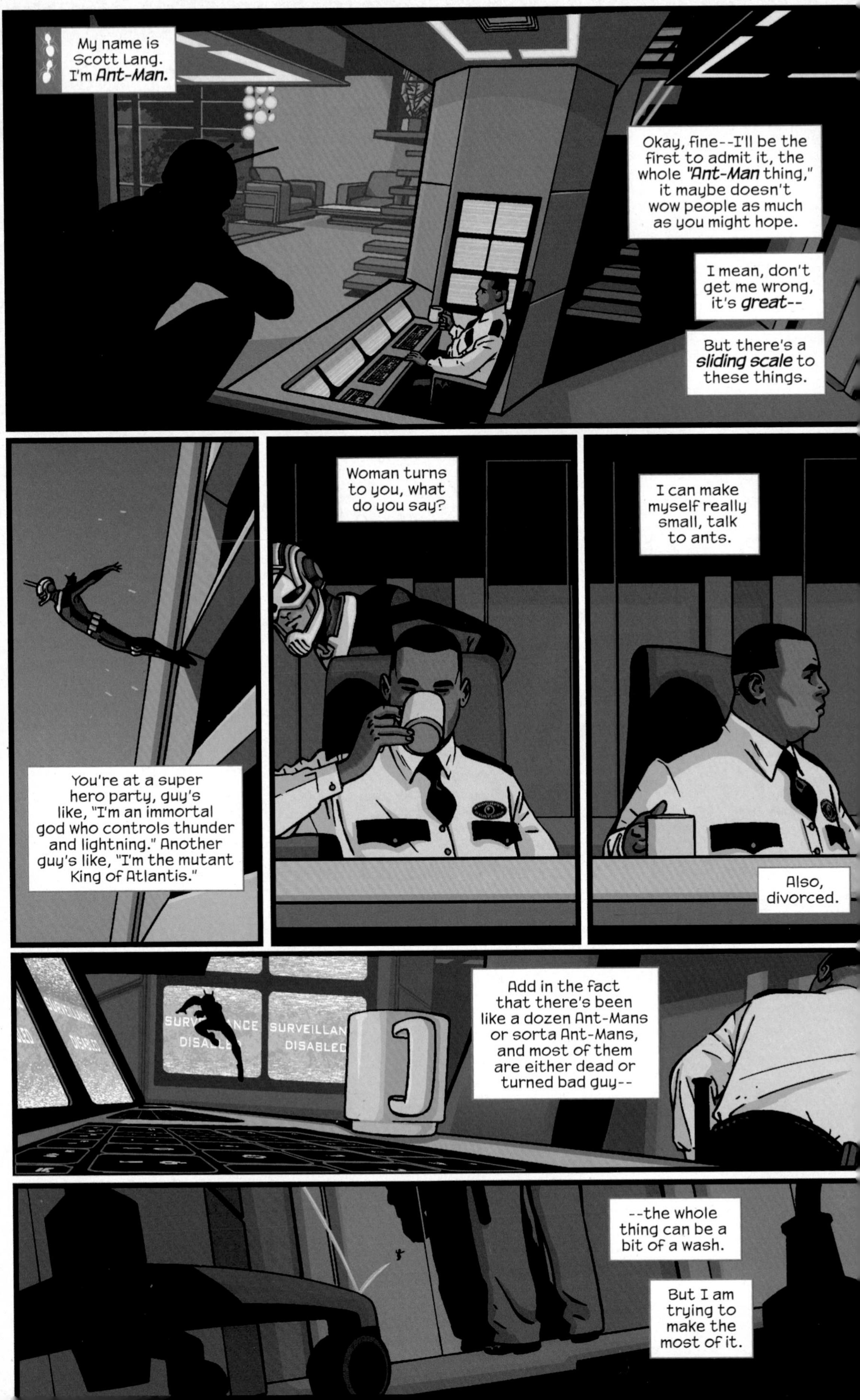
My name is Scott Lang. I'm Ant-Man.
Okay, fine--I'll be the first to admit it, the whole "Ant-Man thing," it maybe doesn't wow people as much as you might hope.
I mean, don't get me wrong, it's great--
But there's a sliding scale to these things.
You're at a super hero party, guy's like, "I'm an immortal god who controls thunder and lightning." Another guy's like, "I'm the mutant King of Atlantis."
Woman turns to you, what do you say?
I can make myself really small, talk to ants.
Also, divorced.
SURVEILLANCE DISABLED
SURVEILLANCE DISABLED
Add in the fact that there's been like a dozen Ant-Mans or sorta Ant-Mans, and most of them are either dead or turned bad guy--
--the whole thing can be a bit of a wash.
But I am trying to make the most of it.

"THE
OSSING."

USER RECOGNIZED. PLEASE SELECT FLOOR.

FIFTY-FOUR, PLEASE.

...THE HELL?!! WHO ARE-- UUNNHHH...

Don't worry, he'll be fine. Just tranq gas. Four hours in the dark and a little short-term memory loss.

Guy's just doing his job, right?

We all got our crosses to bear.

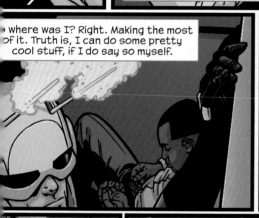

where was I? Right. Making the most of it. Truth is, I can do some pretty cool stuff, if I do say so myself.

Take the ants, for example.

Great

for

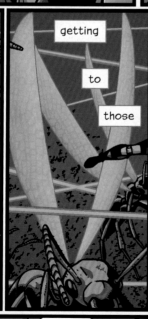

getting

to

those

tough-

to-

reach

places.

GOOD JOB, CHUCK BARRIS.

Yes, I name them. It's important to let your employees know you value them, and believe me--

--these little guys respond to positive reinforcement.

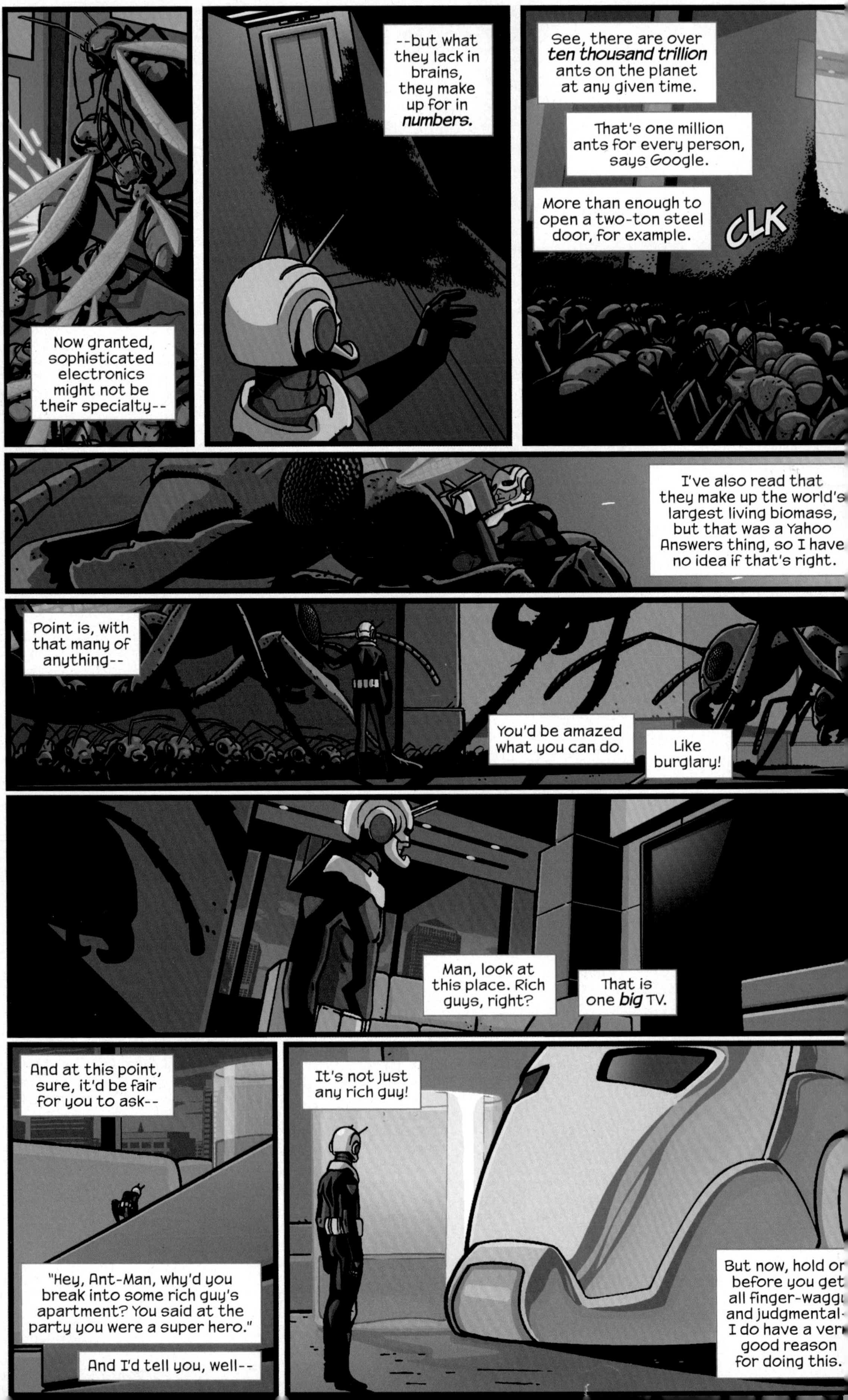

Now granted, sophisticated electronics might not be their specialty--
--but what they lack in brains, they make up for in *numbers.*
See, there are over *ten thousand trillion* ants on the planet at any given time.
That's one million ants for every person, says Google.
More than enough to open a two-ton steel door, for example.
CLK
I've also read that they make up the world's largest living biomass, but that was a Yahoo Answers thing, so I have no idea if that's right.
Point is, with that many of anything--
You'd be amazed what you can do.
Like burglary!
Man, look at this place. Rich guys, right?
That is one *big* TV.
And at this point, sure, it'd be fair for you to ask--
"Hey, Ant-Man, why'd you break into some rich guy's apartment? You said at the party you were a super hero."
And I'd tell you, well--
It's not just any rich guy!
But now, hold on before you get all finger-wagg and judgmental- I do have a ver good reason for doing this.

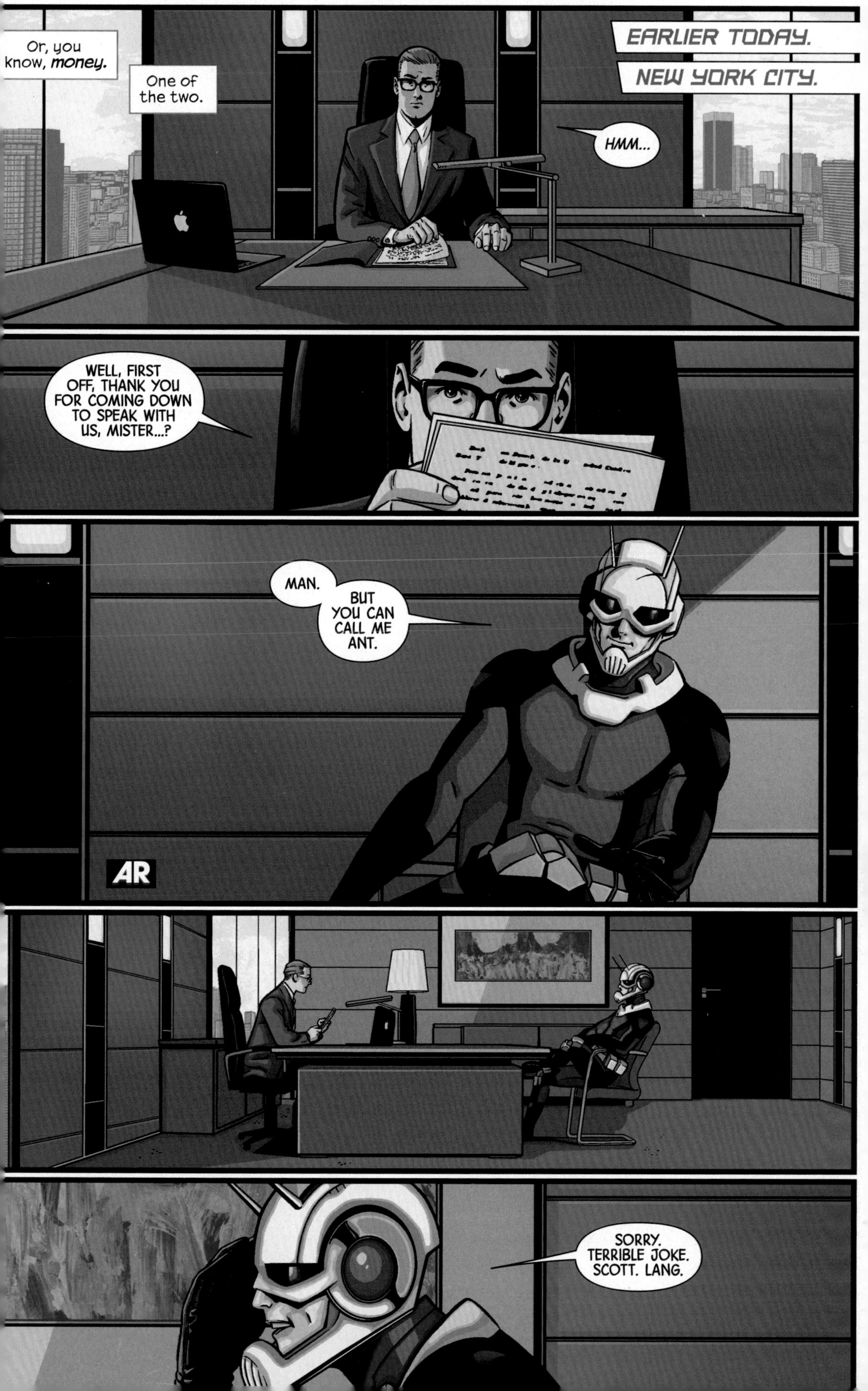
Or, you know, *money.*
One of the two.
EARLIER TODAY.
NEW YORK CITY.
HMM...
WELL, FIRST OFF, THANK YOU FOR COMING DOWN TO SPEAK WITH US, MISTER...?
MAN.
BUT YOU CAN CALL ME ANT.
AR
SORRY. TERRIBLE JOKE. SCOTT. LANG.

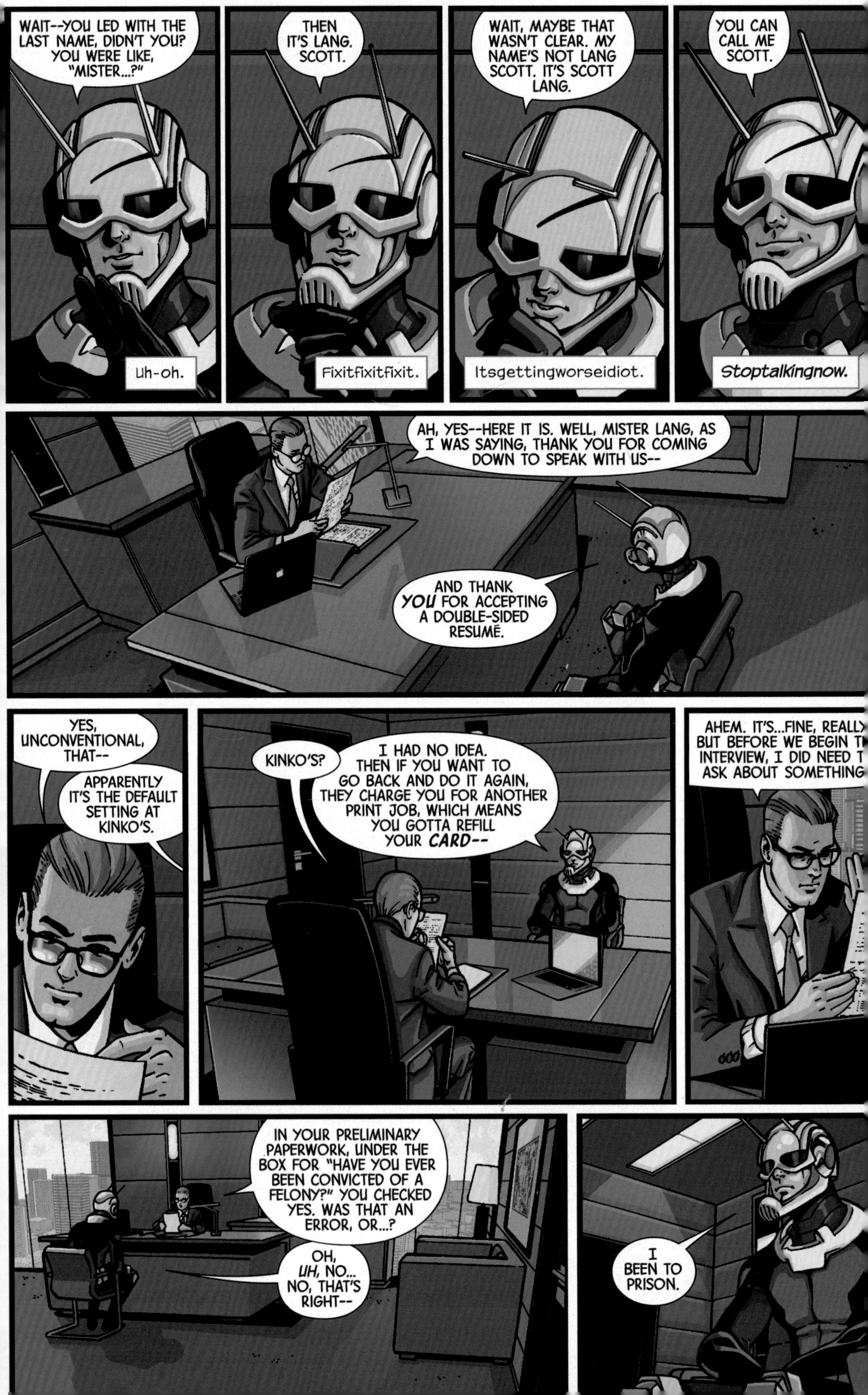
WAIT--YOU LED WITH THE LAST NAME, DIDN'T YOU? YOU WERE LIKE, "MISTER...?"
Uh-oh.
THEN IT'S LANG. SCOTT.
Fixitfixitfixit.
WAIT, MAYBE THAT WASN'T CLEAR. MY NAME'S NOT LANG SCOTT. IT'S SCOTT LANG.
Itsgettingworseidiot.
YOU CAN CALL ME SCOTT.
Stoptalkingnow.
AH, YES--HERE IT IS. WELL, MISTER LANG, AS I WAS SAYING, THANK YOU FOR COMING DOWN TO SPEAK WITH US--
AND THANK YOU FOR ACCEPTING A DOUBLE-SIDED RESUMÉ.
YES, UNCONVENTIONAL, THAT--
APPARENTLY IT'S THE DEFAULT SETTING AT KINKO'S.
KINKO'S?
I HAD NO IDEA. THEN IF YOU WANT TO GO BACK AND DO IT AGAIN, THEY CHARGE YOU FOR ANOTHER PRINT JOB, WHICH MEANS YOU GOTTA REFILL YOUR CARD--
AHEM. IT'S...FINE, REALLY BUT BEFORE WE BEGIN TH INTERVIEW, I DID NEED T ASK ABOUT SOMETHING
IN YOUR PRELIMINARY PAPERWORK, UNDER THE BOX FOR "HAVE YOU EVER BEEN CONVICTED OF A FELONY?" YOU CHECKED YES. WAS THAT AN ERROR, OR...?
OH, UH, NO... NO, THAT'S RIGHT--
I BEEN TO PRISON.

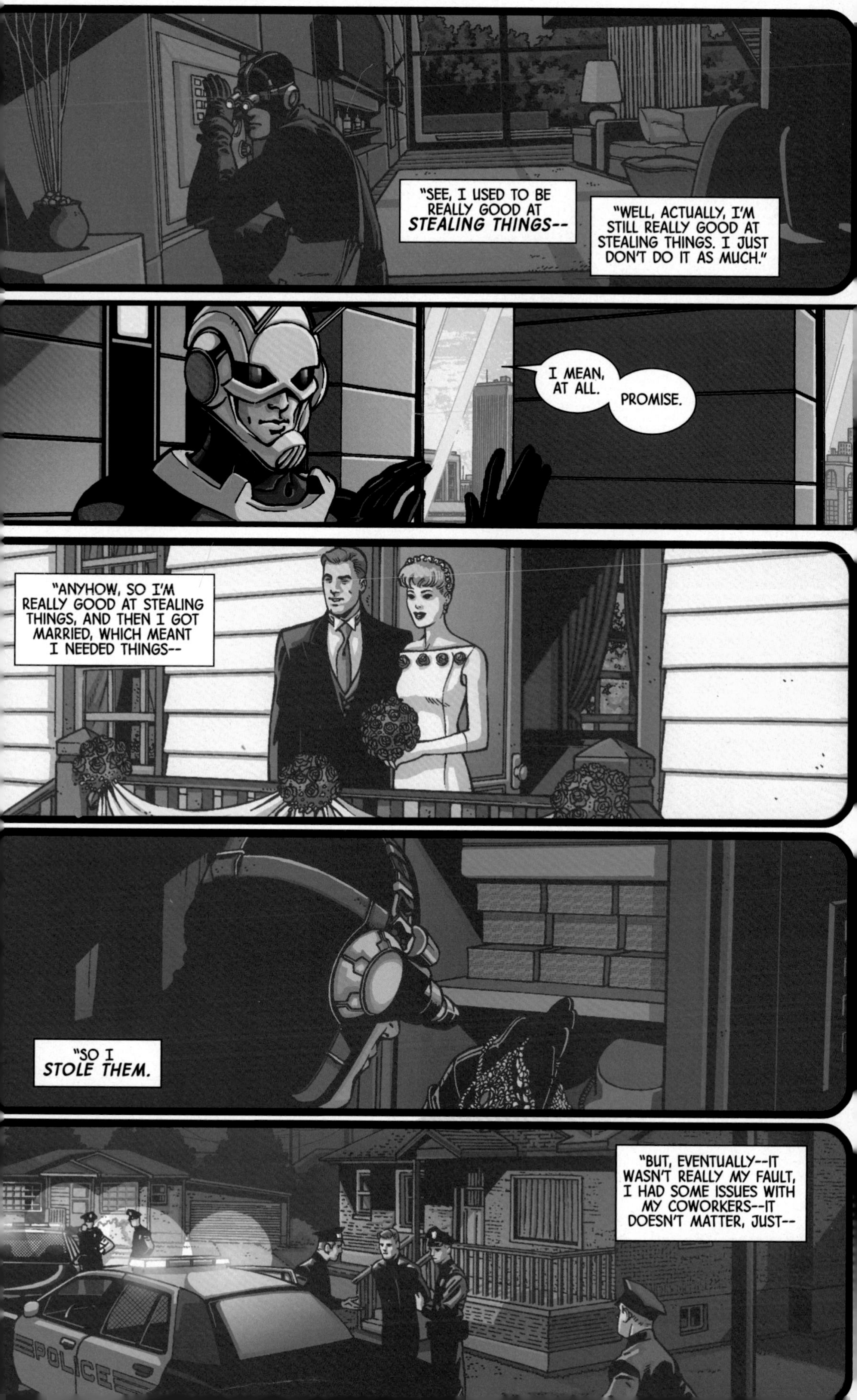
"SEE, I USED TO BE REALLY GOOD AT STEALING THINGS--
"WELL, ACTUALLY, I'M STILL REALLY GOOD AT STEALING THINGS. I JUST DON'T DO IT AS MUCH."
I MEAN, AT ALL.
PROMISE.
"ANYHOW, SO I'M REALLY GOOD AT STEALING THINGS, AND THEN I GOT MARRIED, WHICH MEANT I NEEDED THINGS--
"SO I STOLE THEM.
"BUT, EVENTUALLY--IT WASN'T REALLY MY FAULT, I HAD SOME ISSUES WITH MY COWORKERS--IT DOESN'T MATTER, JUST--
POLICE

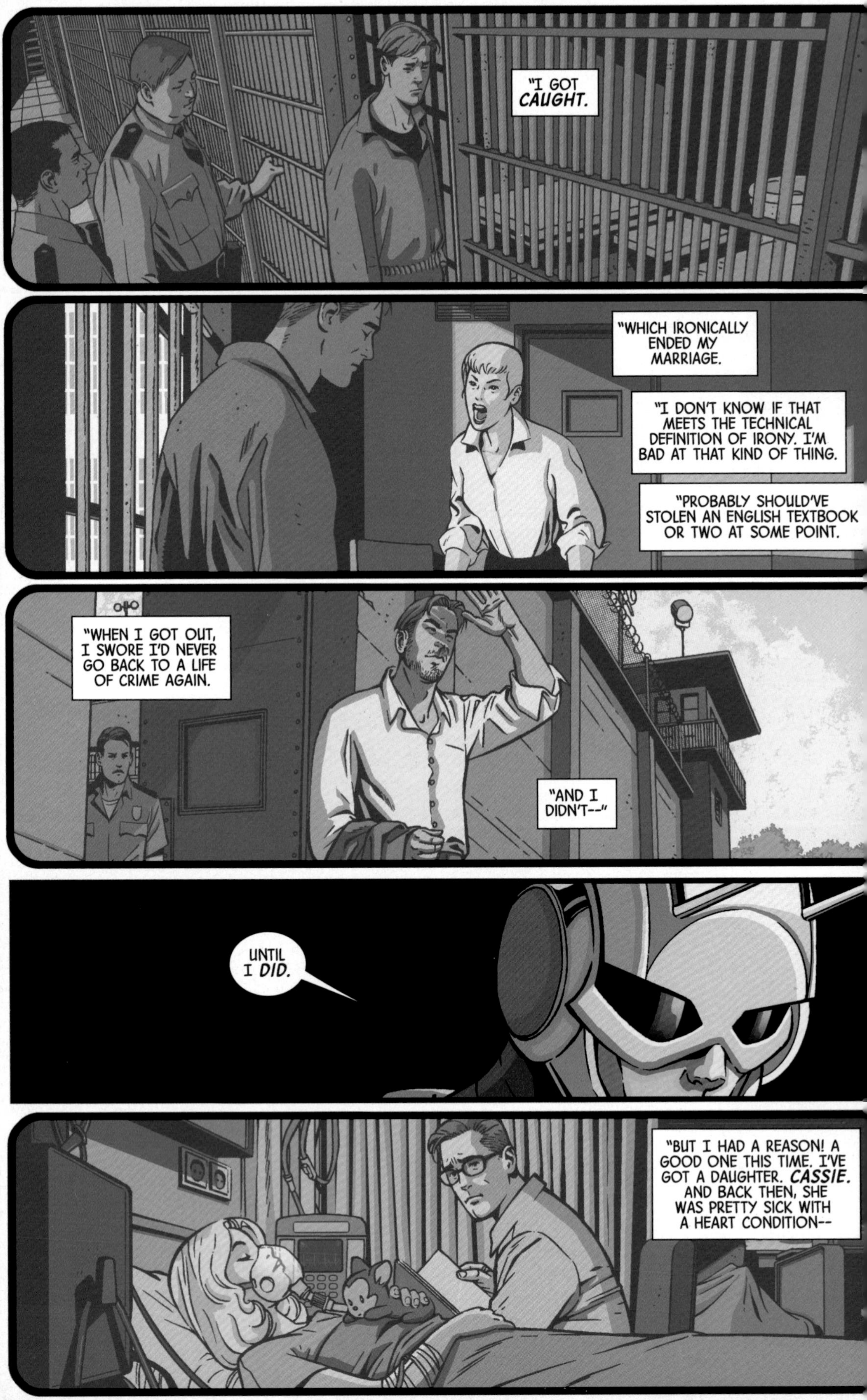

"I GOT *CAUGHT.*
"WHICH IRONICALLY ENDED MY MARRIAGE.
"I DON'T KNOW IF THAT MEETS THE TECHNICAL DEFINITION OF IRONY. I'M BAD AT THAT KIND OF THING.
"PROBABLY SHOULD'VE STOLEN AN ENGLISH TEXTBOOK OR TWO AT SOME POINT.
"WHEN I GOT OUT, I SWORE I'D NEVER GO BACK TO A LIFE OF CRIME AGAIN.
"AND I DIDN'T--"
UNTIL I *DID.*
"BUT I HAD A REASON! A GOOD ONE THIS TIME. I'VE GOT A DAUGHTER. *CASSIE.* AND BACK THEN, SHE WAS PRETTY SICK WITH A HEART CONDITION--

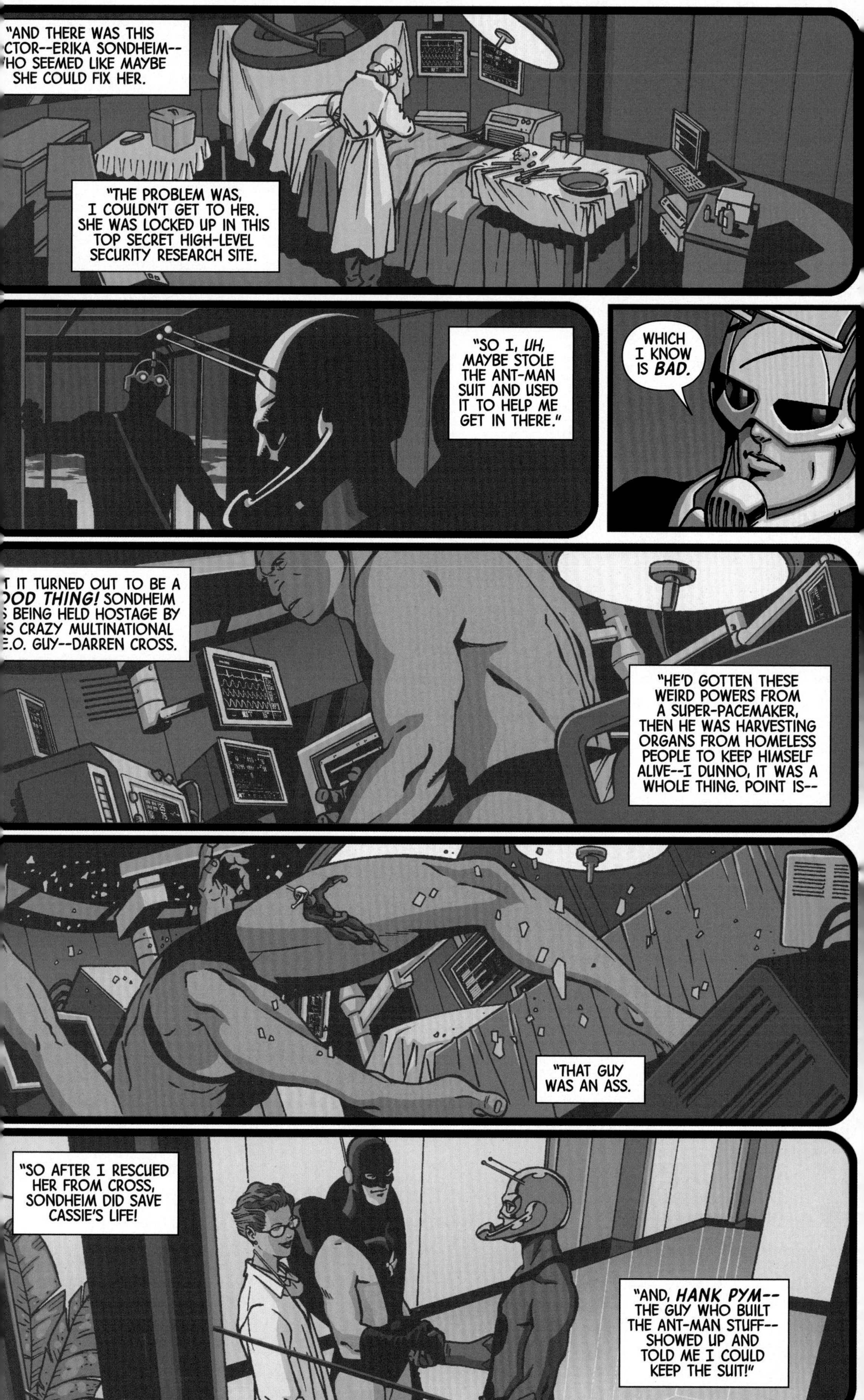
"AND THERE WAS THIS
CTOR--ERIKA SONDHEIM--
HO SEEMED LIKE MAYBE
SHE COULD FIX HER.
"THE PROBLEM WAS, I COULDN'T GET TO HER. SHE WAS LOCKED UP IN THIS TOP SECRET HIGH-LEVEL SECURITY RESEARCH SITE.
"SO I, *UH,* MAYBE STOLE THE ANT-MAN SUIT AND USED IT TO HELP ME GET IN THERE."
WHICH I KNOW IS *BAD.*
T IT TURNED OUT TO BE A
OOD THING! SONDHEIM
S BEING HELD HOSTAGE BY
S CRAZY MULTINATIONAL
E.O. GUY--DARREN CROSS.
"HE'D GOTTEN THESE WEIRD POWERS FROM A SUPER-PACEMAKER, THEN HE WAS HARVESTING ORGANS FROM HOMELESS PEOPLE TO KEEP HIMSELF ALIVE--I DUNNO, IT WAS A WHOLE THING. POINT IS--
"THAT GUY WAS AN ASS.
"SO AFTER I RESCUED HER FROM CROSS, SONDHEIM DID SAVE CASSIE'S LIFE!
"AND, *HANK PYM--* THE GUY WHO BUILT THE ANT-MAN STUFF--SHOWED UP AND TOLD ME I COULD KEEP THE SUIT!"

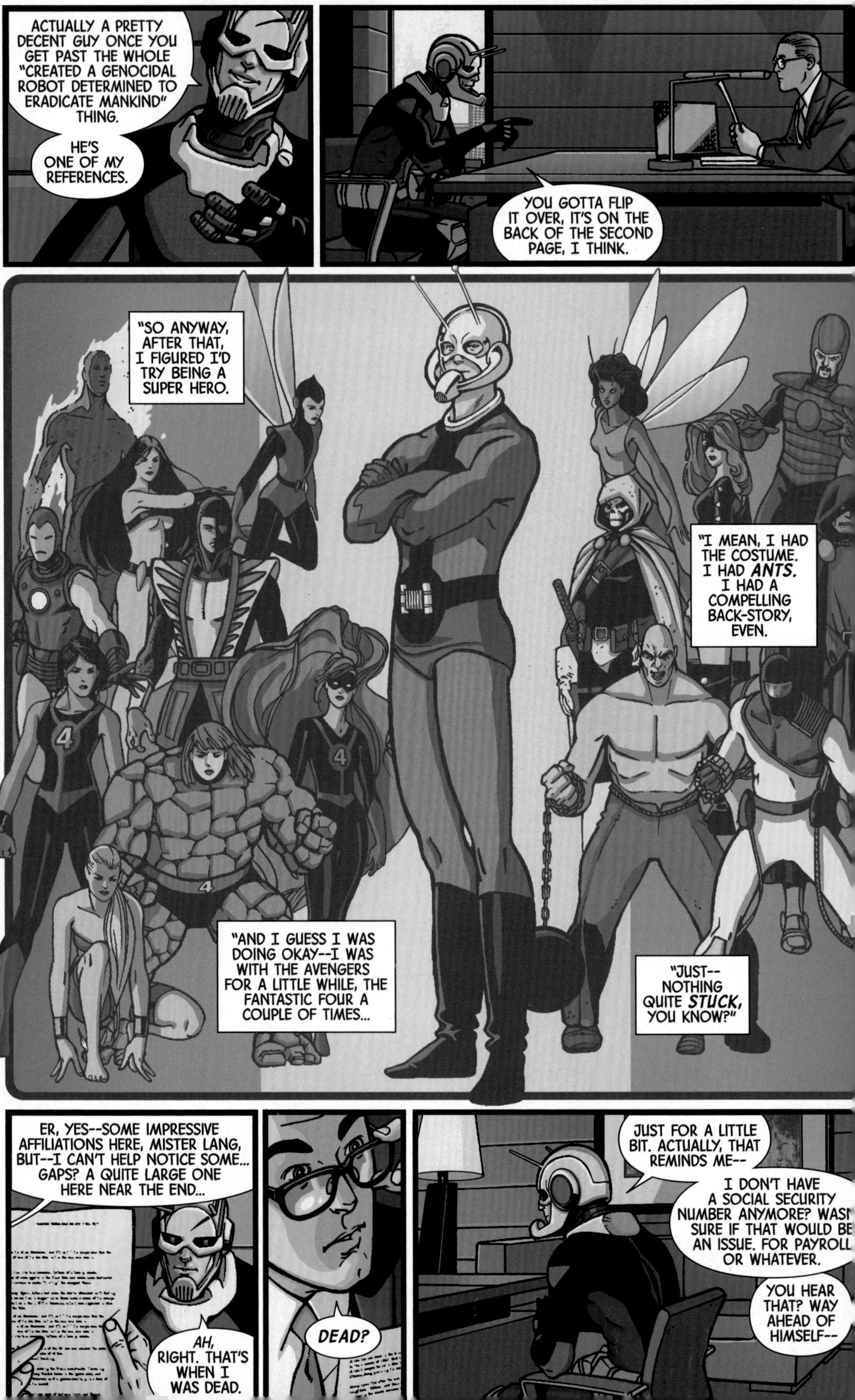
ACTUALLY A PRETTY DECENT GUY ONCE YOU GET PAST THE WHOLE "CREATED A GENOCIDAL ROBOT DETERMINED TO ERADICATE MANKIND" THING.
HE'S ONE OF MY REFERENCES.
YOU GOTTA FLIP IT OVER, IT'S ON THE BACK OF THE SECOND PAGE, I THINK.
"SO ANYWAY, AFTER THAT, I FIGURED I'D TRY BEING A SUPER HERO.
"I MEAN, I HAD THE COSTUME. I HAD ANTS. I HAD A COMPELLING BACK-STORY, EVEN.
"AND I GUESS I WAS DOING OKAY--I WAS WITH THE AVENGERS FOR A LITTLE WHILE, THE FANTASTIC FOUR A COUPLE OF TIMES...
"JUST-- NOTHING QUITE STUCK, YOU KNOW?"
ER, YES--SOME IMPRESSIVE AFFILIATIONS HERE, MISTER LANG, BUT--I CAN'T HELP NOTICE SOME... GAPS? A QUITE LARGE ONE HERE NEAR THE END...
AH, RIGHT. THAT'S WHEN I WAS DEAD.
DEAD?
JUST FOR A LITTLE BIT. ACTUALLY, THAT REMINDS ME--
I DON'T HAVE A SOCIAL SECURITY NUMBER ANYMORE? WASN SURE IF THAT WOULD BE AN ISSUE. FOR PAYROLL OR WHATEVER.
YOU HEAR THAT? WAY AHEAD OF HIMSELF--

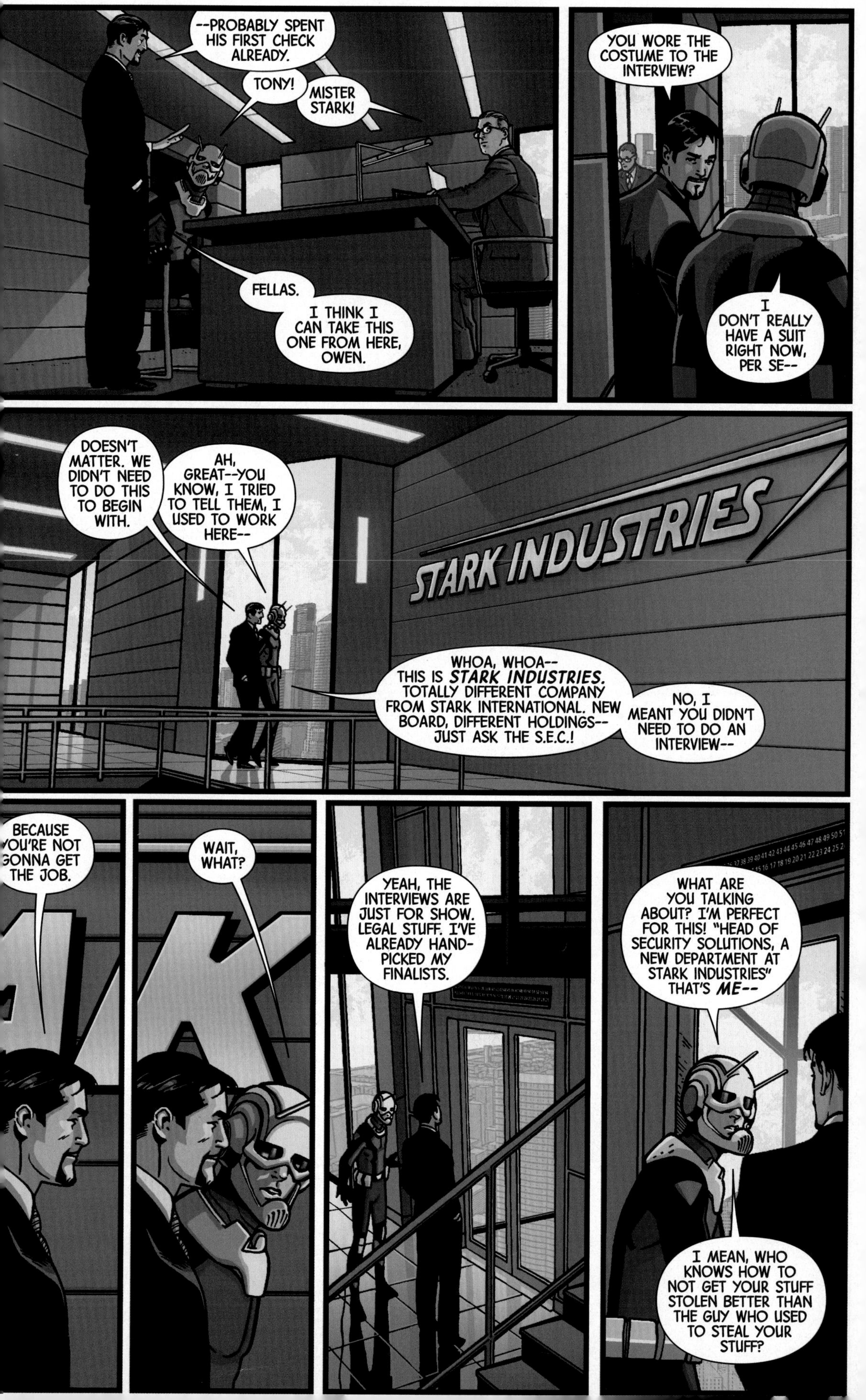
--PROBABLY SPENT HIS FIRST CHECK ALREADY.
TONY!
MISTER STARK!
FELLAS.
I THINK I CAN TAKE THIS ONE FROM HERE, OWEN.
YOU WORE THE COSTUME TO THE INTERVIEW?
I DON'T REALLY HAVE A SUIT RIGHT NOW, PER SE--
DOESN'T MATTER. WE DIDN'T NEED TO DO THIS TO BEGIN WITH.
AH, GREAT--YOU KNOW, I TRIED TO TELL THEM, I USED TO WORK HERE--
STARK INDUSTRIES
WHOA, WHOA-- THIS IS STARK INDUSTRIES. TOTALLY DIFFERENT COMPANY FROM STARK INTERNATIONAL. NEW BOARD, DIFFERENT HOLDINGS-- JUST ASK THE S.E.C.!
NO, I MEANT YOU DIDN'T NEED TO DO AN INTERVIEW--
BECAUSE YOU'RE NOT GONNA GET THE JOB.
WAIT, WHAT?
YEAH, THE INTERVIEWS ARE JUST FOR SHOW. LEGAL STUFF. I'VE ALREADY HAND-PICKED MY FINALISTS.
WHAT ARE YOU TALKING ABOUT? I'M PERFECT FOR THIS! "HEAD OF SECURITY SOLUTIONS, A NEW DEPARTMENT AT STARK INDUSTRIES" THAT'S ME--
I MEAN, WHO KNOWS HOW TO NOT GET YOUR STUFF STOLEN BETTER THAN THE GUY WHO USED TO STEAL YOUR STUFF?

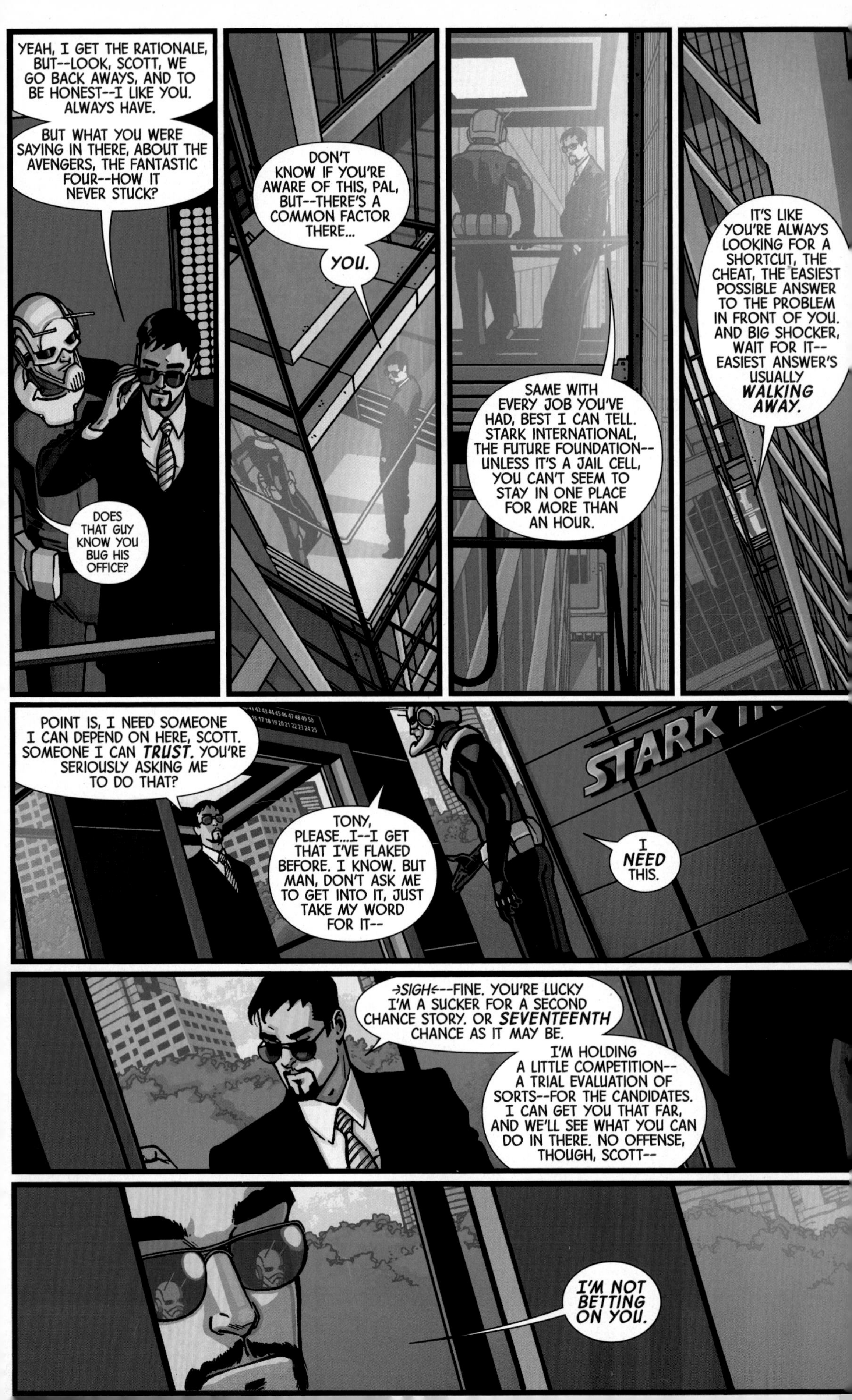
YEAH, I GET THE RATIONALE, BUT--LOOK, SCOTT, WE GO BACK AWAYS, AND TO BE HONEST--I LIKE YOU. ALWAYS HAVE.
BUT WHAT YOU WERE SAYING IN THERE, ABOUT THE AVENGERS, THE FANTASTIC FOUR--HOW IT NEVER STUCK?
DOES THAT GUY KNOW YOU BUG HIS OFFICE?
DON'T KNOW IF YOU'RE AWARE OF THIS, PAL, BUT--THERE'S A COMMON FACTOR THERE...
YOU.
SAME WITH EVERY JOB YOU'VE HAD, BEST I CAN TELL. STARK INTERNATIONAL, THE FUTURE FOUNDATION--UNLESS IT'S A JAIL CELL, YOU CAN'T SEEM TO STAY IN ONE PLACE FOR MORE THAN AN HOUR.
IT'S LIKE YOU'RE ALWAYS LOOKING FOR A SHORTCUT, THE CHEAT, THE EASIEST POSSIBLE ANSWER TO THE PROBLEM IN FRONT OF YOU. AND BIG SHOCKER, WAIT FOR IT--EASIEST ANSWER'S USUALLY WALKING AWAY.
POINT IS, I NEED SOMEONE I CAN DEPEND ON HERE, SCOTT. SOMEONE I CAN TRUST. YOU'RE SERIOUSLY ASKING ME TO DO THAT?
TONY, PLEASE...I--I GET THAT I'VE FLAKED BEFORE. I KNOW. BUT MAN, DON'T ASK ME TO GET INTO IT, JUST TAKE MY WORD FOR IT--
I NEED THIS.
STARK
→SIGH←--FINE. YOU'RE LUCKY I'M A SUCKER FOR A SECOND CHANCE STORY. OR SEVENTEENTH CHANCE AS IT MAY BE.
I'M HOLDING A LITTLE COMPETITION--A TRIAL EVALUATION OF SORTS--FOR THE CANDIDATES. I CAN GET YOU THAT FAR, AND WE'LL SEE WHAT YOU CAN DO IN THERE. NO OFFENSE, THOUGH, SCOTT--
I'M NOT BETTING ON YOU.

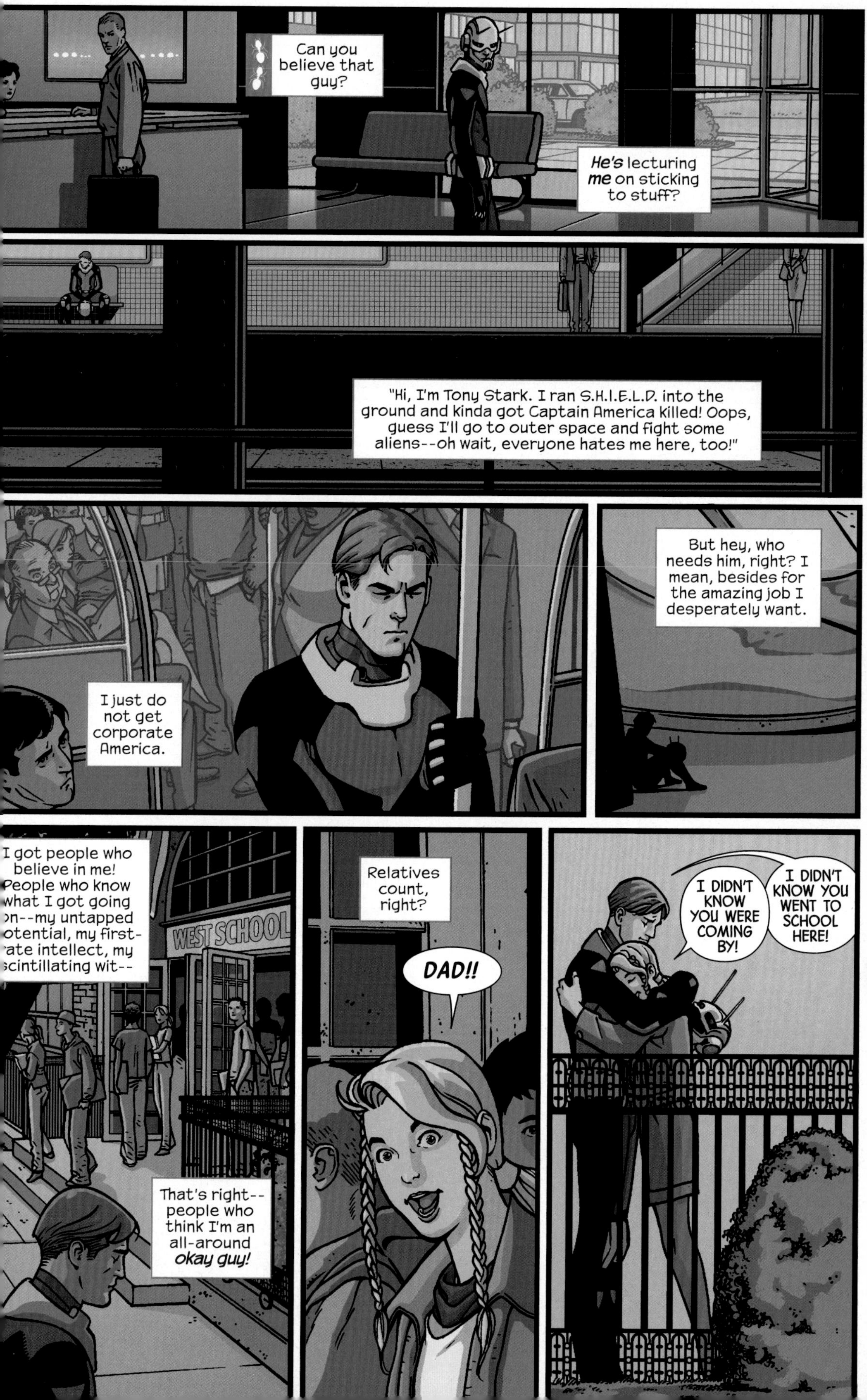
Can you believe that guy?
He's lecturing me on sticking to stuff?
"Hi, I'm Tony Stark. I ran S.H.I.E.L.D. into the ground and kinda got Captain America killed! Oops, guess I'll go to outer space and fight some aliens--oh wait, everyone hates me here, too!"
I just do not get corporate America.
But hey, who needs him, right? I mean, besides for the amazing job I desperately want.
I got people who believe in me! People who know what I got going on--my untapped otential, my first-rate intellect, my scintillating wit--
WEST SCHOOL
That's right--people who think I'm an all-around okay guy!
Relatives count, right?
DAD!!
I DIDN'T KNOW YOU WERE COMING BY!
I DIDN'T KNOW YOU WENT TO SCHOOL HERE!

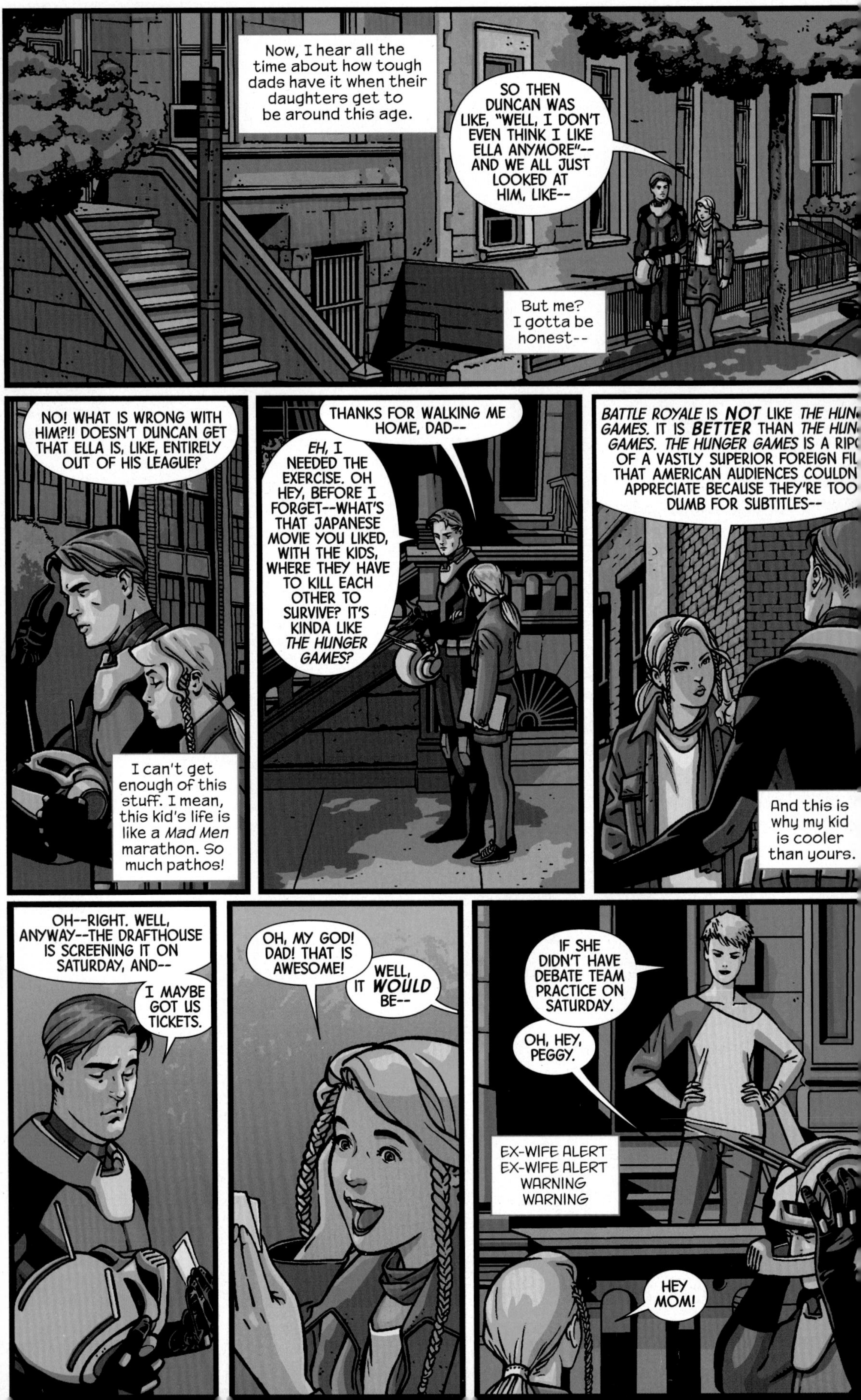
Now, I hear all the time about how tough dads have it when their daughters get to be around this age.
SO THEN DUNCAN WAS LIKE, "WELL, I DON'T EVEN THINK I LIKE ELLA ANYMORE"-- AND WE ALL JUST LOOKED AT HIM, LIKE--
But me? I gotta be honest--
NO! WHAT IS WRONG WITH HIM?!! DOESN'T DUNCAN GET THAT ELLA IS, LIKE, ENTIRELY OUT OF HIS LEAGUE?
I can't get enough of this stuff. I mean, this kid's life is like a *Mad Men* marathon. So much pathos!
THANKS FOR WALKING ME HOME, DAD--
EH, I NEEDED THE EXERCISE. OH HEY, BEFORE I FORGET--WHAT'S THAT JAPANESE MOVIE YOU LIKED, WITH THE KIDS, WHERE THEY HAVE TO KILL EACH OTHER TO SURVIVE? IT'S KINDA LIKE *THE HUNGER GAMES?*
BATTLE ROYALE IS **NOT** LIKE *THE HUN GAMES.* IT IS **BETTER** THAN *THE HUN GAMES. THE HUNGER GAMES* IS A RIP OF A VASTLY SUPERIOR FOREIGN FIL THAT AMERICAN AUDIENCES COULDN APPRECIATE BECAUSE THEY'RE TOO DUMB FOR SUBTITLES--
And this is why my kid is cooler than yours.
OH--RIGHT. WELL, ANYWAY--THE DRAFTHOUSE IS SCREENING IT ON SATURDAY, AND--
I MAYBE GOT US TICKETS.
OH, MY GOD! DAD! THAT IS AWESOME!
WELL, IT **WOULD** BE--
IF SHE DIDN'T HAVE DEBATE TEAM PRACTICE ON SATURDAY.
OH, HEY, PEGGY.
EX-WIFE ALERT
EX-WIFE ALERT
WARNING
WARNING
HEY MOM!

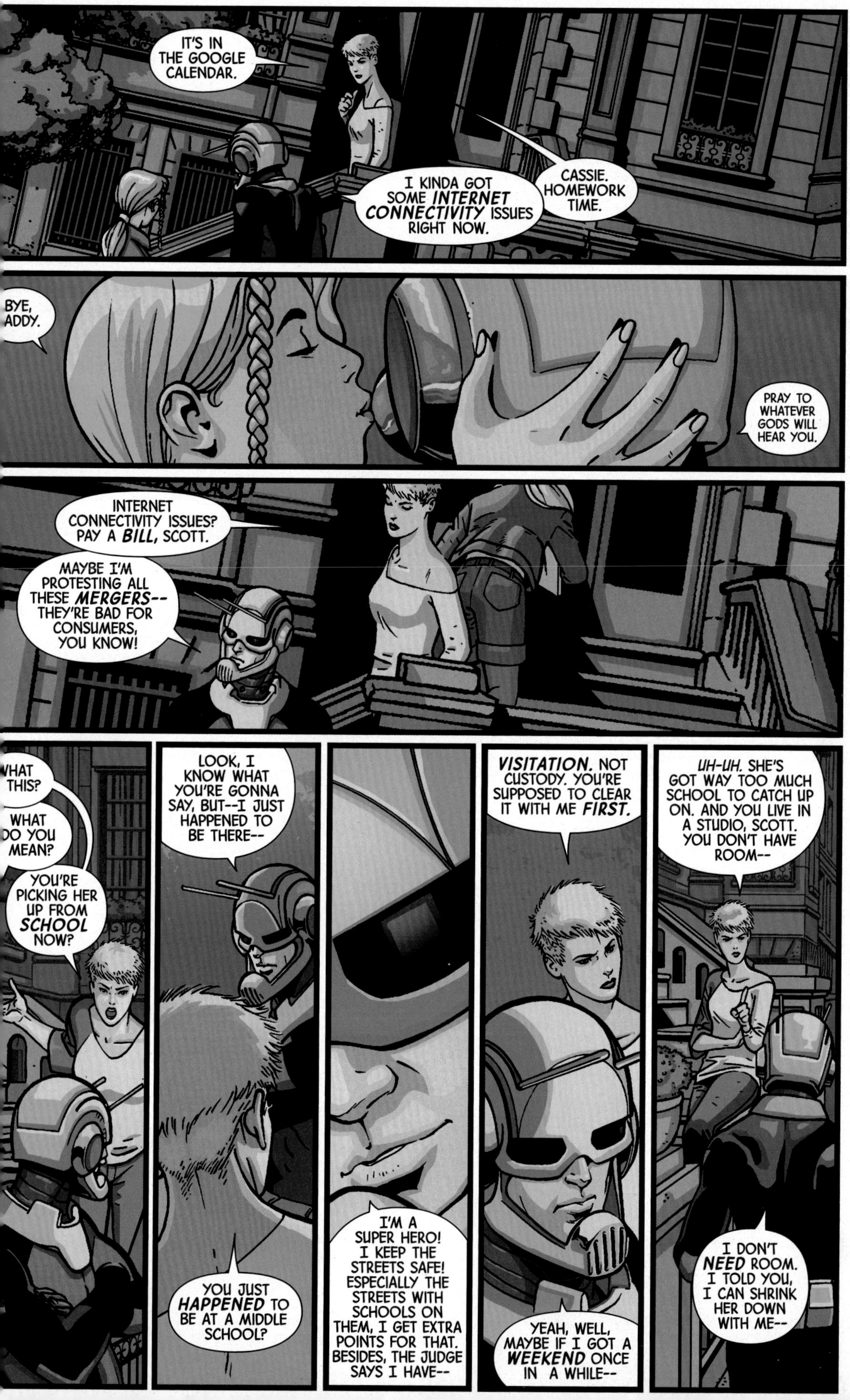
IT'S IN THE GOOGLE CALENDAR.
I KINDA GOT SOME INTERNET CONNECTIVITY ISSUES RIGHT NOW.
CASSIE. HOMEWORK TIME.
BYE, ADDY.
PRAY TO WHATEVER GODS WILL HEAR YOU.
INTERNET CONNECTIVITY ISSUES? PAY A BILL, SCOTT.
MAYBE I'M PROTESTING ALL THESE MERGERS-- THEY'RE BAD FOR CONSUMERS, YOU KNOW!
HAT THIS?
WHAT O YOU MEAN?
YOU'RE PICKING HER UP FROM SCHOOL NOW?
LOOK, I KNOW WHAT YOU'RE GONNA SAY, BUT--I JUST HAPPENED TO BE THERE--
YOU JUST HAPPENED TO BE AT A MIDDLE SCHOOL?
I'M A SUPER HERO! I KEEP THE STREETS SAFE! ESPECIALLY THE STREETS WITH SCHOOLS ON THEM, I GET EXTRA POINTS FOR THAT. BESIDES, THE JUDGE SAYS I HAVE--
VISITATION. NOT CUSTODY. YOU'RE SUPPOSED TO CLEAR IT WITH ME FIRST.
YEAH, WELL, MAYBE IF I GOT A WEEKEND ONCE IN A WHILE--
UH-UH. SHE'S GOT WAY TOO MUCH SCHOOL TO CATCH UP ON. AND YOU LIVE IN A STUDIO, SCOTT. YOU DON'T HAVE ROOM--
I DON'T NEED ROOM. I TOLD YOU, I CAN SHRINK HER DOWN WITH ME--

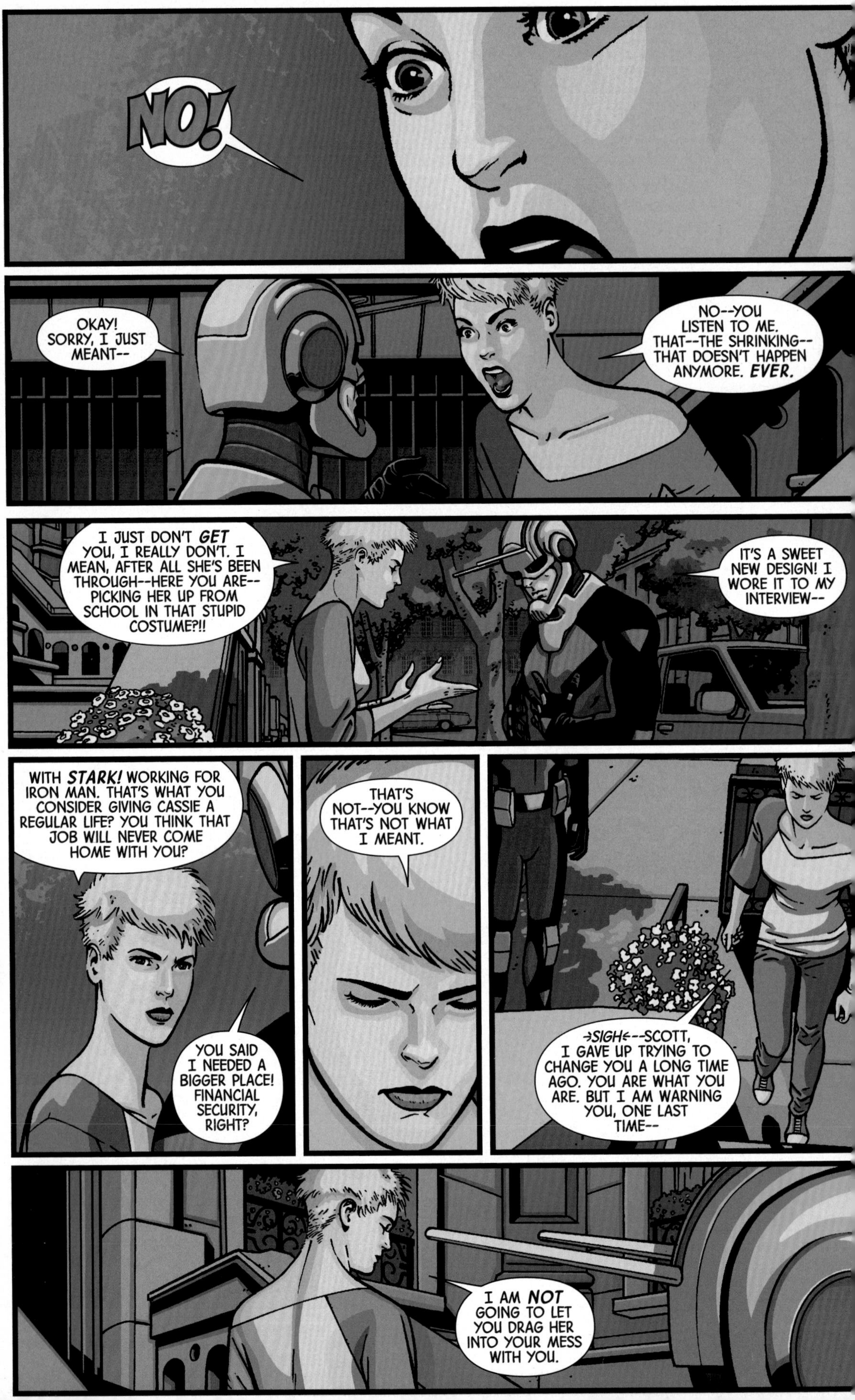
NO!
OKAY! SORRY, I JUST MEANT--
NO--YOU LISTEN TO ME. THAT--THE SHRINKING--THAT DOESN'T HAPPEN ANYMORE. EVER.
I JUST DON'T GET YOU, I REALLY DON'T. I MEAN, AFTER ALL SHE'S BEEN THROUGH--HERE YOU ARE--PICKING HER UP FROM SCHOOL IN THAT STUPID COSTUME?!!
IT'S A SWEET NEW DESIGN! I WORE IT TO MY INTERVIEW--
WITH STARK! WORKING FOR IRON MAN. THAT'S WHAT YOU CONSIDER GIVING CASSIE A REGULAR LIFE? YOU THINK THAT JOB WILL NEVER COME HOME WITH YOU?
YOU SAID I NEEDED A BIGGER PLACE! FINANCIAL SECURITY, RIGHT?
THAT'S NOT--YOU KNOW THAT'S NOT WHAT I MEANT.
→SIGH←--SCOTT, I GAVE UP TRYING TO CHANGE YOU A LONG TIME AGO. YOU ARE WHAT YOU ARE. BUT I AM WARNING YOU, ONE LAST TIME--
I AM NOT GOING TO LET YOU DRAG HER INTO YOUR MESS WITH YOU.

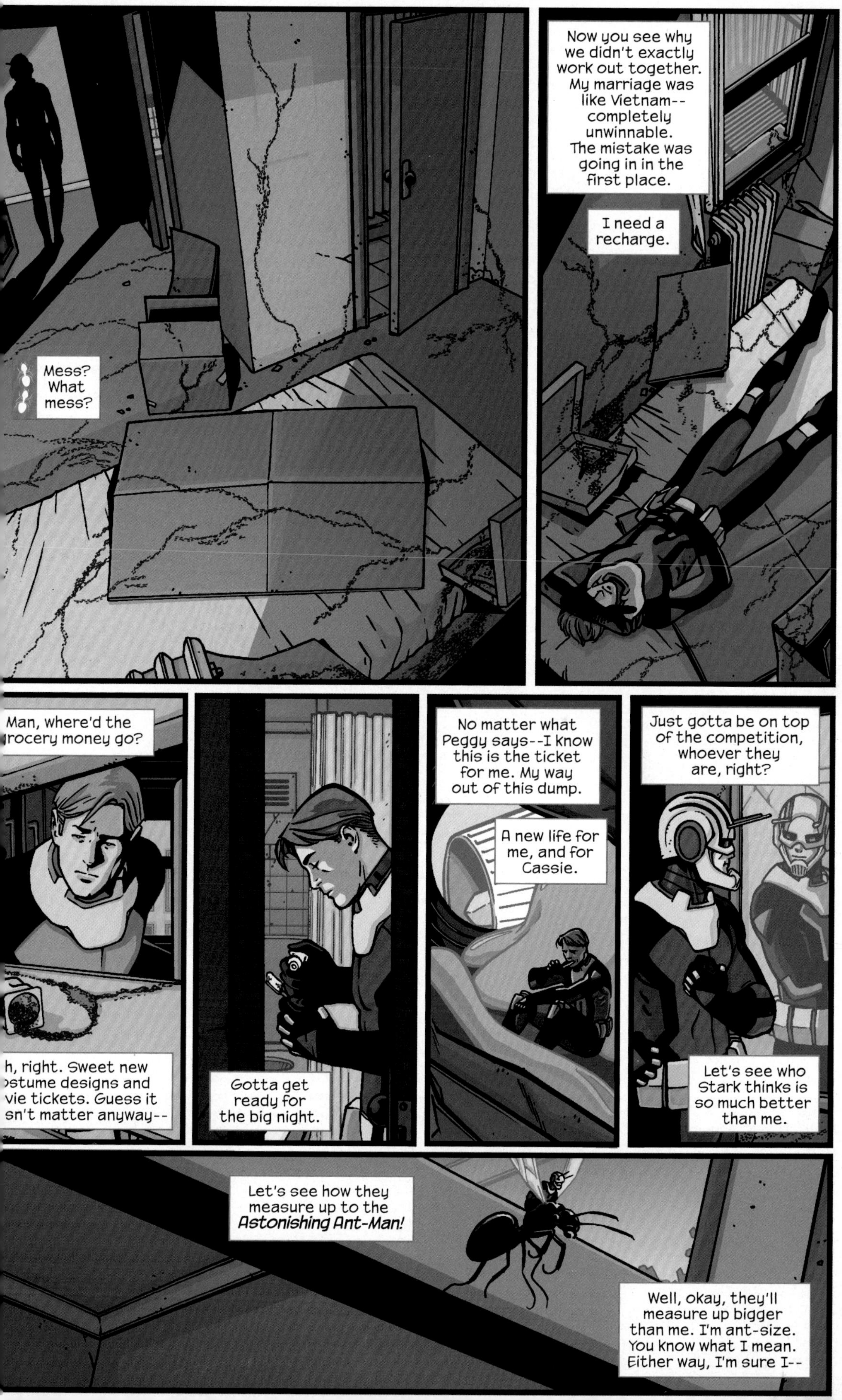

Mess? What mess?
Now you see why we didn't exactly work out together. My marriage was like Vietnam--completely unwinnable. The mistake was going in in the first place.
I need a recharge.
Man, where'd the rocery money go?
h, right. Sweet new ostume designs and vie tickets. Guess it sn't matter anyway--
Gotta get ready for the big night.
No matter what Peggy says--I know this is the ticket for me. My way out of this dump.
A new life for me, and for Cassie.
Just gotta be on top of the competition, whoever they are, right?
Let's see who Stark thinks is so much better than me.
Let's see how they measure up to the *Astonishing Ant-Man!*
Well, okay, they'll measure up bigger than me. I'm ant-size. You know what I mean. Either way, I'm sure I--

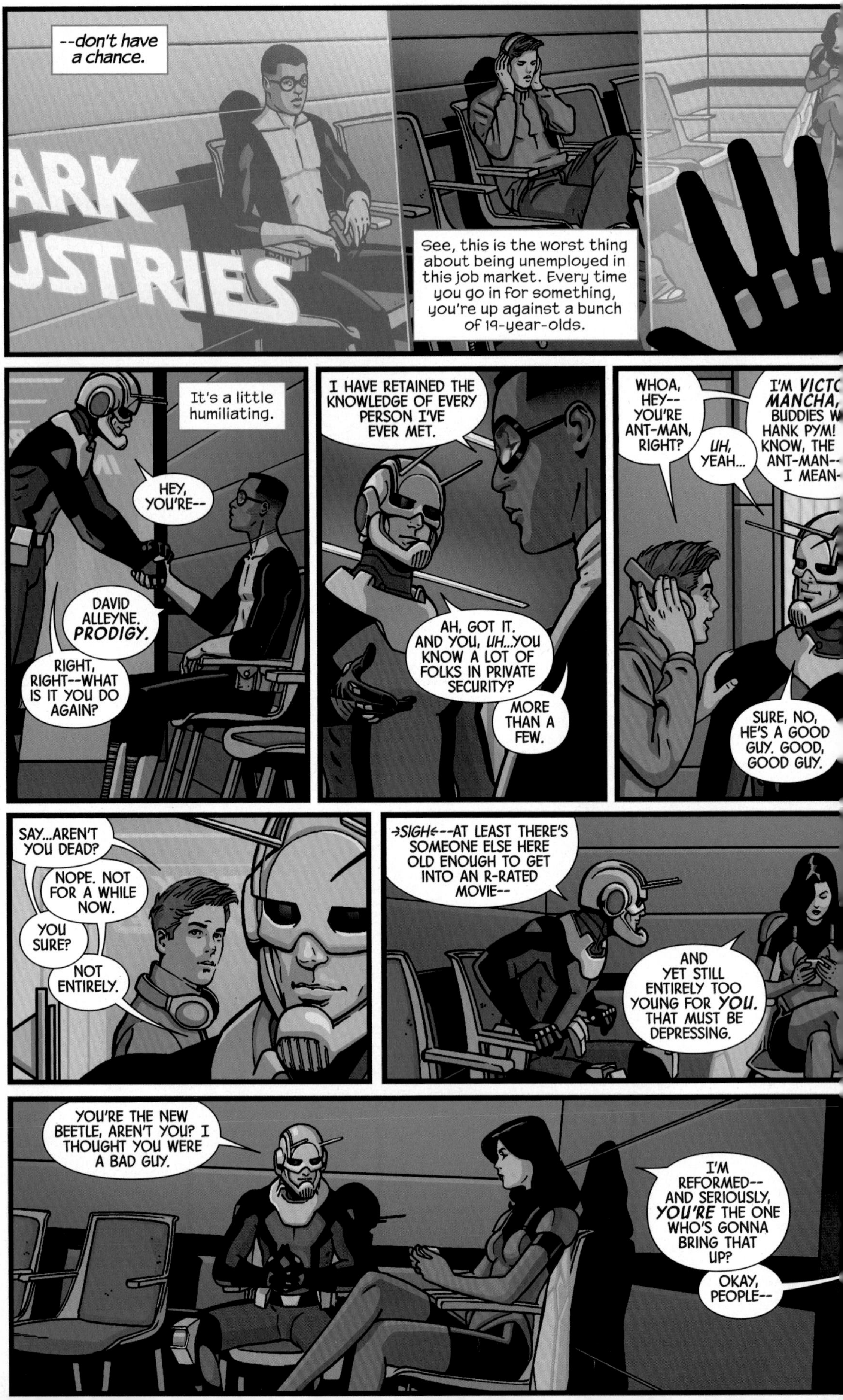
--don't have a chance.
ARK
USTRIES
See, this is the worst thing about being unemployed in this job market. Every time you go in for something, you're up against a bunch of 19-year-olds.
It's a little humiliating.
HEY, YOU'RE--
DAVID ALLEYNE. PRODIGY.
RIGHT, RIGHT--WHAT IS IT YOU DO AGAIN?
I HAVE RETAINED THE KNOWLEDGE OF EVERY PERSON I'VE EVER MET.
AH, GOT IT. AND YOU, UH...YOU KNOW A LOT OF FOLKS IN PRIVATE SECURITY?
MORE THAN A FEW.
WHOA, HEY-- YOU'RE ANT-MAN, RIGHT?
UH, YEAH...
I'M VICTO MANCHA, BUDDIES W HANK PYM! KNOW, THE ANT-MAN-- I MEAN-
SURE, NO, HE'S A GOOD GUY. GOOD, GOOD GUY.
SAY...AREN'T YOU DEAD?
NOPE. NOT FOR A WHILE NOW.
YOU SURE?
NOT ENTIRELY.
→SIGH←--AT LEAST THERE'S SOMEONE ELSE HERE OLD ENOUGH TO GET INTO AN R-RATED MOVIE--
AND YET STILL ENTIRELY TOO YOUNG FOR YOU. THAT MUST BE DEPRESSING.
YOU'RE THE NEW BEETLE, AREN'T YOU? I THOUGHT YOU WERE A BAD GUY.
I'M REFORMED-- AND SERIOUSLY, YOU'RE THE ONE WHO'S GONNA BRING THAT UP?
OKAY, PEOPLE--

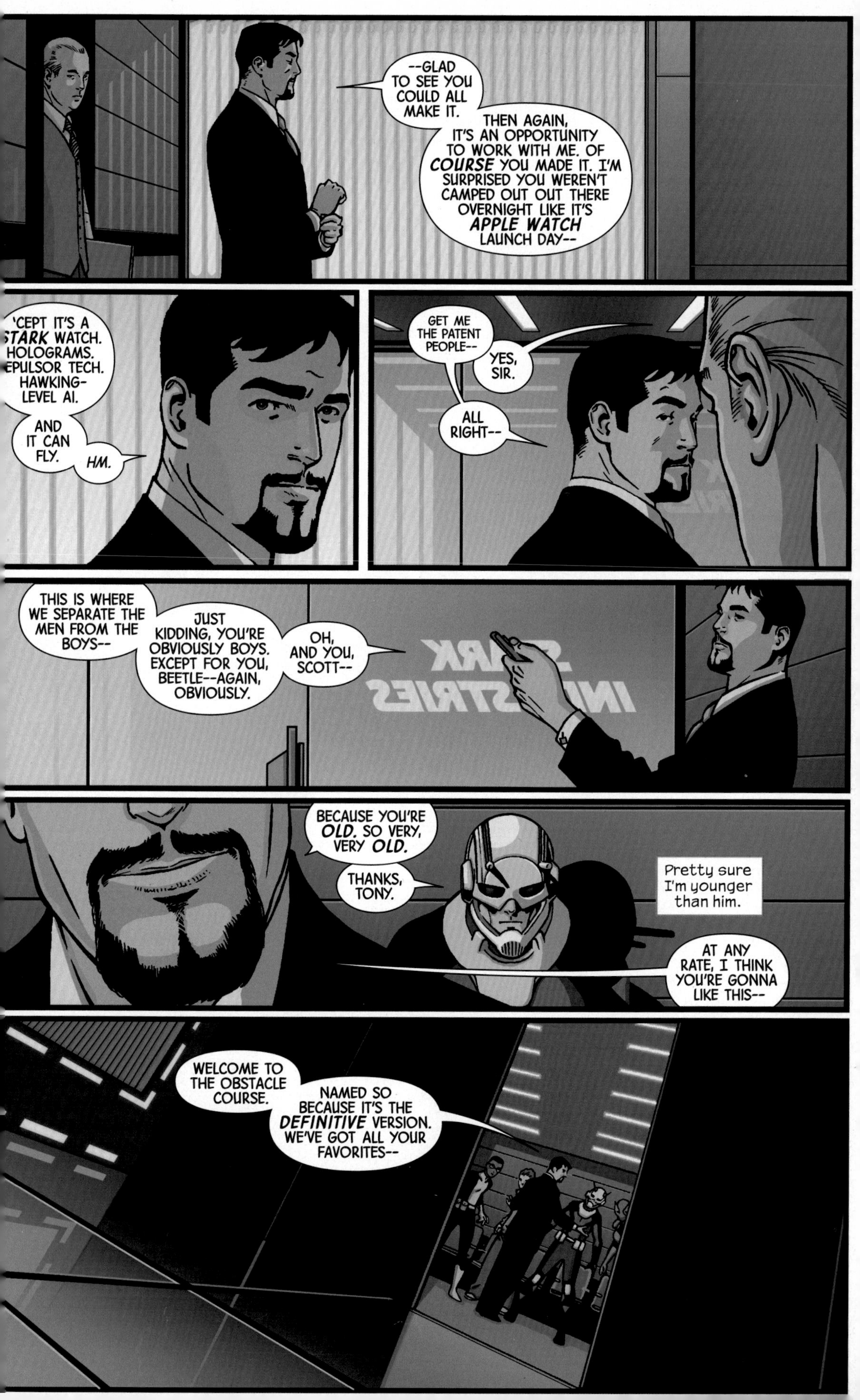
--GLAD TO SEE YOU COULD ALL MAKE IT.
THEN AGAIN, IT'S AN OPPORTUNITY TO WORK WITH ME. OF COURSE YOU MADE IT. I'M SURPRISED YOU WEREN'T CAMPED OUT OUT THERE OVERNIGHT LIKE IT'S APPLE WATCH LAUNCH DAY--
'CEPT IT'S A STARK WATCH. HOLOGRAMS. EPULSOR TECH. HAWKING-LEVEL AI.
AND IT CAN FLY.
HM.
GET ME THE PATENT PEOPLE--
YES, SIR.
ALL RIGHT--
THIS IS WHERE WE SEPARATE THE MEN FROM THE BOYS--
JUST KIDDING, YOU'RE OBVIOUSLY BOYS. EXCEPT FOR YOU, BEETLE--AGAIN, OBVIOUSLY.
OH, AND YOU, SCOTT--
BECAUSE YOU'RE OLD. SO VERY, VERY OLD.
THANKS, TONY.
Pretty sure I'm younger than him.
AT ANY RATE, I THINK YOU'RE GONNA LIKE THIS--
WELCOME TO THE OBSTACLE COURSE.
NAMED SO BECAUSE IT'S THE DEFINITIVE VERSION. WE'VE GOT ALL YOUR FAVORITES--

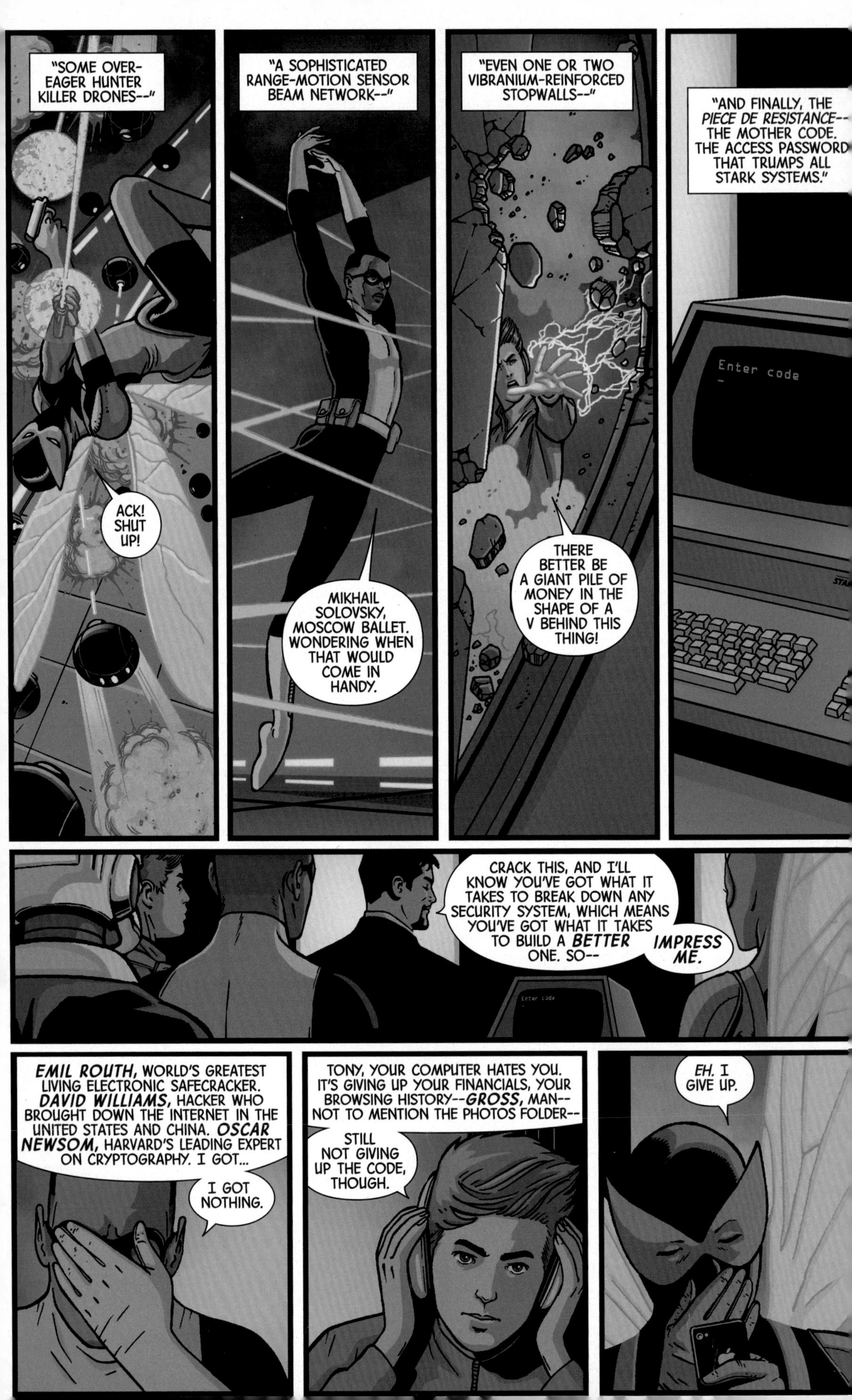
"SOME OVER-EAGER HUNTER KILLER DRONES--"
ACK! SHUT UP!
"A SOPHISTICATED RANGE-MOTION SENSOR BEAM NETWORK--"
MIKHAIL SOLOVSKY, MOSCOW BALLET. WONDERING WHEN THAT WOULD COME IN HANDY.
"EVEN ONE OR TWO VIBRANIUM-REINFORCED STOPWALLS--"
THERE BETTER BE A GIANT PILE OF MONEY IN THE SHAPE OF A V BEHIND THIS THING!
"AND FINALLY, THE PIECE DE RESISTANCE--THE MOTHER CODE. THE ACCESS PASSWORD THAT TRUMPS ALL STARK SYSTEMS."
Enter code
CRACK THIS, AND I'LL KNOW YOU'VE GOT WHAT IT TAKES TO BREAK DOWN ANY SECURITY SYSTEM, WHICH MEANS YOU'VE GOT WHAT IT TAKES TO BUILD A BETTER ONE. SO--
IMPRESS ME.
EMIL ROUTH, WORLD'S GREATEST LIVING ELECTRONIC SAFECRACKER. DAVID WILLIAMS, HACKER WHO BROUGHT DOWN THE INTERNET IN THE UNITED STATES AND CHINA. OSCAR NEWSOM, HARVARD'S LEADING EXPERT ON CRYPTOGRAPHY. I GOT...
I GOT NOTHING.
TONY, YOUR COMPUTER HATES YOU. IT'S GIVING UP YOUR FINANCIALS, YOUR BROWSING HISTORY--GROSS, MAN--NOT TO MENTION THE PHOTOS FOLDER--
STILL NOT GIVING UP THE CODE, THOUGH.
EH. I GIVE UP.

ELL, SCOTT-- OU GONNA HOW THESE DS HOW IT'S DONE?

WITH *PLEASURE*, TONY.

Or deep, unrelenting agony.

I mean, if Knows Everything Kid and Living Computer Lad can't do this, how the hell am I supposed to?

Luckily I do have one secret super-power none of the others have--

Enter code

The power to fake *sick*.

See, with the Pym Particles, I can actually shrink individual parts of my body. Now this is not something most guys are usually in a rush to do, but in the case of the *digestive* system--

an come n handy.

BLERGH!!

EWW!

OH MAN--

INSIDE THE HELMET!

OKAY, THAT'S ENOUGH--

TONY, I'M SORRY, --I SHOULD'VE SAID ETHING. BEEN DEALING H A STOMACH FLU-- HOUGHT I COULD TOUGH IT OUT--

→SIGH←-- IT'S FINE--

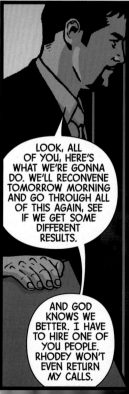

LOOK, ALL OF YOU, HERE'S WHAT WE'RE GONNA DO. WE'LL RECONVENE TOMORROW MORNING AND GO THROUGH ALL OF THIS AGAIN, SEE IF WE GET SOME DIFFERENT RESULTS.

AND GOD KNOWS WE BETTER. I HAVE TO HIRE ONE OF YOU PEOPLE. RHODEY WON'T EVEN RETURN MY CALLS.

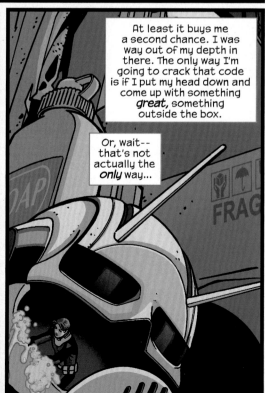

At least it buys me a second chance. I was way out of my depth in there. The only way I'm going to crack that code is if I put my head down and come up with something *great*, something outside the box.

Or, wait-- that's not actually the *only* way...

FRAG

So yeah, this is how I ended up breaking into Tony Stark's apartment.

Y'know, on second thought--

Judge away.

Because if this is what I gotta do to give Cassie a better life, so be it. I know exactly where he'll have stored the mother code- localized on his helmet. With the right gear, it's easy pickings.

I am in it to--

OH, TONY!!

Oh, come on!!

Beetle's hooking up with Stark now?!!

I can't believe this. That's totally cheating

I mean, yeah, sure, this is cheating too, but this is different. In ways that are difficult to expres

OPYING FILES 90 PERCENT

I HOPE YOU DON'T THIN THIS WILL GET Y FAVORABLE TREAT/ TOMORROW AT COMPETITION.

IF I THOUGHT THAT WAS SOMET YOU COULD CONT I WOULDN'T BE H

Whatever. Tomorrow we'll see how her unmerited advantage does against my...unmerited advantage. For now, I just need to get out of here--

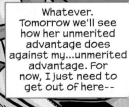

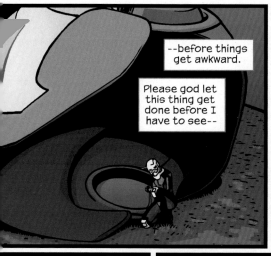

--before things get awkward.

Please god let this thing get done before I have to see--

Too late.

Always too late.

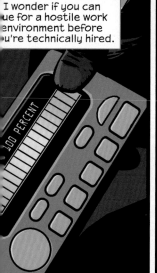

I wonder if you can [s]ue for a hostile work [e]nvironment before [yo]u're technically hired.

100 PERCENT

Either way, this better have been worth it. Let's see what the mother code is--man, this thing is loading slow--

Huh?

CONGRATULATIONS!

CLAP

CLAP

CLAP

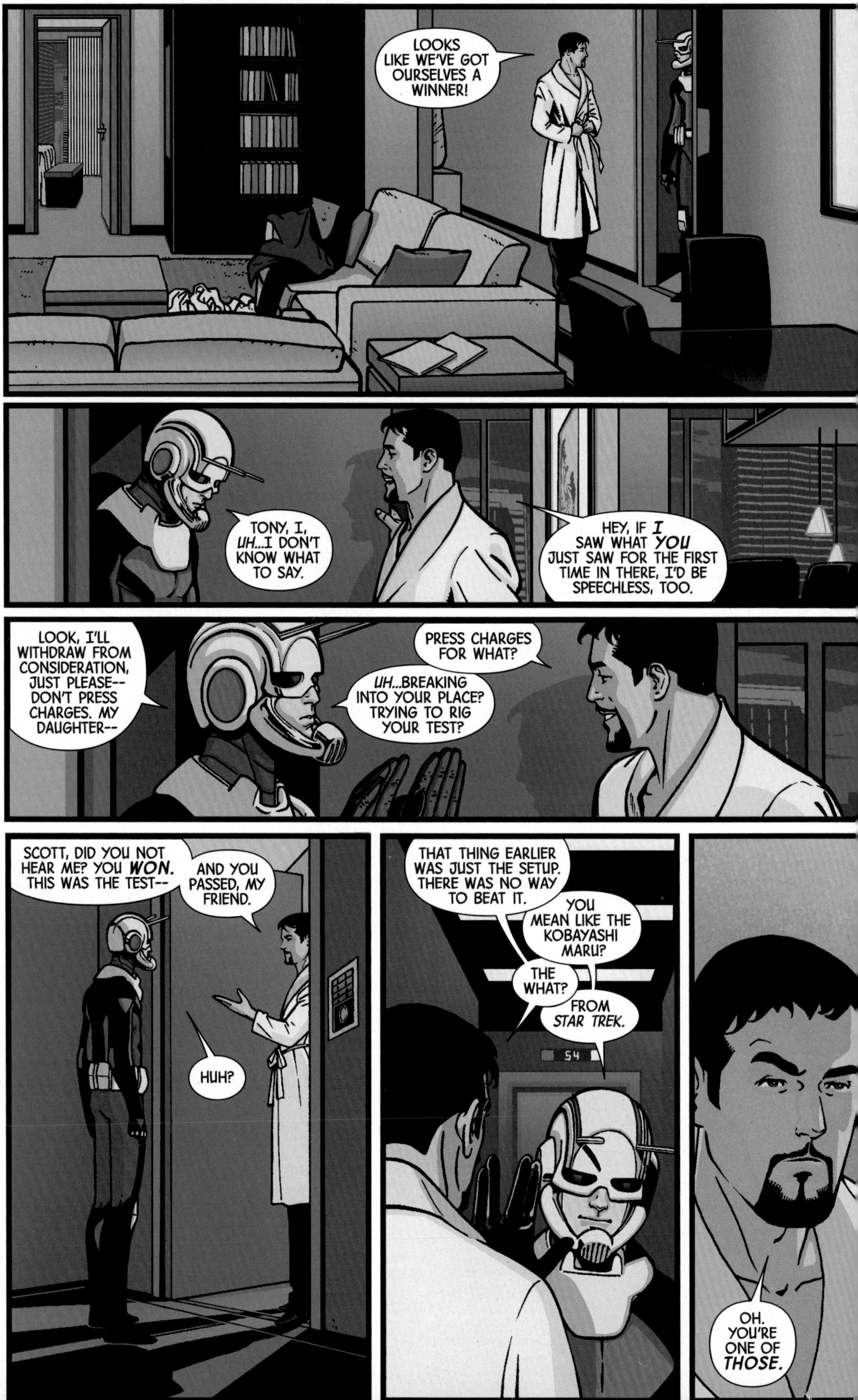
LOOKS LIKE WE'VE GOT OURSELVES A WINNER!
TONY, I, UH...I DON'T KNOW WHAT TO SAY.
HEY, IF I SAW WHAT YOU JUST SAW FOR THE FIRST TIME IN THERE, I'D BE SPEECHLESS, TOO.
LOOK, I'LL WITHDRAW FROM CONSIDERATION, JUST PLEASE-- DON'T PRESS CHARGES. MY DAUGHTER--
PRESS CHARGES FOR WHAT?
UH...BREAKING INTO YOUR PLACE? TRYING TO RIG YOUR TEST?
SCOTT, DID YOU NOT HEAR ME? YOU WON. THIS WAS THE TEST--
AND YOU PASSED, MY FRIEND.
HUH?
THAT THING EARLIER WAS JUST THE SETUP. THERE WAS NO WAY TO BEAT IT.
YOU MEAN LIKE THE KOBAYASHI MARU?
THE WHAT?
FROM STAR TREK.
54
OH. YOU'RE ONE OF THOSE.

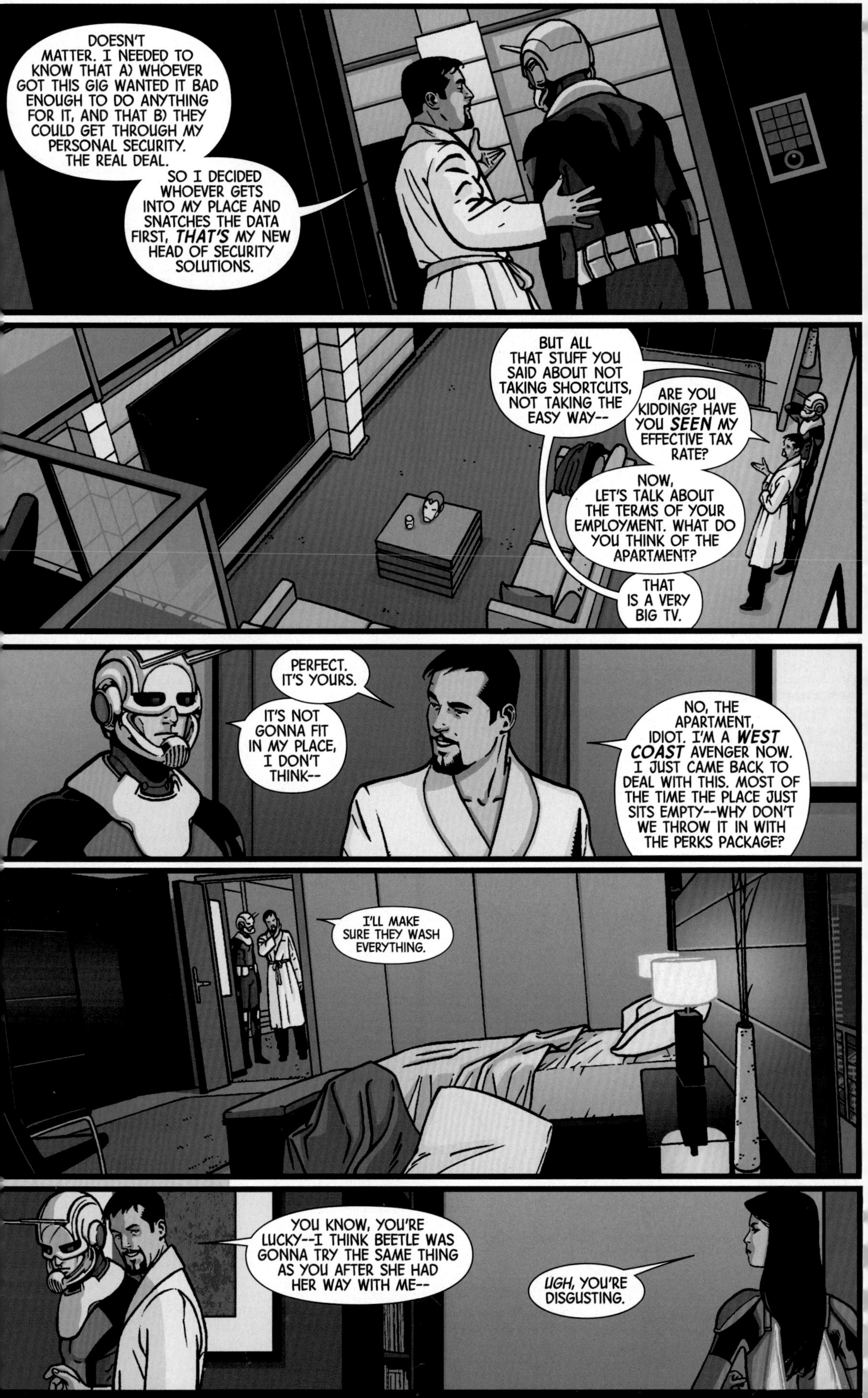
DOESN'T MATTER. I NEEDED TO KNOW THAT A) WHOEVER GOT THIS GIG WANTED IT BAD ENOUGH TO DO ANYTHING FOR IT, AND THAT B) THEY COULD GET THROUGH MY PERSONAL SECURITY. THE REAL DEAL.
SO I DECIDED WHOEVER GETS INTO MY PLACE AND SNATCHES THE DATA FIRST, THAT'S MY NEW HEAD OF SECURITY SOLUTIONS.
BUT ALL THAT STUFF YOU SAID ABOUT NOT TAKING SHORTCUTS, NOT TAKING THE EASY WAY--
ARE YOU KIDDING? HAVE YOU SEEN MY EFFECTIVE TAX RATE?
NOW, LET'S TALK ABOUT THE TERMS OF YOUR EMPLOYMENT. WHAT DO YOU THINK OF THE APARTMENT?
THAT IS A VERY BIG TV.
PERFECT. IT'S YOURS.
IT'S NOT GONNA FIT IN MY PLACE, I DON'T THINK--
NO, THE APARTMENT, IDIOT. I'M A WEST COAST AVENGER NOW. I JUST CAME BACK TO DEAL WITH THIS. MOST OF THE TIME THE PLACE JUST SITS EMPTY--WHY DON'T WE THROW IT IN WITH THE PERKS PACKAGE?
I'LL MAKE SURE THEY WASH EVERYTHING.
YOU KNOW, YOU'RE LUCKY--I THINK BEETLE WAS GONNA TRY THE SAME THING AS YOU AFTER SHE HAD HER WAY WITH ME--
UGH, YOU'RE DISGUSTING.

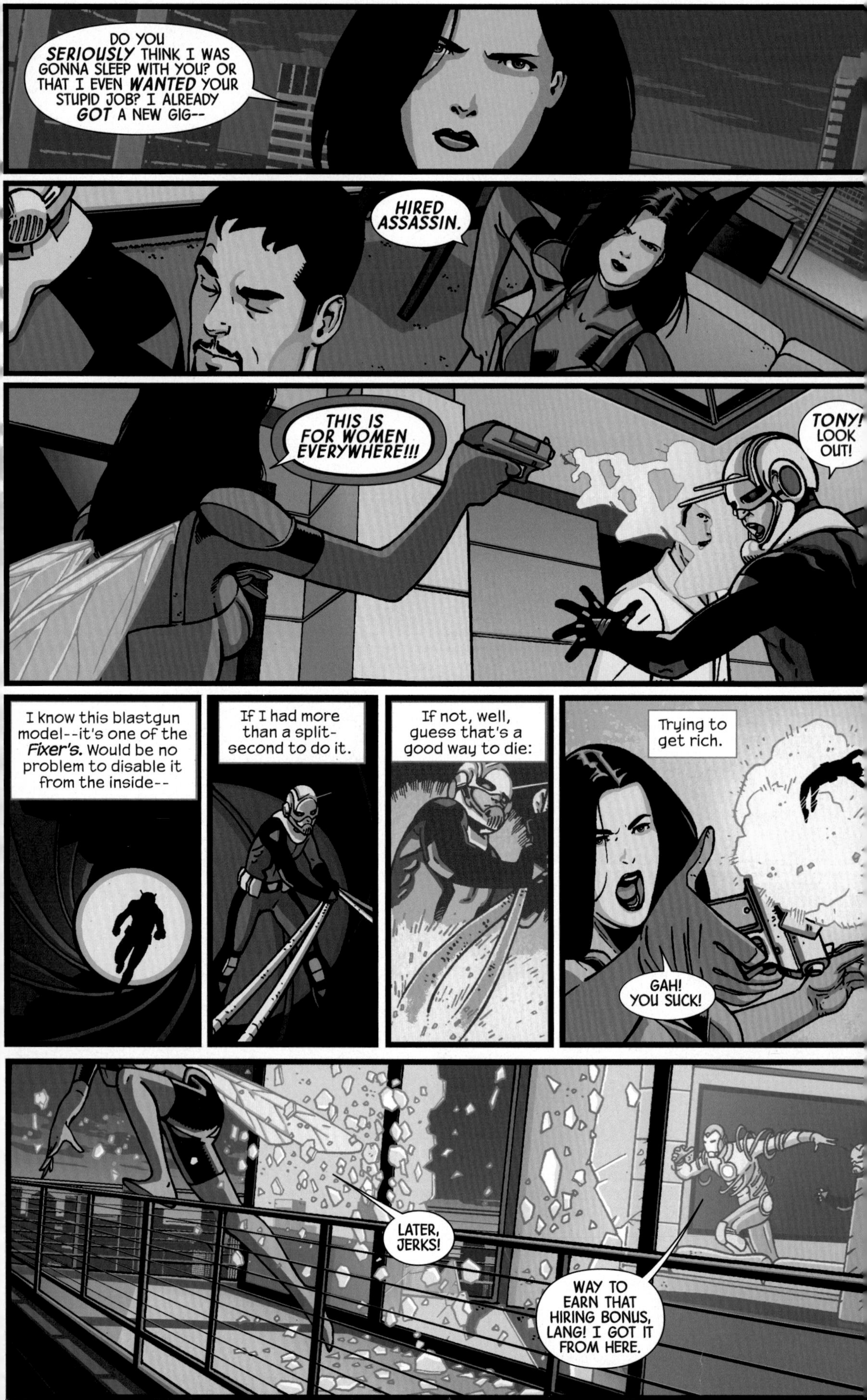
DO YOU SERIOUSLY THINK I WAS GONNA SLEEP WITH YOU? OR THAT I EVEN WANTED YOUR STUPID JOB? I ALREADY GOT A NEW GIG--
HIRED ASSASSIN.
THIS IS FOR WOMEN EVERYWHERE!!!
TONY! LOOK OUT!
I know this blastgun model--it's one of the Fixer's. Would be no problem to disable it from the inside--
If I had more than a split-second to do it.
If not, well, guess that's a good way to die:
Trying to get rich.
GAH! YOU SUCK!
LATER, JERKS!
WAY TO EARN THAT HIRING BONUS, LANG! I GOT IT FROM HERE.

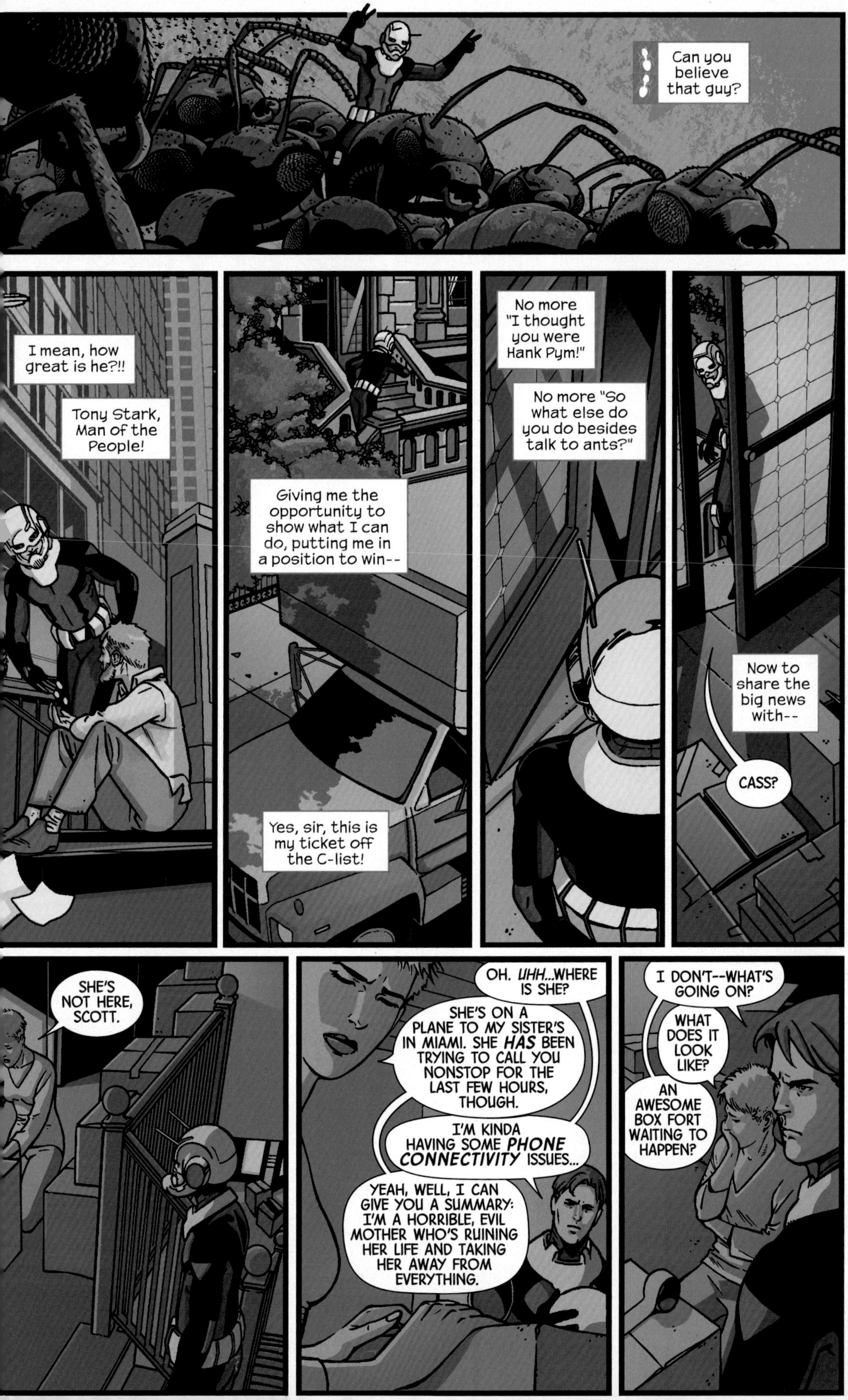

Can you believe that guy?
I mean, how great is he?!!
Tony Stark, Man of the People!
Giving me the opportunity to show what I can do, putting me in a position to win--
Yes, sir, this is my ticket off the C-list!
No more "I thought you were Hank Pym!"
No more "So what else do you do besides talk to ants?"
Now to share the big news with--
CASS?
SHE'S NOT HERE, SCOTT.
OH. *UHH*...WHERE IS SHE?
SHE'S ON A PLANE TO MY SISTER'S IN MIAMI. SHE *HAS* BEEN TRYING TO CALL YOU NONSTOP FOR THE LAST FEW HOURS, THOUGH.
I'M KINDA HAVING SOME *PHONE CONNECTIVITY* ISSUES...
YEAH, WELL, I CAN GIVE YOU A SUMMARY: I'M A HORRIBLE, EVIL MOTHER WHO'S RUINING HER LIFE AND TAKING HER AWAY FROM EVERYTHING.
I DON'T--WHAT'S GOING ON?
WHAT DOES IT LOOK LIKE?
AN AWESOME BOX FORT WAITING TO HAPPEN?

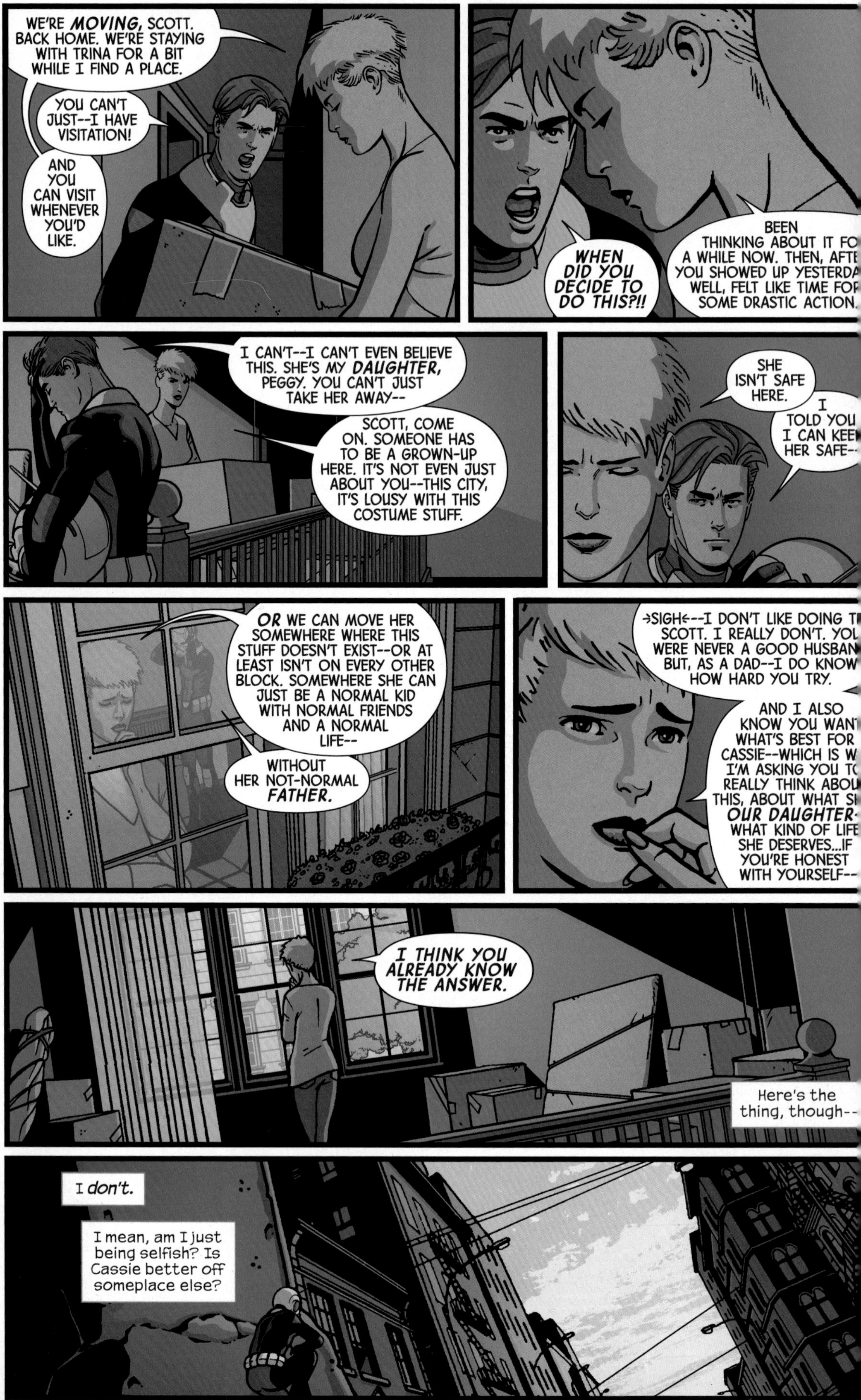
WE'RE MOVING, SCOTT. BACK HOME. WE'RE STAYING WITH TRINA FOR A BIT WHILE I FIND A PLACE.
YOU CAN'T JUST--I HAVE VISITATION!
AND YOU CAN VISIT WHENEVER YOU'D LIKE.
WHEN DID YOU DECIDE TO DO THIS?!!
BEEN THINKING ABOUT IT FO A WHILE NOW. THEN, AFTE YOU SHOWED UP YESTERDA WELL, FELT LIKE TIME FOR SOME DRASTIC ACTION.
I CAN'T--I CAN'T EVEN BELIEVE THIS. SHE'S MY DAUGHTER, PEGGY. YOU CAN'T JUST TAKE HER AWAY--
SCOTT, COME ON. SOMEONE HAS TO BE A GROWN-UP HERE. IT'S NOT EVEN JUST ABOUT YOU--THIS CITY, IT'S LOUSY WITH THIS COSTUME STUFF.
SHE ISN'T SAFE HERE.
I TOLD YOU I CAN KEE HER SAFE--
OR WE CAN MOVE HER SOMEWHERE WHERE THIS STUFF DOESN'T EXIST--OR AT LEAST ISN'T ON EVERY OTHER BLOCK. SOMEWHERE SHE CAN JUST BE A NORMAL KID WITH NORMAL FRIENDS AND A NORMAL LIFE--
WITHOUT HER NOT-NORMAL FATHER.
→SIGH←--I DON'T LIKE DOING T SCOTT. I REALLY DON'T. YO WERE NEVER A GOOD HUSBAN BUT, AS A DAD--I DO KNOW HOW HARD YOU TRY.
AND I ALSO KNOW YOU WAN WHAT'S BEST FOR CASSIE--WHICH IS W I'M ASKING YOU T REALLY THINK ABOU THIS, ABOUT WHAT S OUR DAUGHTER WHAT KIND OF LIFE SHE DESERVES...IF YOU'RE HONEST WITH YOURSELF--
I THINK YOU ALREADY KNOW THE ANSWER.
Here's the thing, though--
I don't.
I mean, am I just being selfish? Is Cassie better off someplace else?

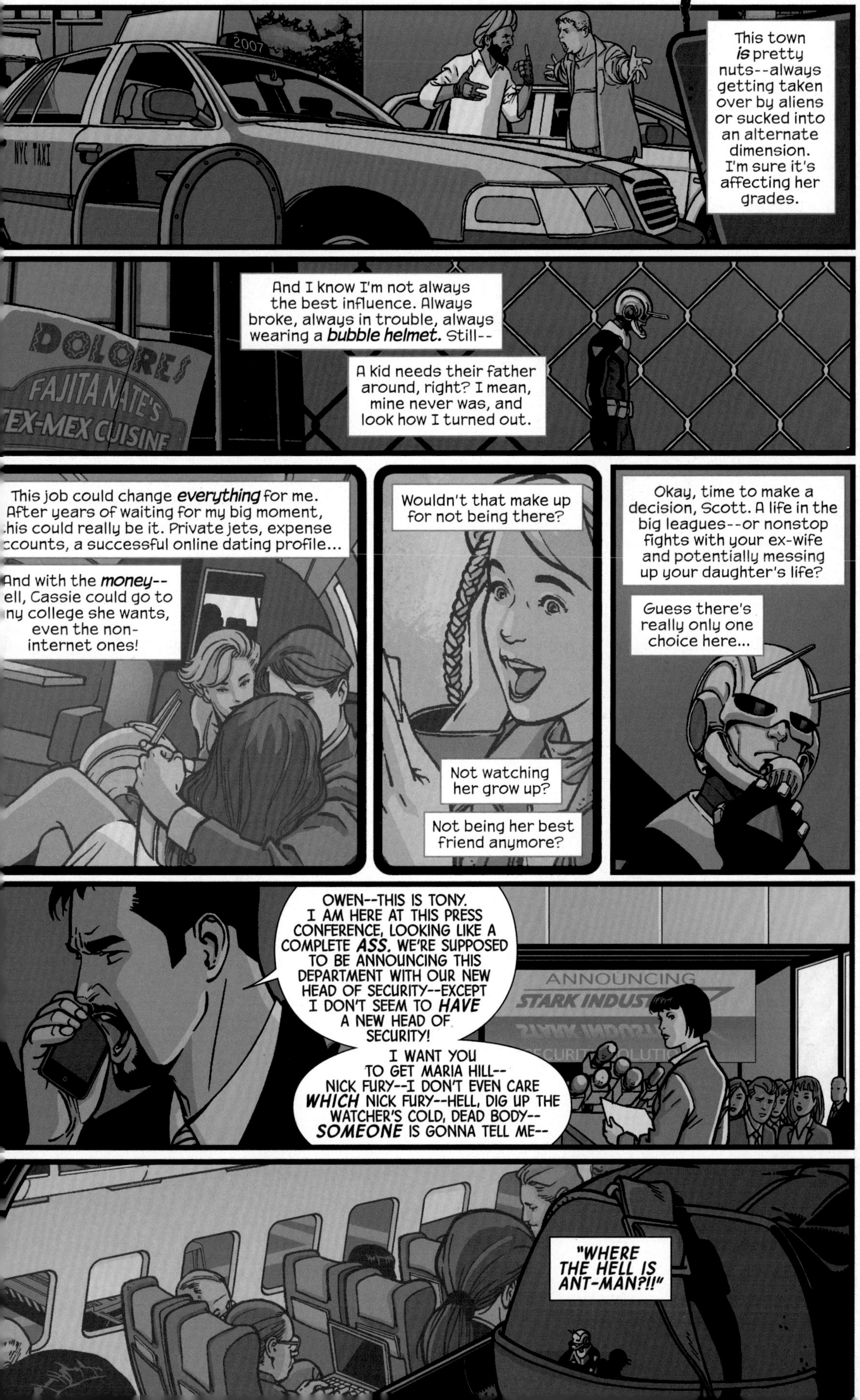
2007
NYC TAXI
This town *is* pretty nuts--always getting taken over by aliens or sucked into an alternate dimension. I'm sure it's affecting her grades.
DOLORES
FAJITA NATE'S
TEX-MEX CUISINE
And I know I'm not always the best influence. Always broke, always in trouble, always wearing a *bubble helmet.* Still--
A kid needs their father around, right? I mean, mine never was, and look how I turned out.
This job could change *everything* for me. After years of waiting for my big moment, his could really be it. Private jets, expense ccounts, a successful online dating profile...
And with the *money*-- ell, Cassie could go to ny college she wants, even the non-internet ones!
Wouldn't that make up for not being there?
Not watching her grow up?
Not being her best friend anymore?
Okay, time to make a decision, Scott. A life in the big leagues--or nonstop fights with your ex-wife and potentially messing up your daughter's life?
Guess there's really only one choice here...
OWEN--THIS IS TONY. I AM HERE AT THIS PRESS CONFERENCE, LOOKING LIKE A COMPLETE *ASS.* WE'RE SUPPOSED TO BE ANNOUNCING THIS DEPARTMENT WITH OUR NEW HEAD OF SECURITY--EXCEPT I DON'T SEEM TO *HAVE* A NEW HEAD OF SECURITY!
ANNOUNCING
I WANT YOU TO GET MARIA HILL-- NICK FURY--I DON'T EVEN CARE *WHICH* NICK FURY--HELL, DIG UP THE WATCHER'S COLD, DEAD BODY-- *SOMEONE* IS GONNA TELL ME--
"WHERE THE HELL IS ANT-MAN?!!"

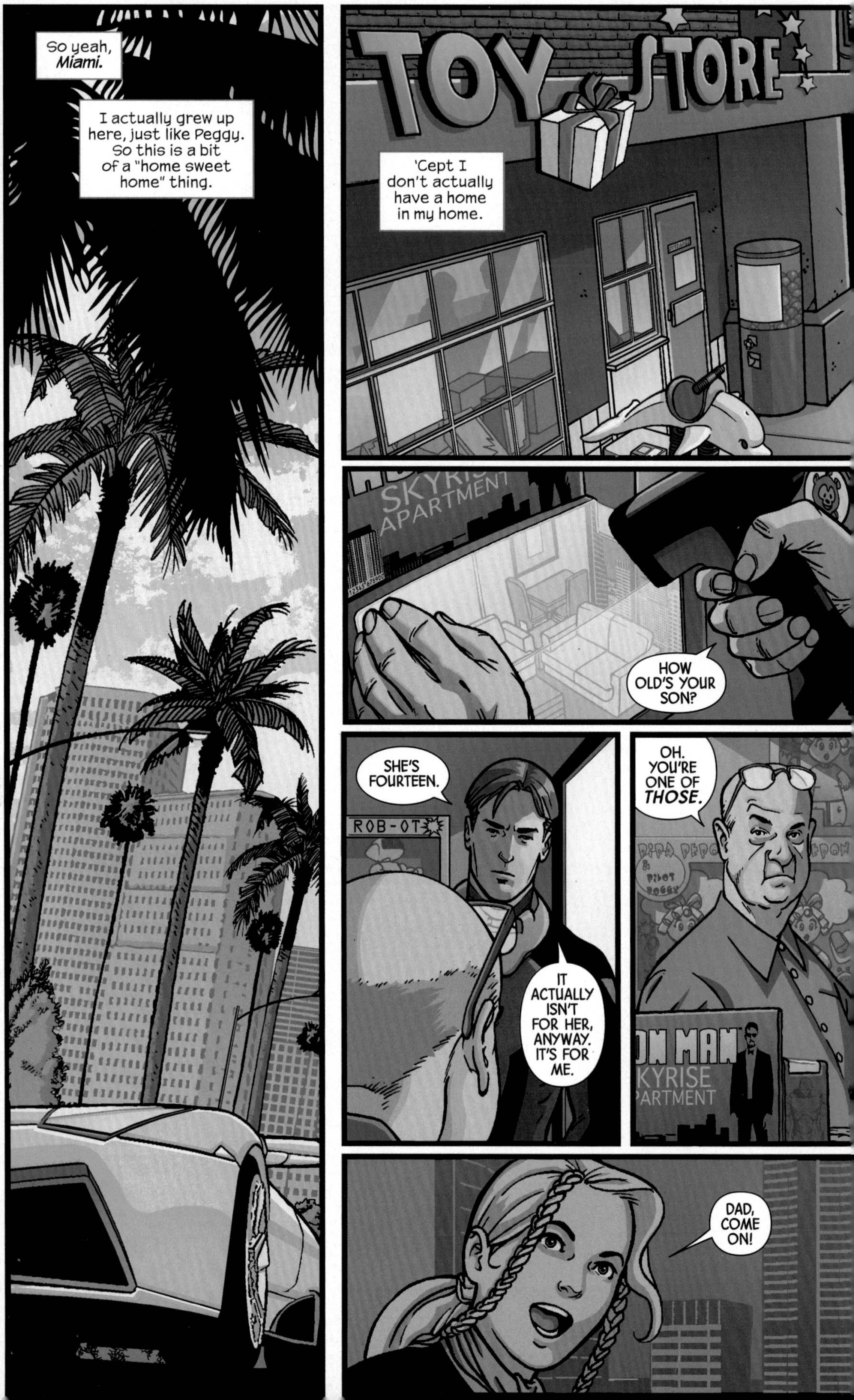
So yeah, *Miami.*
I actually grew up here, just like Peggy. So this is a bit of a "home sweet home" thing.
TOY STORE
'Cept I don't actually have a home in my home.
SKYRISE APARTMENT
HOW OLD'S YOUR SON?
SHE'S FOURTEEN.
ROB-OT
IT ACTUALLY ISN'T FOR HER, ANYWAY. IT'S FOR ME.
OH. YOU'RE ONE OF *THOSE.*
ON MAN KYRISE PARTMENT
DAD, COME ON!

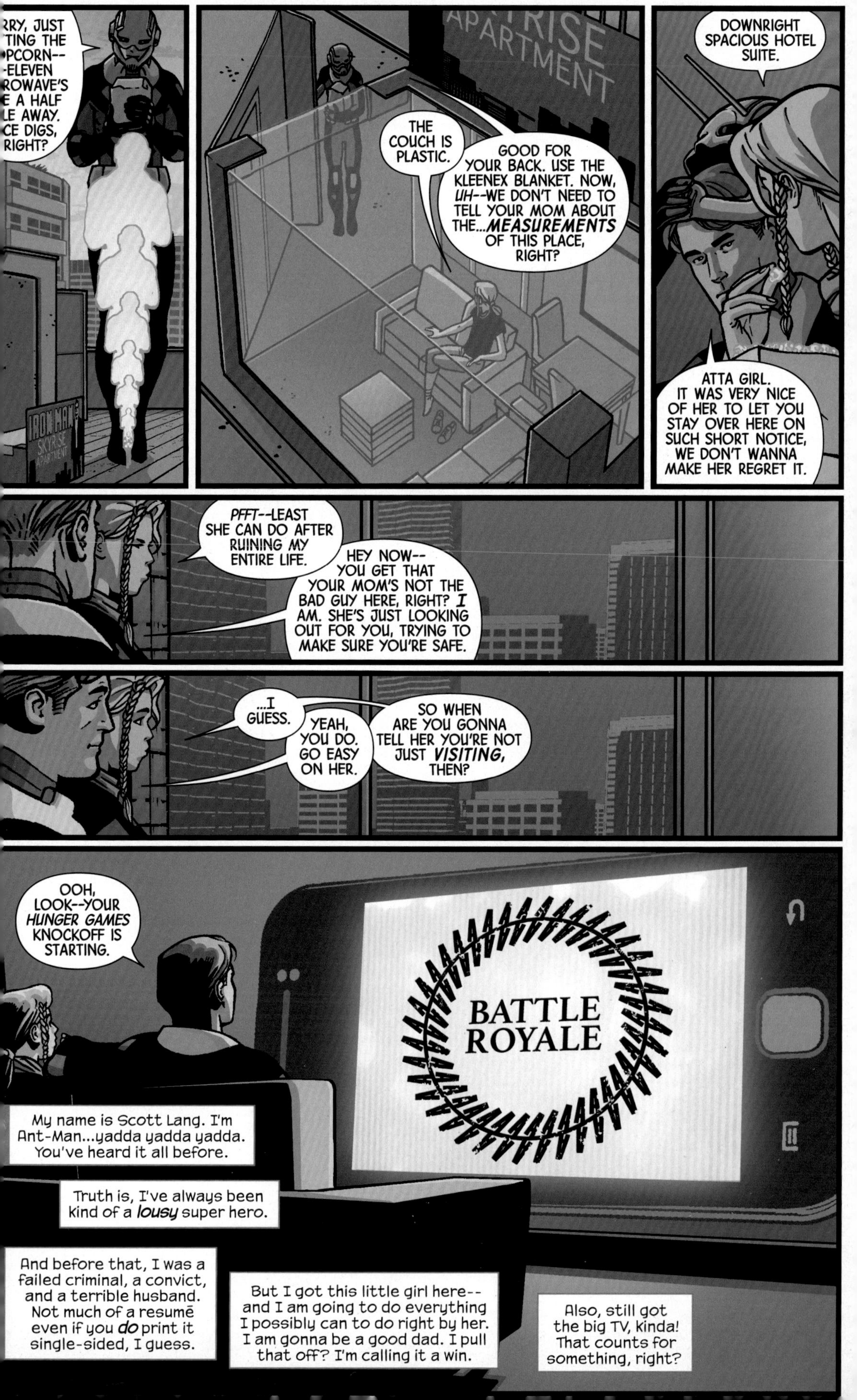

RRY, JUST
TING THE
PCORN--
-ELEVEN
ROWAVE'S
E A HALF
LE AWAY.
CE DIGS,
RIGHT?
IRON MAN SKYRISE APARTMENT
RISE APARTMENT
THE COUCH IS PLASTIC.
GOOD FOR YOUR BACK. USE THE KLEENEX BLANKET. NOW, UH--WE DON'T NEED TO TELL YOUR MOM ABOUT THE...MEASUREMENTS OF THIS PLACE, RIGHT?
DOWNRIGHT SPACIOUS HOTEL SUITE.
ATTA GIRL. IT WAS VERY NICE OF HER TO LET YOU STAY OVER HERE ON SUCH SHORT NOTICE, WE DON'T WANNA MAKE HER REGRET IT.
PFFT--LEAST SHE CAN DO AFTER RUINING MY ENTIRE LIFE.
HEY NOW--YOU GET THAT YOUR MOM'S NOT THE BAD GUY HERE, RIGHT? I AM. SHE'S JUST LOOKING OUT FOR YOU, TRYING TO MAKE SURE YOU'RE SAFE.
...I GUESS.
YEAH, YOU DO. GO EASY ON HER.
SO WHEN ARE YOU GONNA TELL HER YOU'RE NOT JUST VISITING, THEN?
OOH, LOOK--YOUR HUNGER GAMES KNOCKOFF IS STARTING.
BATTLE ROYALE
My name is Scott Lang. I'm Ant-Man...yadda yadda yadda. You've heard it all before.
Truth is, I've always been kind of a lousy super hero.
And before that, I was a failed criminal, a convict, and a terrible husband. Not much of a resumé even if you do print it single-sided, I guess.
But I got this little girl here--and I am going to do everything I possibly can to do right by her. I am gonna be a good dad. I pull that off? I'm calling it a win.
Also, still got the big TV, kinda! That counts for something, right?

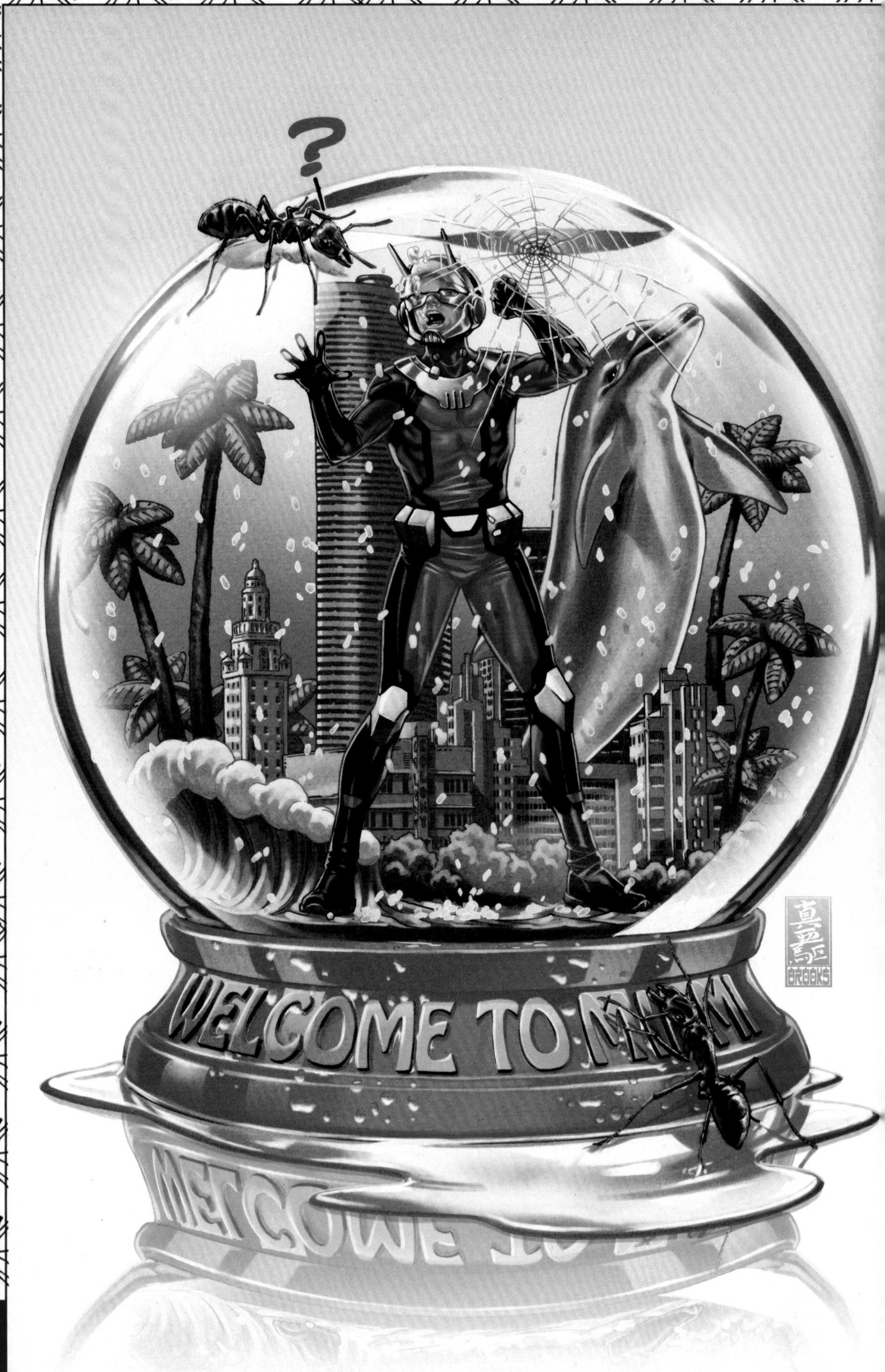
?
WELCOME TO
BROOKS

#2

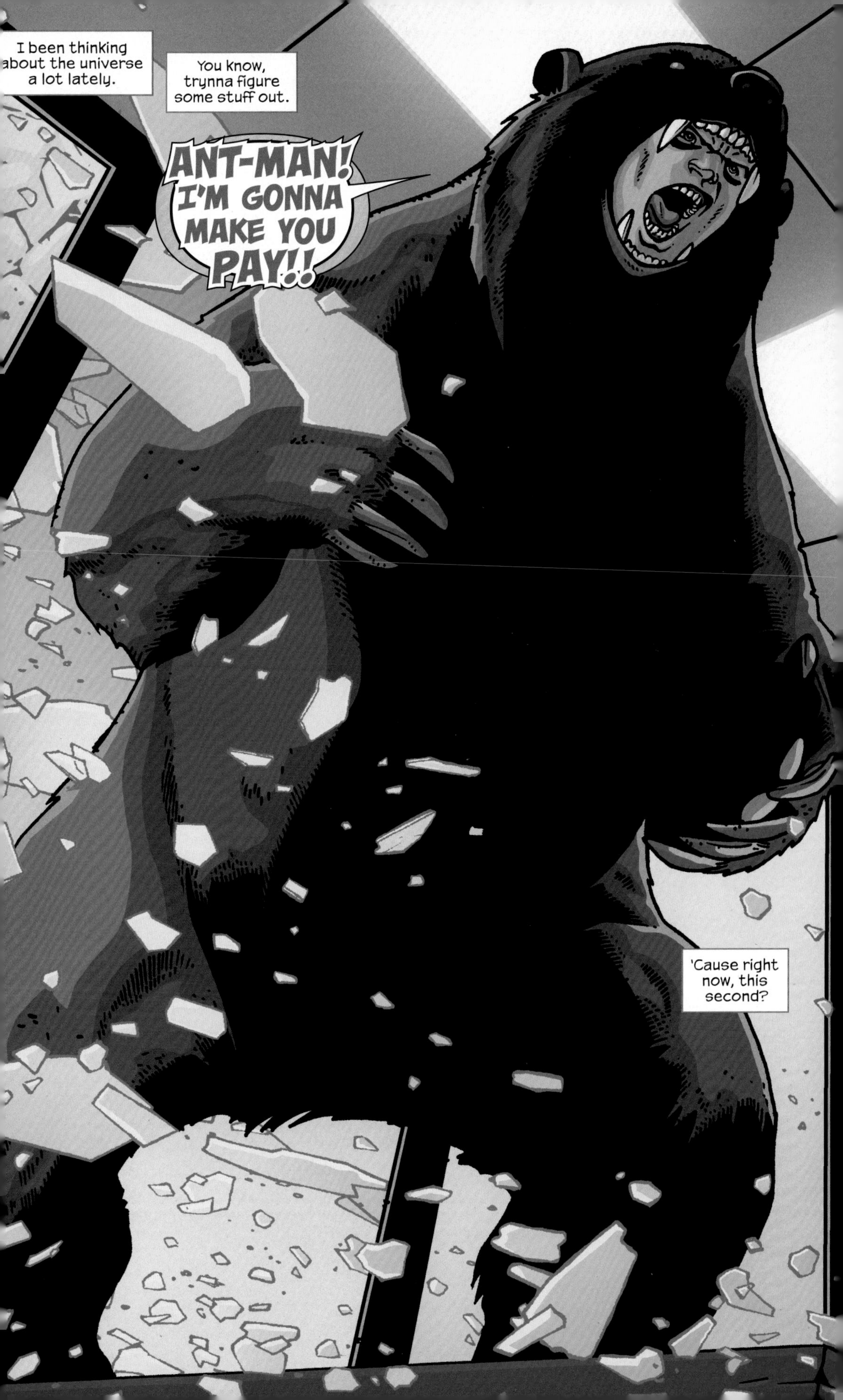
I been thinking about the universe a lot lately.
You know, trynna figure some stuff out.
ANT-MAN! I'M GONNA MAKE YOU PAY!!
'Cause right now, this second?

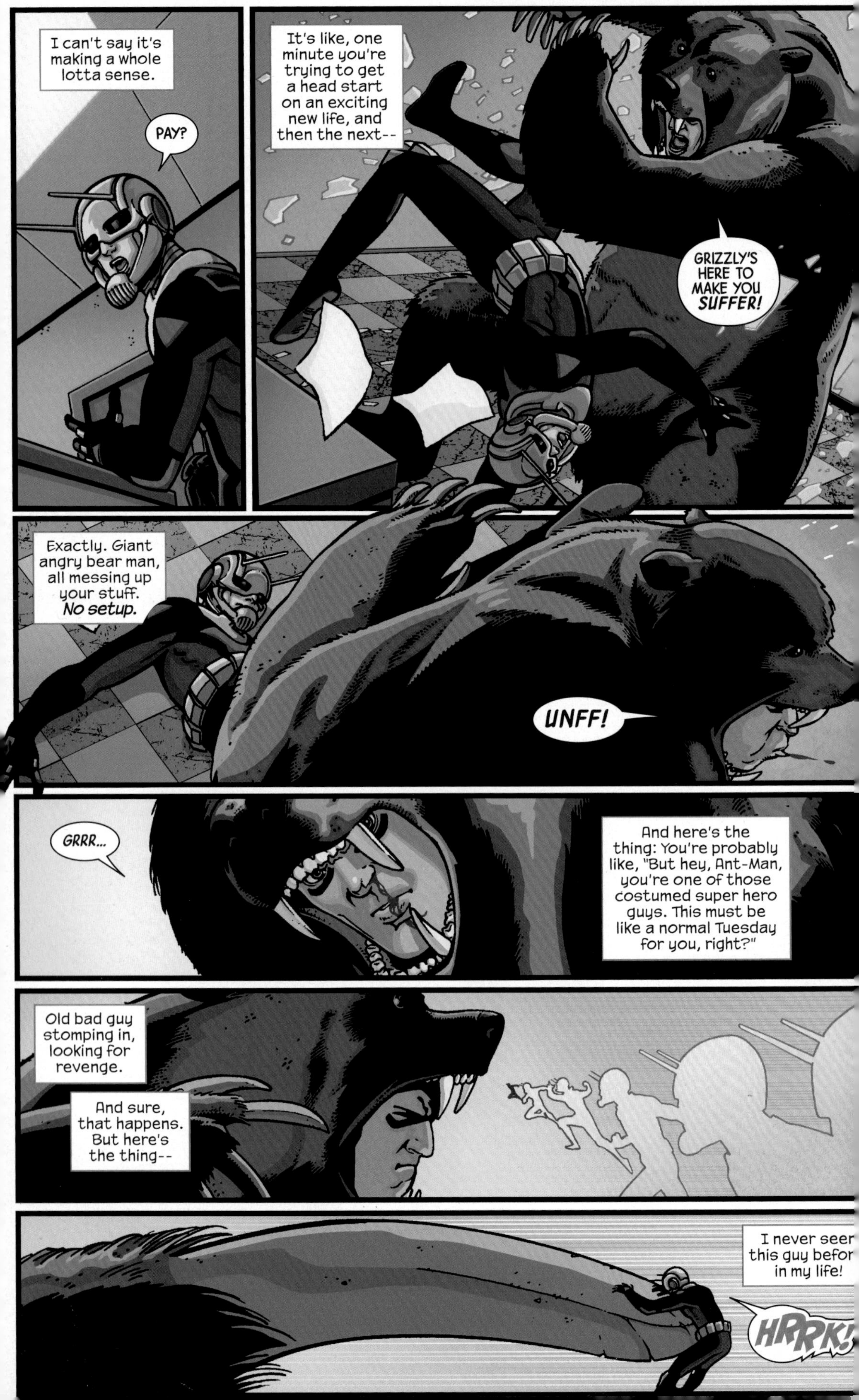
I can't say it's making a whole lotta sense.
PAY?
It's like, one minute you're trying to get a head start on an exciting new life, and then the next--
GRIZZLY'S HERE TO MAKE YOU SUFFER!
Exactly. Giant angry bear man, all messing up your stuff. No setup.
UNFF!
GRRR...
And here's the thing: You're probably like, "But hey, Ant-Man, you're one of those costumed super hero guys. This must be like a normal Tuesday for you, right?"
Old bad guy stomping in, looking for revenge.
And sure, that happens. But here's the thing--
I never seen this guy before in my life!
HRRK!

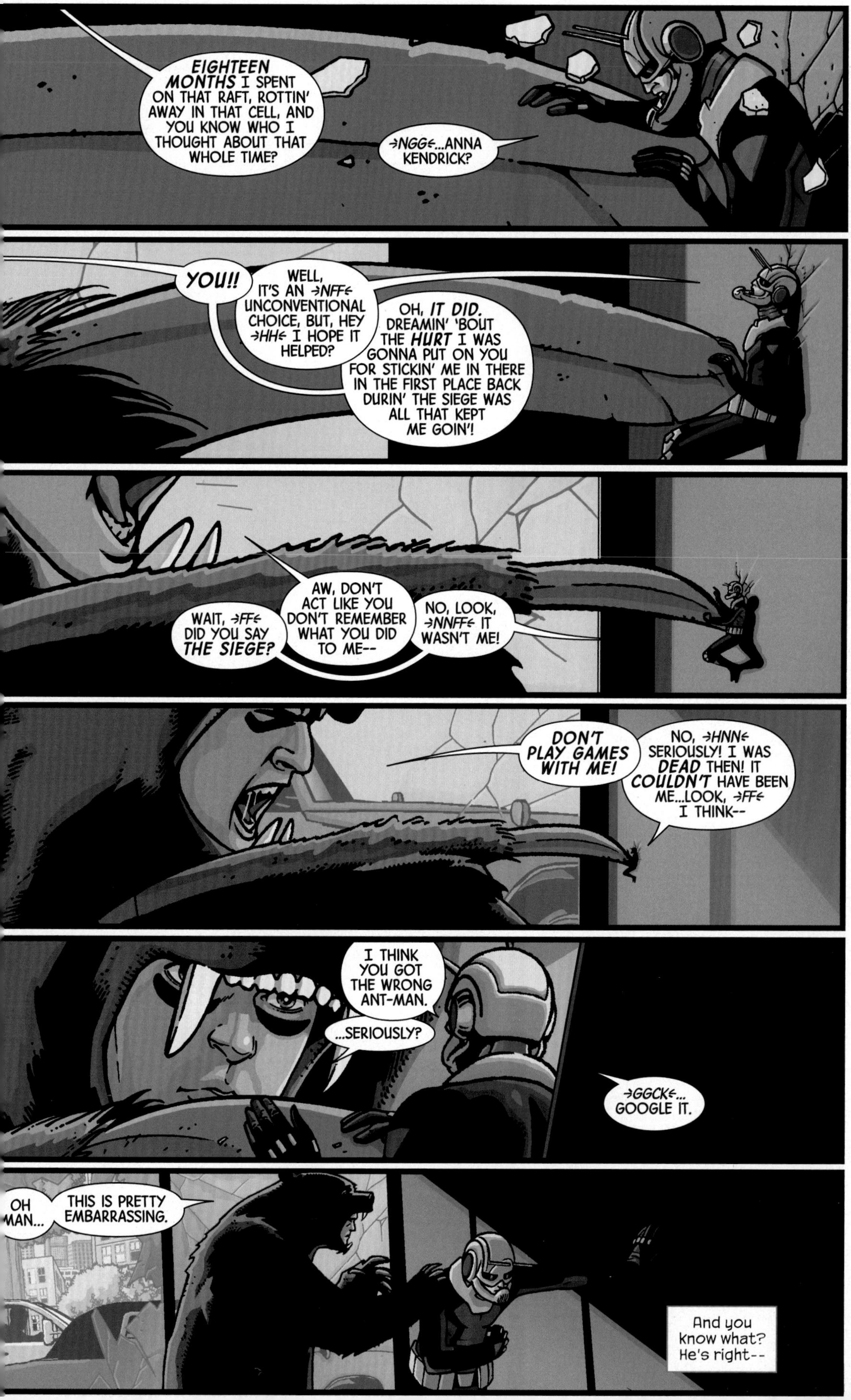
EIGHTEEN MONTHS I SPENT ON THAT RAFT, ROTTIN' AWAY IN THAT CELL, AND YOU KNOW WHO I THOUGHT ABOUT THAT WHOLE TIME?
→NGG←...ANNA KENDRICK?
YOU!!
WELL, IT'S AN →NFF← UNCONVENTIONAL CHOICE, BUT, HEY →HH← I HOPE IT HELPED?
OH, IT DID. DREAMIN' 'BOUT THE HURT I WAS GONNA PUT ON YOU FOR STICKIN' ME IN THERE IN THE FIRST PLACE BACK DURIN' THE SIEGE WAS ALL THAT KEPT ME GOIN'!
WAIT, →FF← DID YOU SAY THE SIEGE?
AW, DON'T ACT LIKE YOU DON'T REMEMBER WHAT YOU DID TO ME--
NO, LOOK, →NNFF← IT WASN'T ME!
DON'T PLAY GAMES WITH ME!
NO, →HNN← SERIOUSLY! I WAS DEAD THEN! IT COULDN'T HAVE BEEN ME...LOOK, →FF← I THINK--
I THINK YOU GOT THE WRONG ANT-MAN.
...SERIOUSLY?
→GGCK←... GOOGLE IT.
OH MAN...
THIS IS PRETTY EMBARRASSING.
And you know what? He's right--

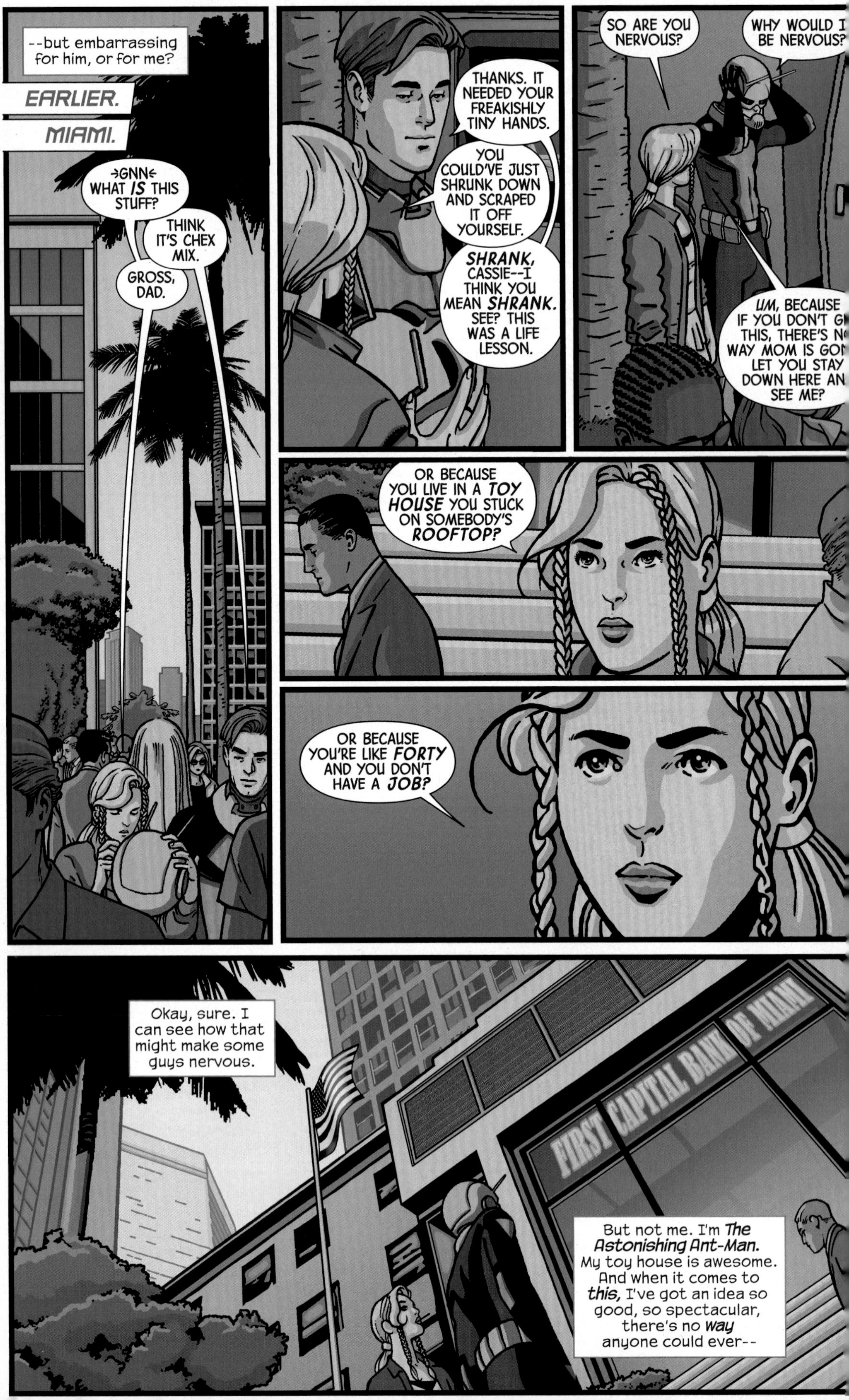
--but embarrassing for him, or for me?
EARLIER.
MIAMI.
>GNN< WHAT IS THIS STUFF?
THINK IT'S CHEX MIX.
GROSS, DAD.
THANKS. IT NEEDED YOUR FREAKISHLY TINY HANDS.
YOU COULD'VE JUST SHRUNK DOWN AND SCRAPED IT OFF YOURSELF.
SHRANK, CASSIE--I THINK YOU MEAN SHRANK. SEE? THIS WAS A LIFE LESSON.
SO ARE YOU NERVOUS?
WHY WOULD I BE NERVOUS?
UM, BECAUSE IF YOU DON'T G THIS, THERE'S N WAY MOM IS GO LET YOU STAY DOWN HERE AN SEE ME?
OR BECAUSE YOU LIVE IN A TOY HOUSE YOU STUCK ON SOMEBODY'S ROOFTOP?
OR BECAUSE YOU'RE LIKE FORTY AND YOU DON'T HAVE A JOB?
Okay, sure. I can see how that might make some guys nervous.
FIRST CAPITAL BANK OF MIAMI
But not me. I'm The Astonishing Ant-Man. My toy house is awesome. And when it comes to this, I've got an idea so good, so spectacular, there's no way anyone could ever--

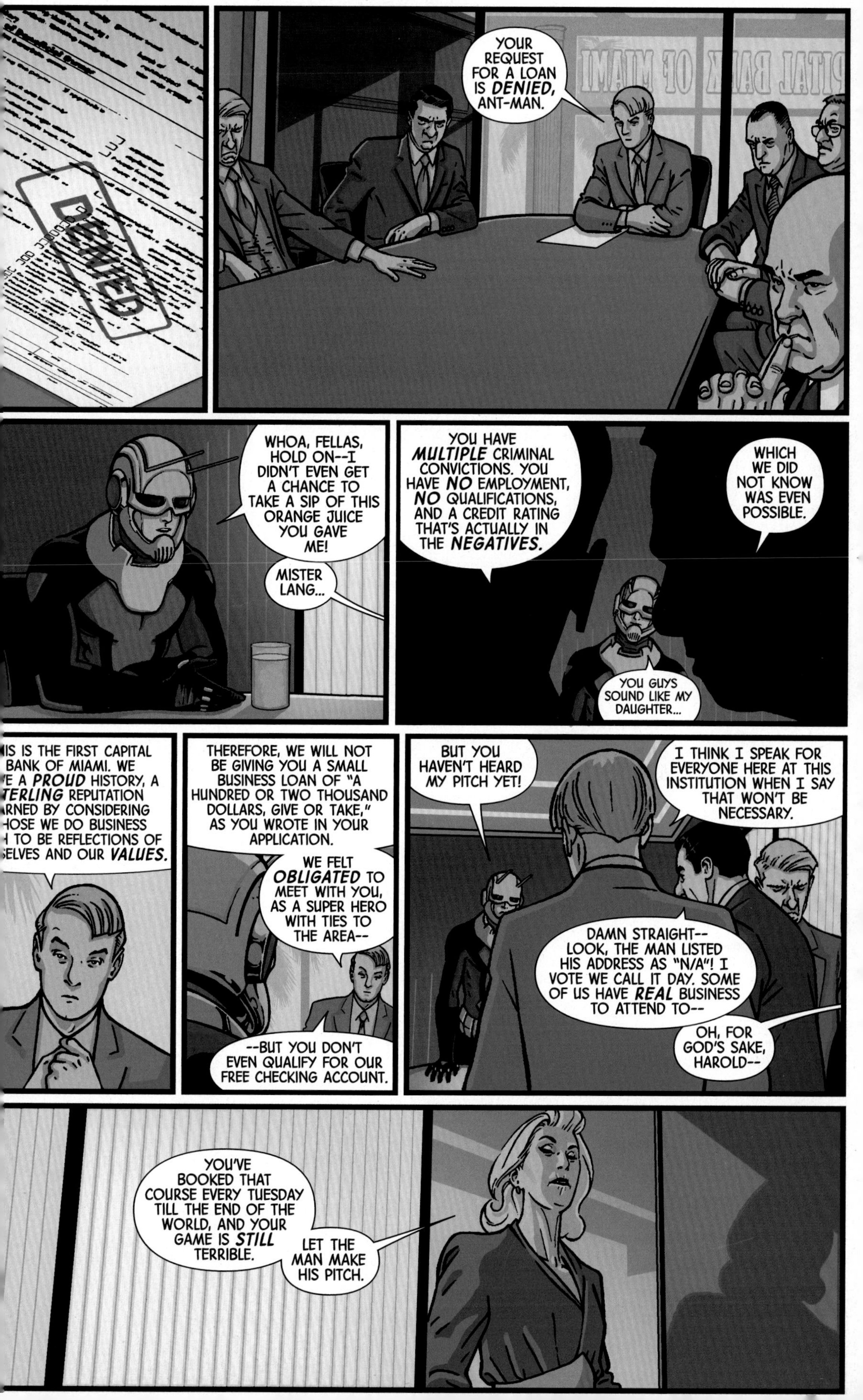
DENIED
CAPITAL BANK OF MIAMI
YOUR REQUEST FOR A LOAN IS DENIED, ANT-MAN.
WHOA, FELLAS, HOLD ON--I DIDN'T EVEN GET A CHANCE TO TAKE A SIP OF THIS ORANGE JUICE YOU GAVE ME!
MISTER LANG...
YOU HAVE MULTIPLE CRIMINAL CONVICTIONS. YOU HAVE NO EMPLOYMENT, NO QUALIFICATIONS, AND A CREDIT RATING THAT'S ACTUALLY IN THE NEGATIVES.
WHICH WE DID NOT KNOW WAS EVEN POSSIBLE.
YOU GUYS SOUND LIKE MY DAUGHTER...
IS IS THE FIRST CAPITAL BANK OF MIAMI. WE E A PROUD HISTORY, A TERLING REPUTATION RNED BY CONSIDERING HOSE WE DO BUSINESS H TO BE REFLECTIONS OF SELVES AND OUR VALUES.
THEREFORE, WE WILL NOT BE GIVING YOU A SMALL BUSINESS LOAN OF "A HUNDRED OR TWO THOUSAND DOLLARS, GIVE OR TAKE," AS YOU WROTE IN YOUR APPLICATION.
WE FELT OBLIGATED TO MEET WITH YOU, AS A SUPER HERO WITH TIES TO THE AREA--
--BUT YOU DON'T EVEN QUALIFY FOR OUR FREE CHECKING ACCOUNT.
BUT YOU HAVEN'T HEARD MY PITCH YET!
I THINK I SPEAK FOR EVERYONE HERE AT THIS INSTITUTION WHEN I SAY THAT WON'T BE NECESSARY.
DAMN STRAIGHT-- LOOK, THE MAN LISTED HIS ADDRESS AS "N/A"! I VOTE WE CALL IT DAY. SOME OF US HAVE REAL BUSINESS TO ATTEND TO--
OH, FOR GOD'S SAKE, HAROLD--
YOU'VE BOOKED THAT COURSE EVERY TUESDAY TILL THE END OF THE WORLD, AND YOUR GAME IS STILL TERRIBLE.
LET THE MAN MAKE HIS PITCH.

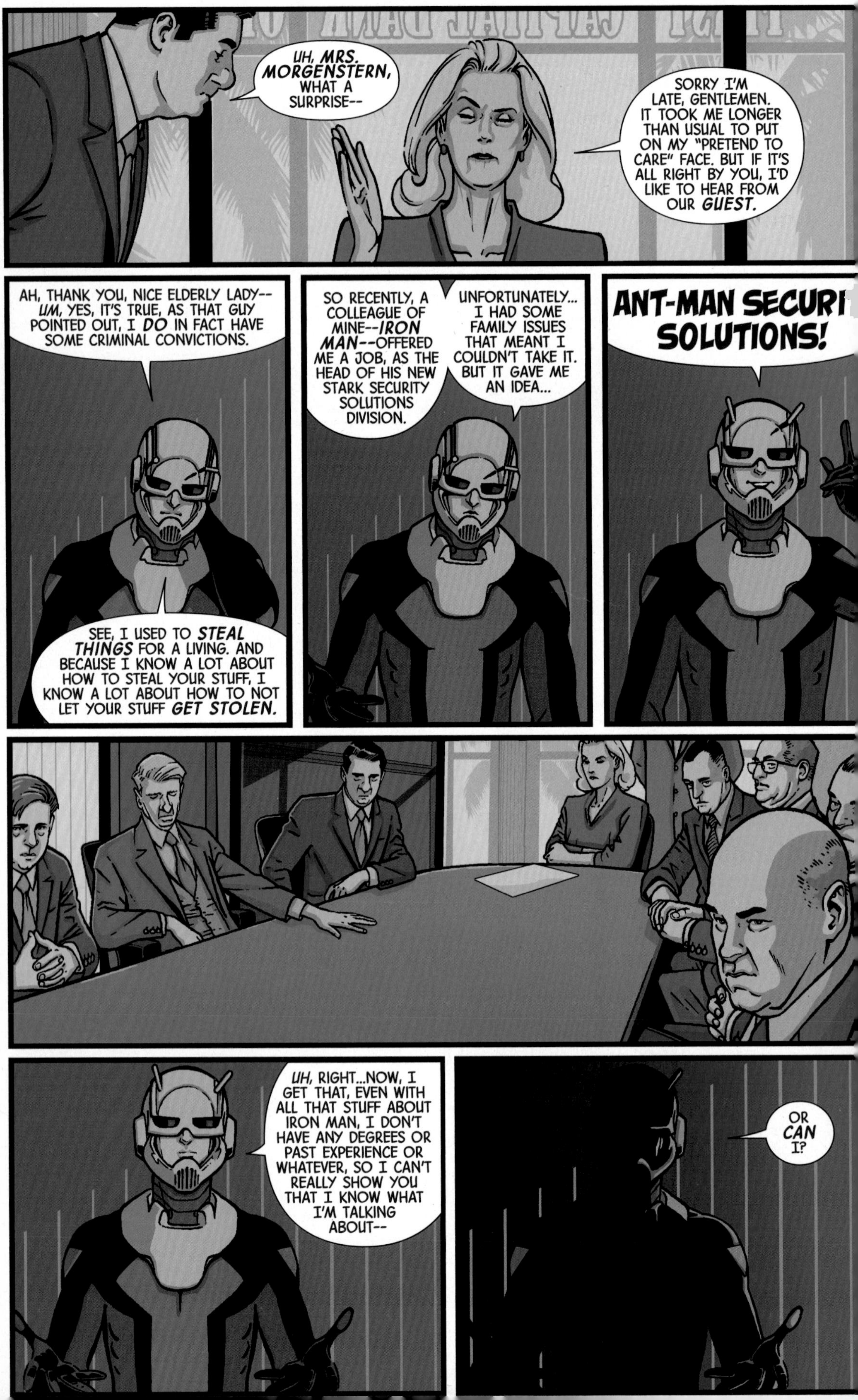
UH, MRS. MORGENSTERN, WHAT A SURPRISE--
SORRY I'M LATE, GENTLEMEN. IT TOOK ME LONGER THAN USUAL TO PUT ON MY "PRETEND TO CARE" FACE. BUT IF IT'S ALL RIGHT BY YOU, I'D LIKE TO HEAR FROM OUR GUEST.
AH, THANK YOU, NICE ELDERLY LADY-- UM, YES, IT'S TRUE, AS THAT GUY POINTED OUT, I DO IN FACT HAVE SOME CRIMINAL CONVICTIONS.
SEE, I USED TO STEAL THINGS FOR A LIVING. AND BECAUSE I KNOW A LOT ABOUT HOW TO STEAL YOUR STUFF, I KNOW A LOT ABOUT HOW TO NOT LET YOUR STUFF GET STOLEN.
SO RECENTLY, A COLLEAGUE OF MINE--IRON MAN--OFFERED ME A JOB, AS THE HEAD OF HIS NEW STARK SECURITY SOLUTIONS DIVISION.
UNFORTUNATELY... I HAD SOME FAMILY ISSUES THAT MEANT I COULDN'T TAKE IT. BUT IT GAVE ME AN IDEA...
ANT-MAN SECURI SOLUTIONS!
UH, RIGHT...NOW, I GET THAT, EVEN WITH ALL THAT STUFF ABOUT IRON MAN, I DON'T HAVE ANY DEGREES OR PAST EXPERIENCE OR WHATEVER, SO I CAN'T REALLY SHOW YOU THAT I KNOW WHAT I'M TALKING ABOUT--
OR CAN I?

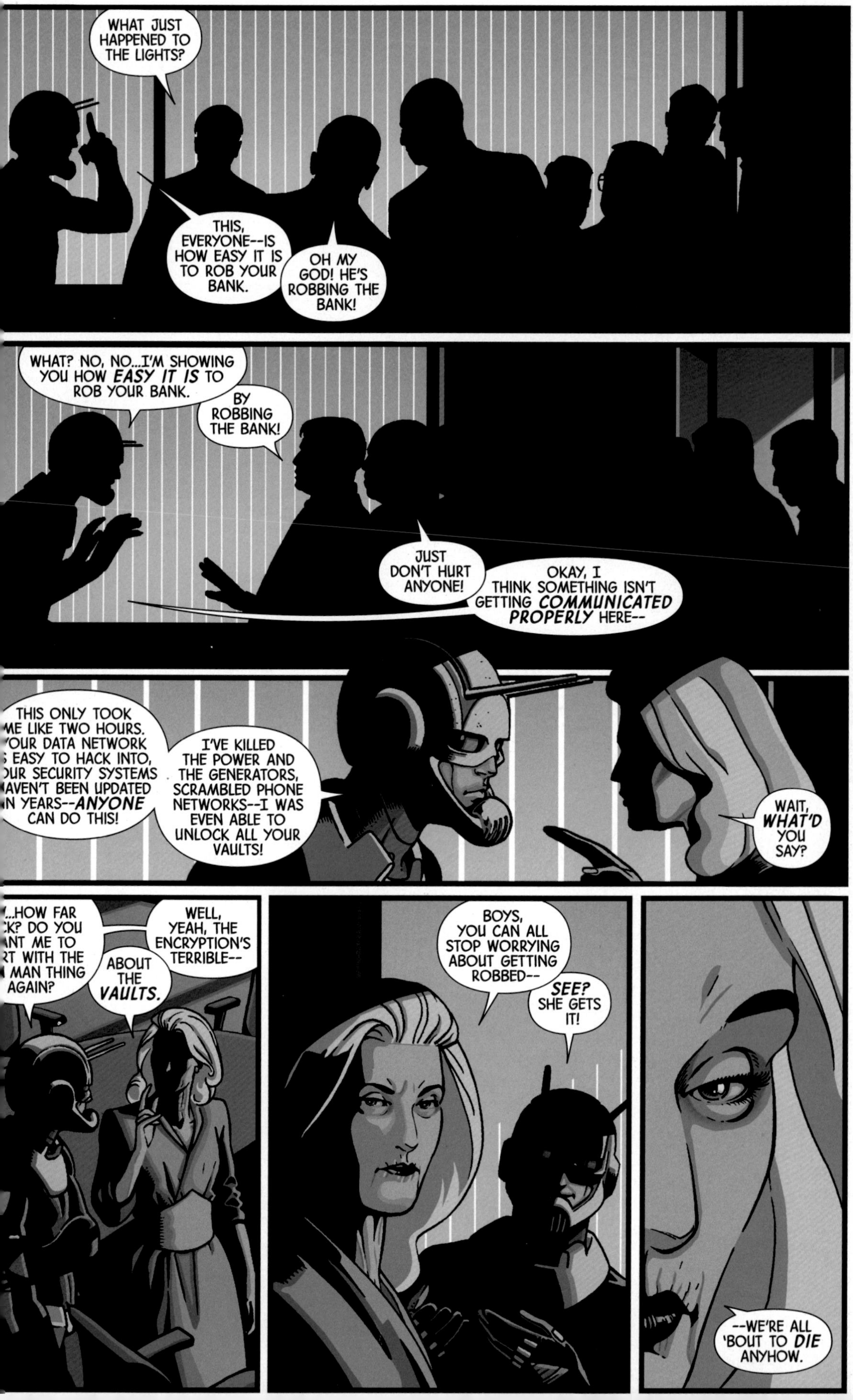
WHAT JUST HAPPENED TO THE LIGHTS?
THIS, EVERYONE--IS HOW EASY IT IS TO ROB YOUR BANK.
OH MY GOD! HE'S ROBBING THE BANK!
WHAT? NO, NO...I'M SHOWING YOU HOW *EASY IT IS* TO ROB YOUR BANK.
BY ROBBING THE BANK!
JUST DON'T HURT ANYONE!
OKAY, I THINK SOMETHING ISN'T GETTING *COMMUNICATED PROPERLY* HERE--
THIS ONLY TOOK ME LIKE TWO HOURS. OUR DATA NETWORK S EASY TO HACK INTO, UR SECURITY SYSTEMS AVEN'T BEEN UPDATED N YEARS--*ANYONE* CAN DO THIS!
I'VE KILLED THE POWER AND THE GENERATORS, SCRAMBLED PHONE NETWORKS--I WAS EVEN ABLE TO UNLOCK ALL YOUR VAULTS!
WAIT, *WHAT'D* YOU SAY?
WELL, YEAH, THE ENCRYPTION'S TERRIBLE--
ABOUT THE *VAULTS.*
...HOW FAR K? DO YOU NT ME TO RT WITH THE MAN THING AGAIN?
BOYS, YOU CAN ALL STOP WORRYING ABOUT GETTING ROBBED--
SEE? SHE GETS IT!
--WE'RE ALL 'BOUT TO *DIE* ANYHOW.

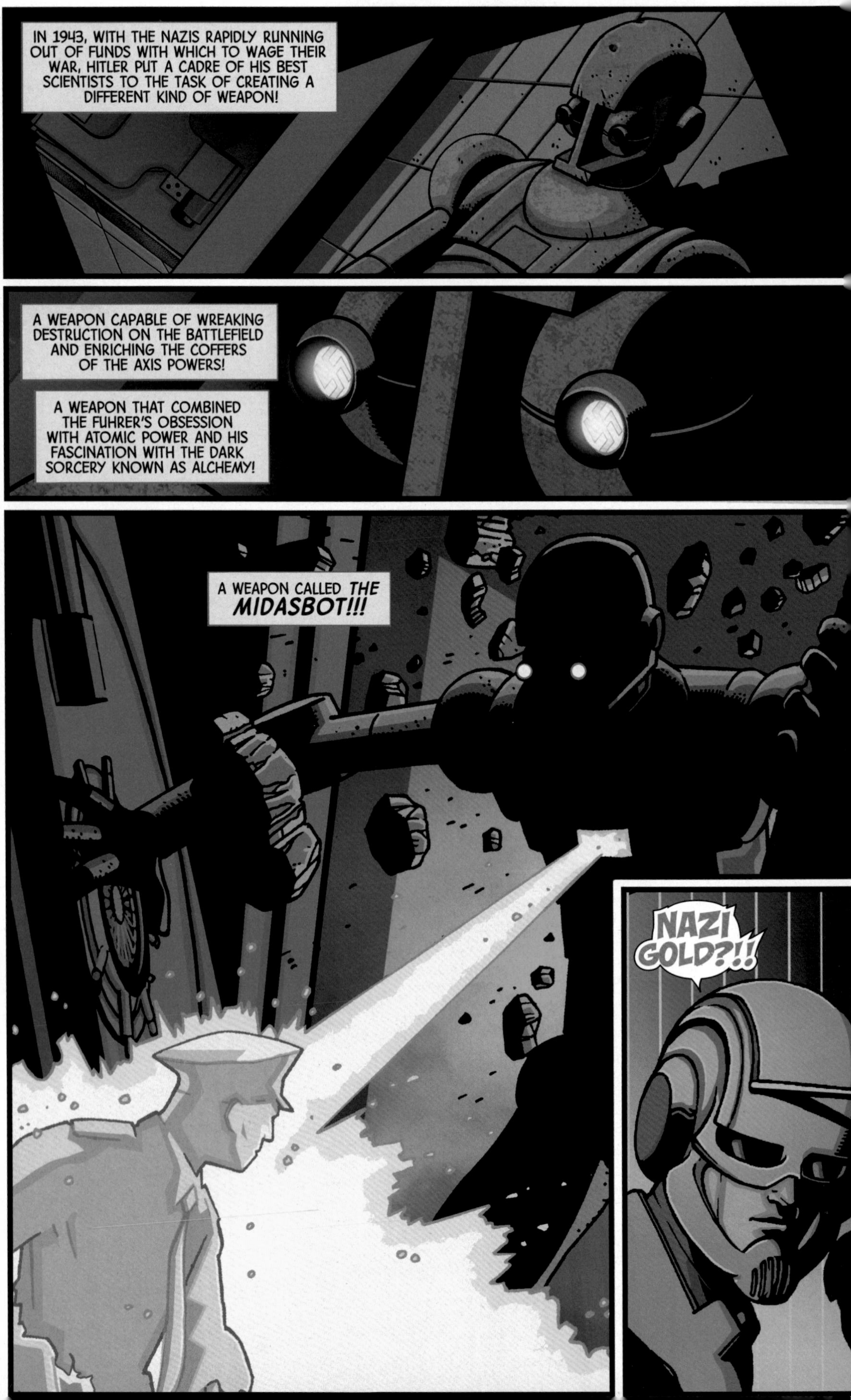
IN 1943, WITH THE NAZIS RAPIDLY RUNNING OUT OF FUNDS WITH WHICH TO WAGE THEIR WAR, HITLER PUT A CADRE OF HIS BEST SCIENTISTS TO THE TASK OF CREATING A DIFFERENT KIND OF WEAPON!
A WEAPON CAPABLE OF WREAKING DESTRUCTION ON THE BATTLEFIELD AND ENRICHING THE COFFERS OF THE AXIS POWERS!
A WEAPON THAT COMBINED THE FUHRER'S OBSESSION WITH ATOMIC POWER AND HIS FASCINATION WITH THE DARK SORCERY KNOWN AS ALCHEMY!
A WEAPON CALLED THE MIDASBOT!!!
NAZI GOLD?!!

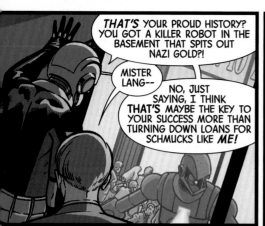

THAT'S YOUR PROUD HISTORY? YOU GOT A KILLER ROBOT IN THE BASEMENT THAT SPITS OUT NAZI GOLD?!

MISTER LANG--

NO, JUST SAYING, I THINK THAT'S MAYBE THE KEY TO YOUR SUCCESS MORE THAN TURNING DOWN LOANS FOR SCHMUCKS LIKE ME!

WAIT-- WHAT ARE YOU DOING?!!

WHAT DOES IT LOOK LIKE? HIDING!

BUT AREN'T YOU A SUPER HERO?! ISN'T DEALING WITH THIS SORT OF THING SUPPOSED TO BE YOUR JOB?!!

WELL, NO, SEE-- IT ISN'T ACTUALLY A JOB. IT'S MORE LIKE A VOLUNTEER THING. I DON'T HAVE A REAL JOB. I HAD AN IDEA FOR ONE--MY OWN BUSINESS, I MEAN--BUT I HAVEN'T BEEN ABLE TO SECURE THE FINANCING.

NOW, IF YOU GUYS WERE TO RECONSIDER ON THAT FRONT...

CELEBRITY ENDORSEMENT

NOT REALLY A CELEBRITY IS HE

LEAST HE'S NOT A MUTANT

GOD YOU'RE SO RACIST HAROLD

OKAY, WE'LL AGREE TO NOT PRESS CHARGES AGAINST YOU FOR LETTING THAT THING OUT.

OR FOR TRYING TO ROB OUR BANK!

I WASN'T TRYING TO--

HELP!!! SOMEBODY HELP ME!!!

→SIGH← FINE.

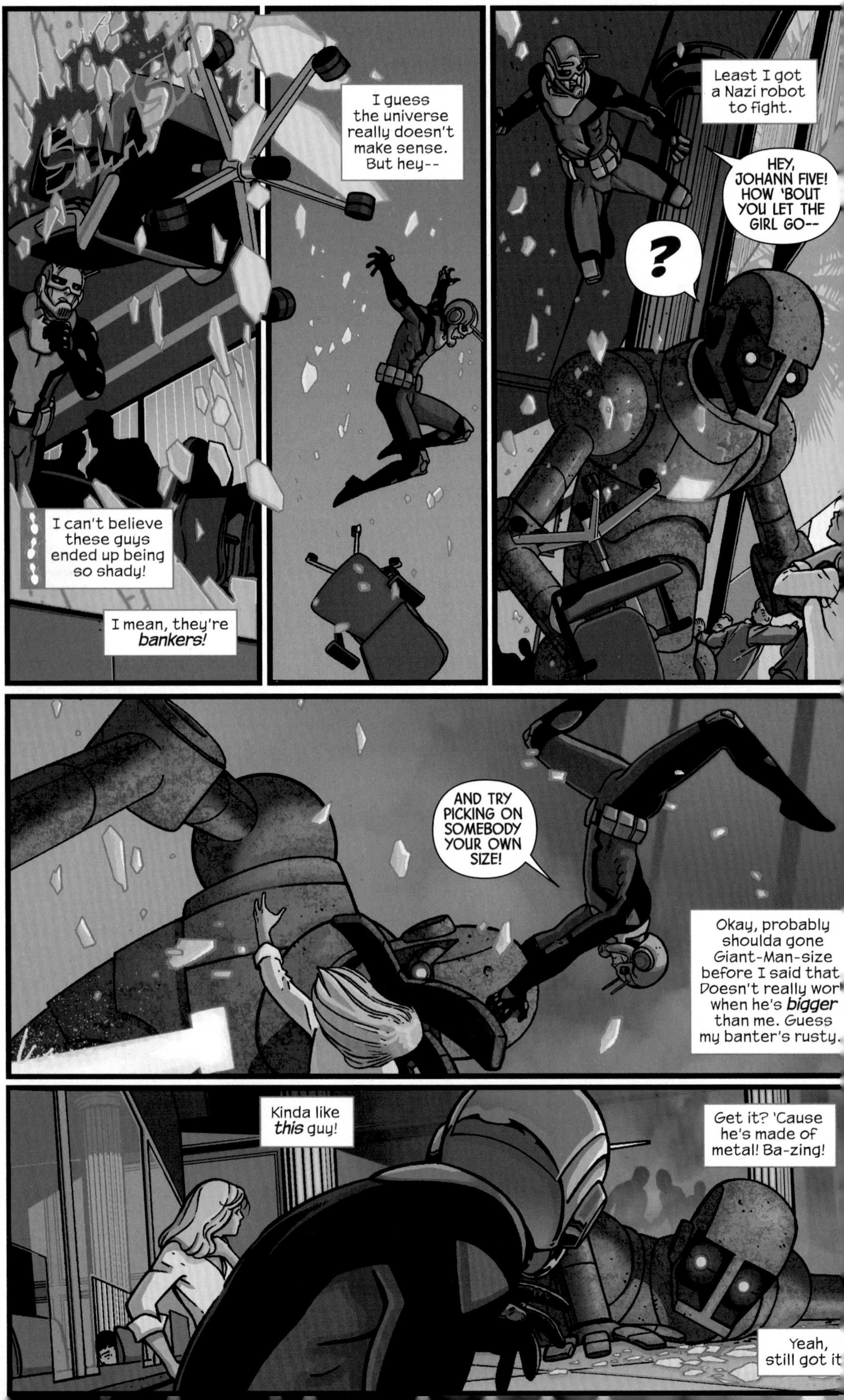
SMASH
I can't believe these guys ended up being so shady!
I mean, they're *bankers!*
I guess the universe really doesn't make sense. But hey--
Least I got a Nazi robot to fight.
HEY, JOHANN FIVE! HOW 'BOUT YOU LET THE GIRL GO--
?
AND TRY PICKING ON SOMEBODY YOUR OWN SIZE!
Okay, probably shoulda gone Giant-Man-size before I said that. Doesn't really wor when he's *bigger* than me. Guess my banter's rusty.
Kinda like *this* guy!
Get it? 'Cause he's made of metal! Ba-zing!
Yeah, still got it

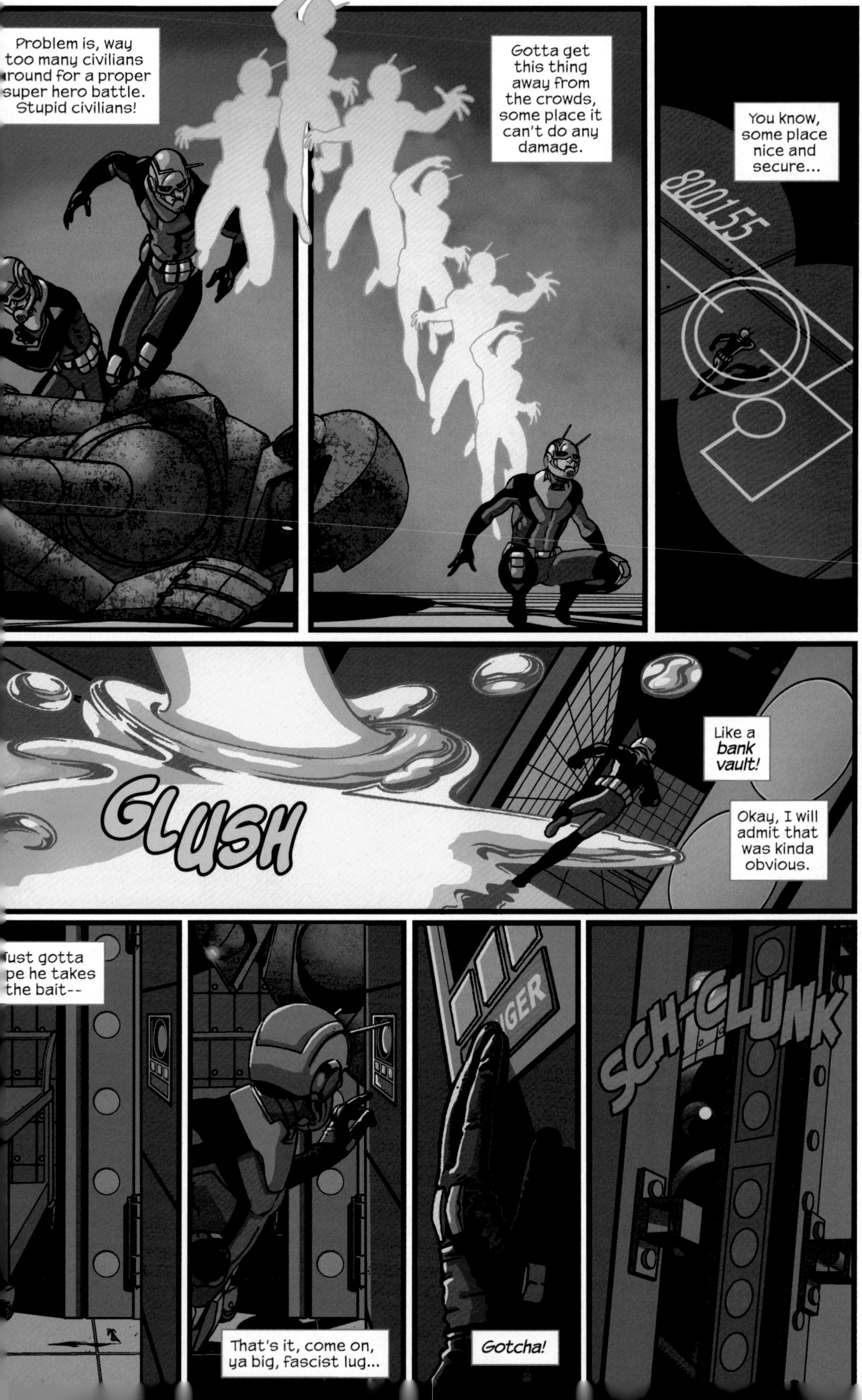

Problem is, way too many civilians around for a proper super hero battle. Stupid civilians!
Gotta get this thing away from the crowds, some place it can't do any damage.
You know, some place nice and secure...
800155
GLUSH
Like a *bank vault!*
Okay, I will admit that was kinda obvious.
Just gotta hope he takes the bait--
That's it, come on, ya big, fascist lug...
Gotcha!
SCHICLUNK

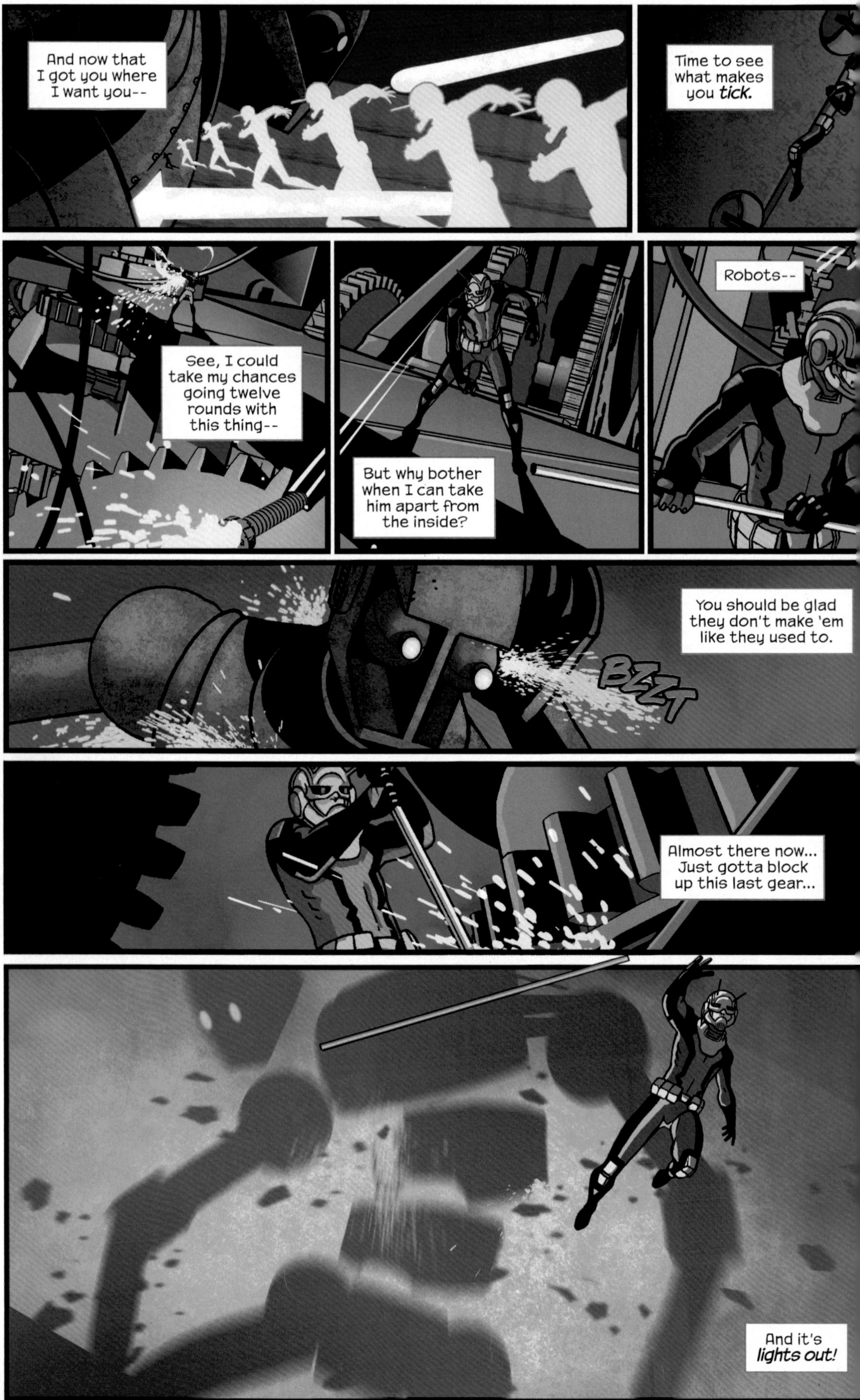

And now that I got you where I want you--
Time to see what makes you *tick.*
See, I could take my chances going twelve rounds with this thing--
But why bother when I can take him apart from the inside?
Robots--
You should be glad they don't make 'em like they used to.
BZZT
Almost there now... Just gotta block up this last gear...
And it's *lights out!*

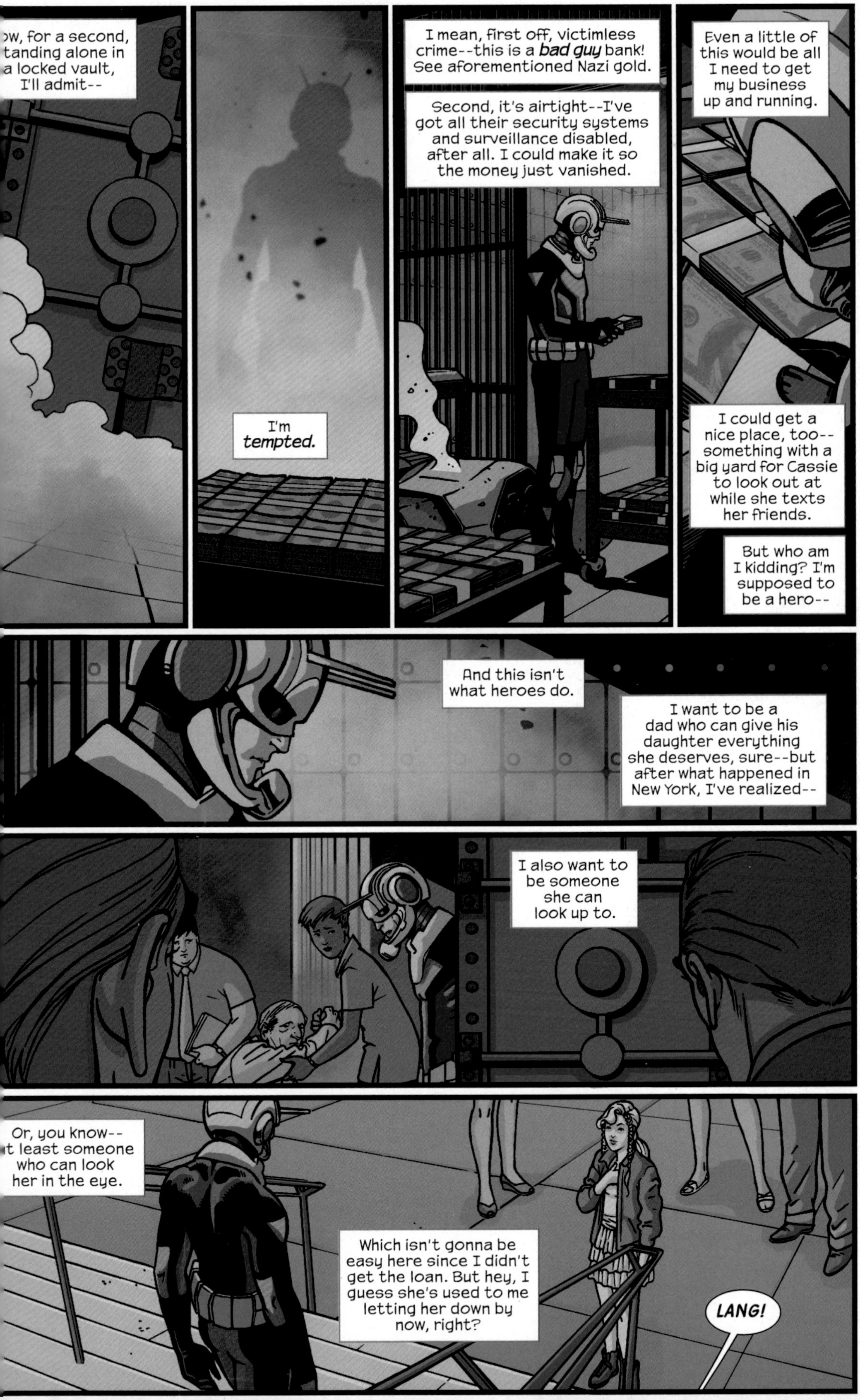
w, for a second, tanding alone in a locked vault, I'll admit--
I'm *tempted.*
I mean, first off, victimless crime--this is a ***bad guy*** bank! See aforementioned Nazi gold.
Second, it's airtight--I've got all their security systems and surveillance disabled, after all. I could make it so the money just vanished.
Even a little of this would be all I need to get my business up and running.
I could get a nice place, too--something with a big yard for Cassie to look out at while she texts her friends.
But who am I kidding? I'm supposed to be a hero--
And this isn't what heroes do.
I want to be a dad who can give his daughter everything she deserves, sure--but after what happened in New York, I've realized--
I also want to be someone she can look up to.
Or, you know--t least someone who can look her in the eye.
Which isn't gonna be easy here since I didn't get the loan. But hey, I guess she's used to me letting her down by now, right?
LANG!

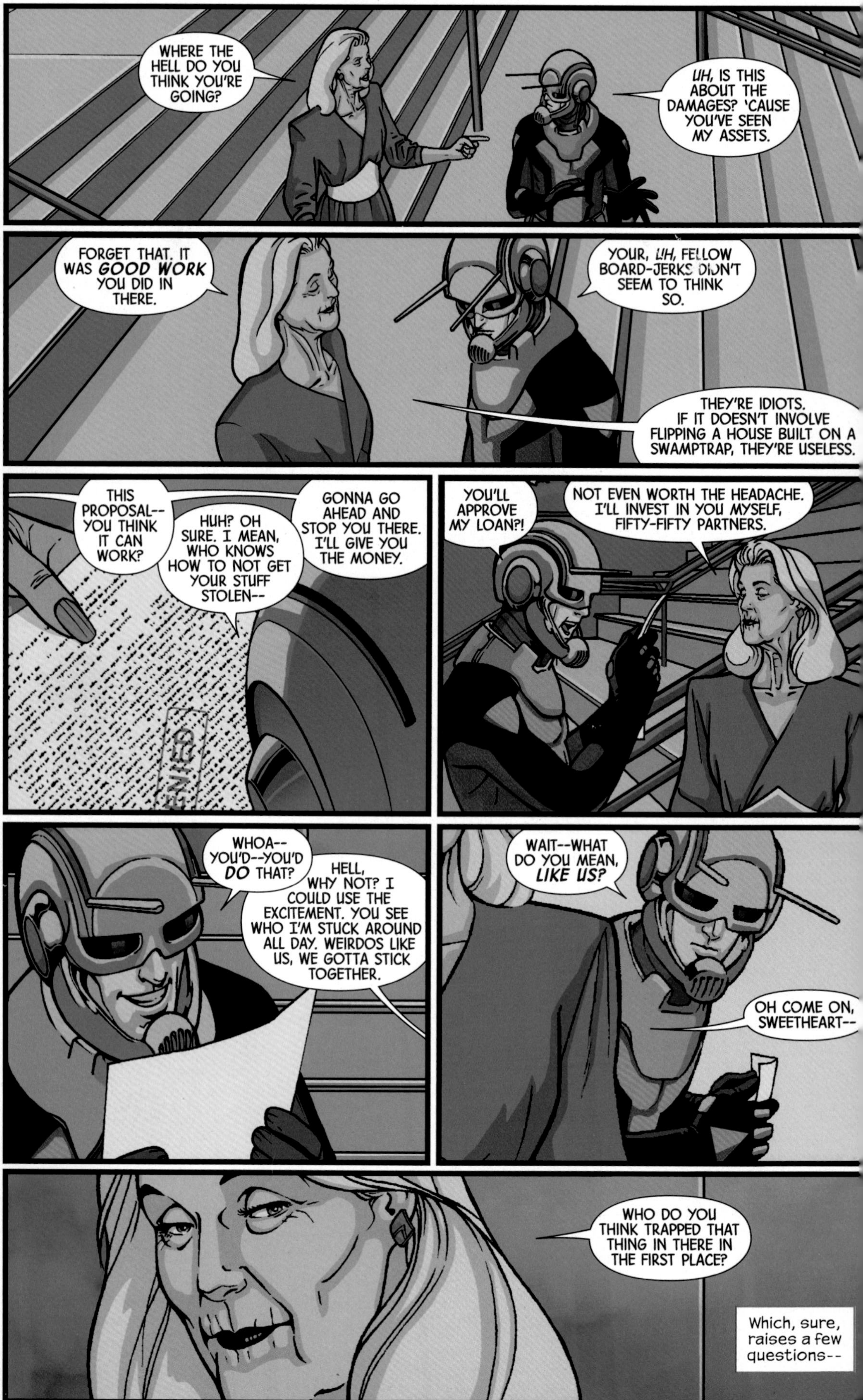
WHERE THE HELL DO YOU THINK YOU'RE GOING?
UH, IS THIS ABOUT THE DAMAGES? 'CAUSE YOU'VE SEEN MY ASSETS.
FORGET THAT. IT WAS GOOD WORK YOU DID IN THERE.
YOUR, UH, FELLOW BOARD-JERKS DIDN'T SEEM TO THINK SO.
THEY'RE IDIOTS. IF IT DOESN'T INVOLVE FLIPPING A HOUSE BUILT ON A SWAMPTRAP, THEY'RE USELESS.
THIS PROPOSAL-- YOU THINK IT CAN WORK?
HUH? OH SURE. I MEAN, WHO KNOWS HOW TO NOT GET YOUR STUFF STOLEN--
GONNA GO AHEAD AND STOP YOU THERE. I'LL GIVE YOU THE MONEY.
YOU'LL APPROVE MY LOAN?!
NOT EVEN WORTH THE HEADACHE. I'LL INVEST IN YOU MYSELF, FIFTY-FIFTY PARTNERS.
WHOA-- YOU'D--YOU'D DO THAT?
HELL, WHY NOT? I COULD USE THE EXCITEMENT. YOU SEE WHO I'M STUCK AROUND ALL DAY. WEIRDOS LIKE US, WE GOTTA STICK TOGETHER.
WAIT--WHAT DO YOU MEAN, LIKE US?
OH COME ON, SWEETHEART--
WHO DO YOU THINK TRAPPED THAT THING IN THERE IN THE FIRST PLACE?
Which, sure, raises a few questions--

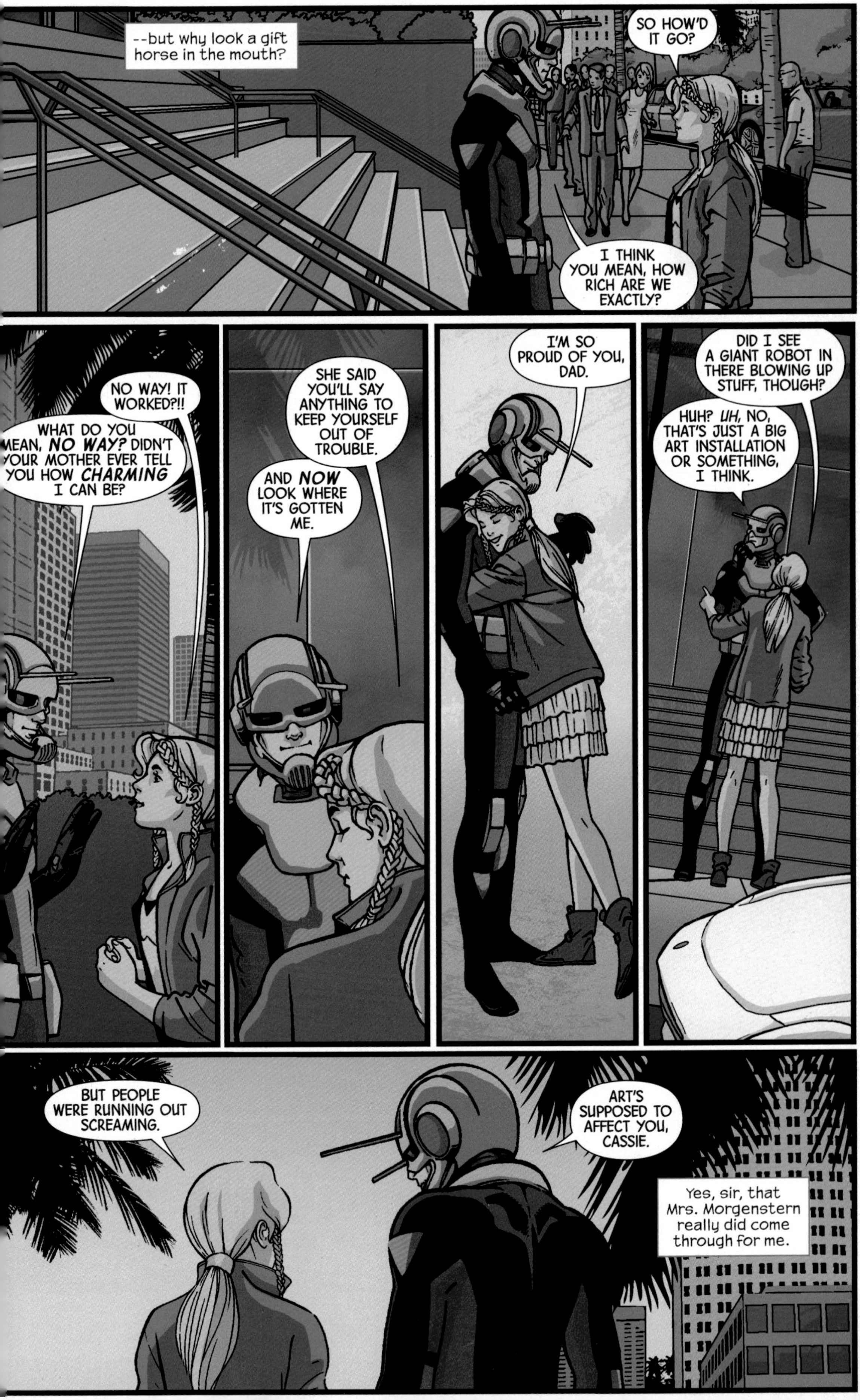
--but why look a gift horse in the mouth?
SO HOW'D IT GO?
I THINK YOU MEAN, HOW RICH ARE WE EXACTLY?
NO WAY! IT WORKED?!!
WHAT DO YOU MEAN, NO WAY? DIDN'T YOUR MOTHER EVER TELL YOU HOW CHARMING I CAN BE?
SHE SAID YOU'LL SAY ANYTHING TO KEEP YOURSELF OUT OF TROUBLE.
AND NOW LOOK WHERE IT'S GOTTEN ME.
I'M SO PROUD OF YOU, DAD.
DID I SEE A GIANT ROBOT IN THERE BLOWING UP STUFF, THOUGH?
HUH? UH, NO, THAT'S JUST A BIG ART INSTALLATION OR SOMETHING, I THINK.
BUT PEOPLE WERE RUNNING OUT SCREAMING.
ART'S SUPPOSED TO AFFECT YOU, CASSIE.
Yes, sir, that Mrs. Morgenstern really did come through for me.

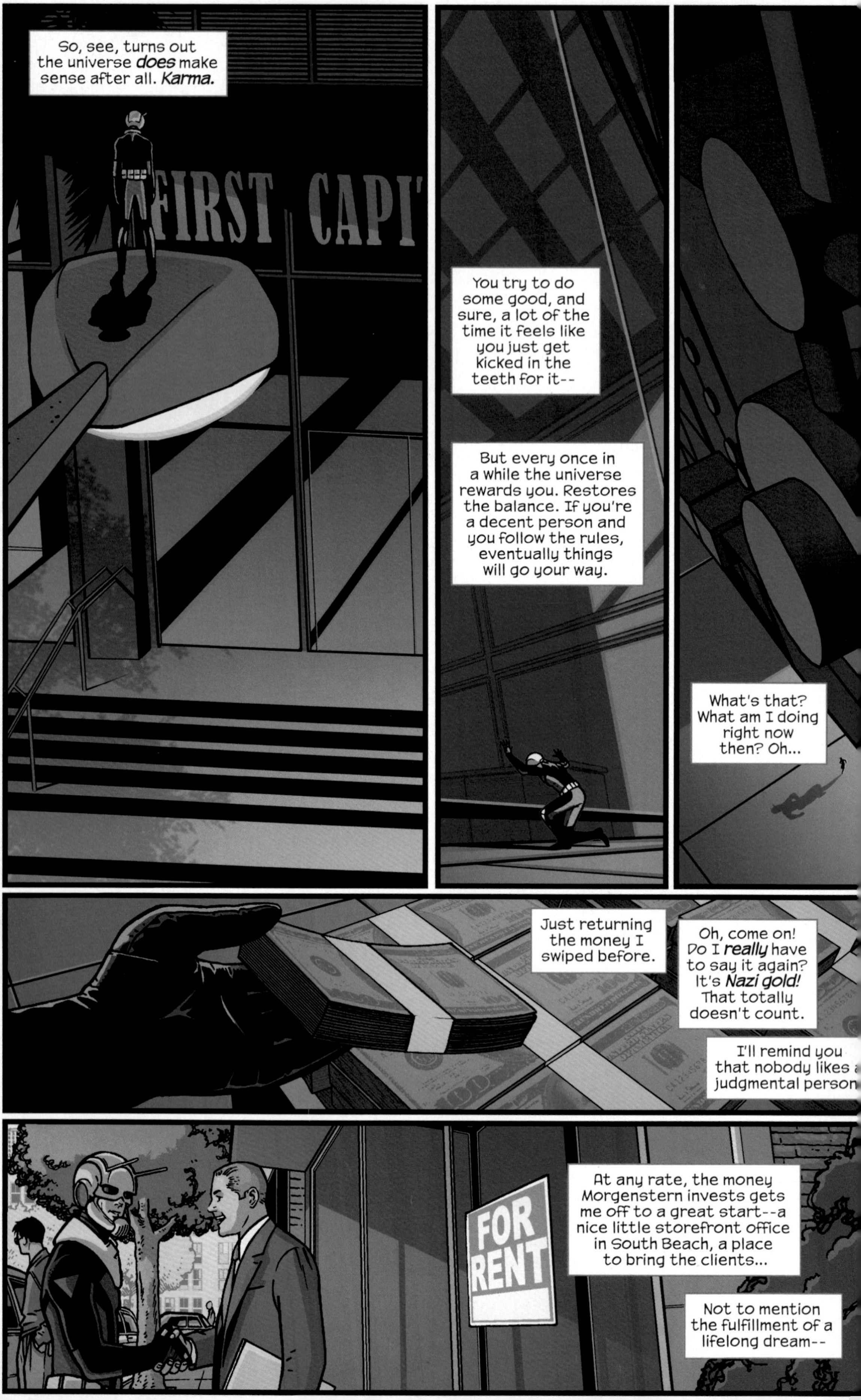
So, see, turns out the universe *does* make sense after all. *Karma.*
FIRST CAPI
You try to do some good, and sure, a lot of the time it feels like you just get kicked in the teeth for it--
But every once in a while the universe rewards you. Restores the balance. If you're a decent person and you follow the rules, eventually things will go your way.
What's that? What am I doing right now then? Oh...
Just returning the money I swiped before.
Oh, come on! Do I *really* have to say it again? It's *Nazi gold!* That totally doesn't count.
I'll remind you that nobody likes a judgmental person
At any rate, the money Morgenstern invests gets me off to a great start--a nice little storefront office in South Beach, a place to bring the clients...
FOR RENT
Not to mention the fulfillment of a lifelong dream--

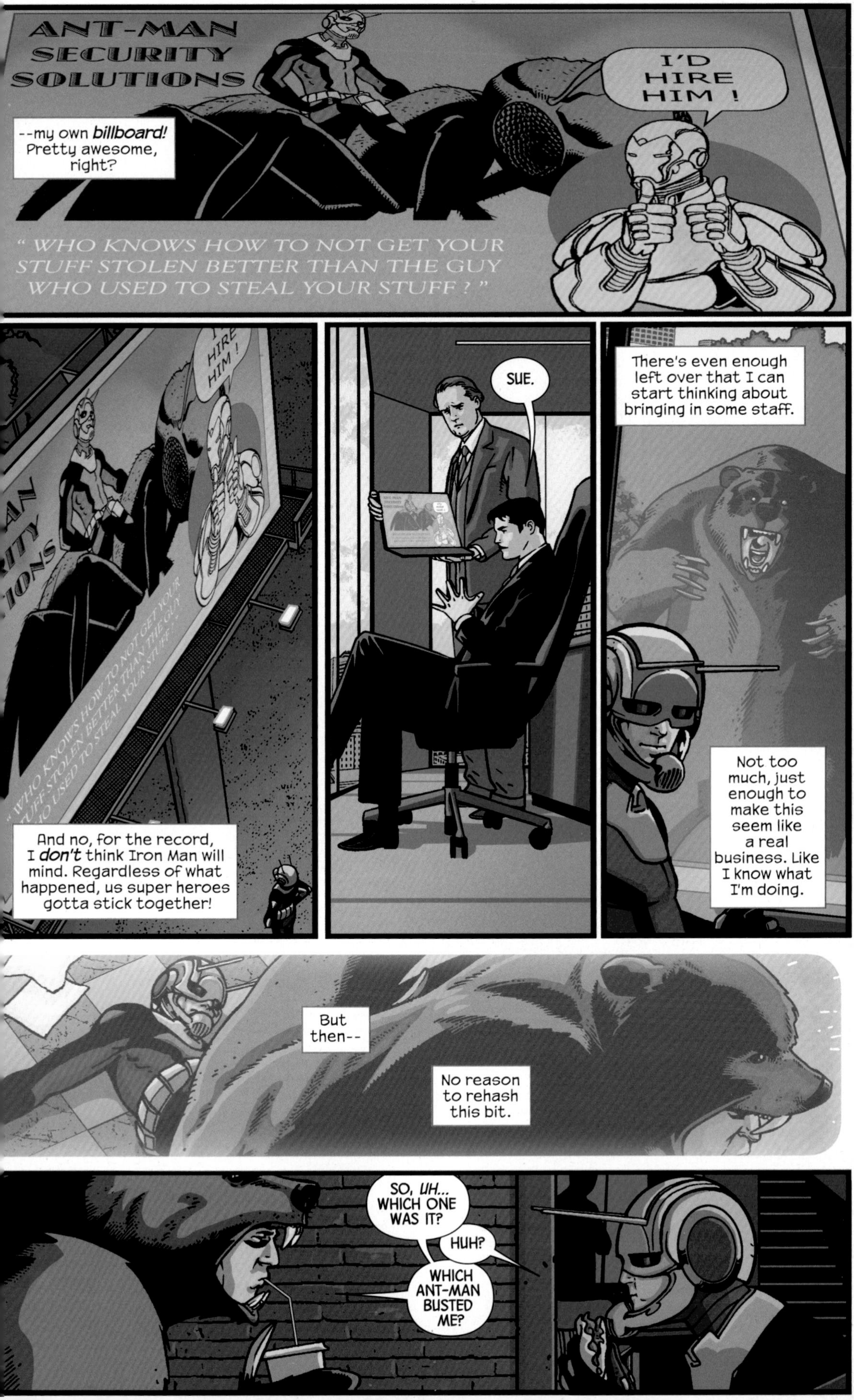
ANT-MAN SECURITY SOLUTIONS
I'D HIRE HIM !
--my own *billboard!* Pretty awesome, right?
" WHO KNOWS HOW TO NOT GET YOUR STUFF STOLEN BETTER THAN THE GUY WHO USED TO STEAL YOUR STUFF ? "
And no, for the record, I *don't* think Iron Man will mind. Regardless of what happened, us super heroes gotta stick together!
SUE.
There's even enough left over that I can start thinking about bringing in some staff.
Not too much, just enough to make this seem like a real business. Like I know what I'm doing.
But then--
No reason to rehash this bit.
SO, *UH*... WHICH ONE WAS IT?
HUH?
WHICH ANT-MAN BUSTED ME?

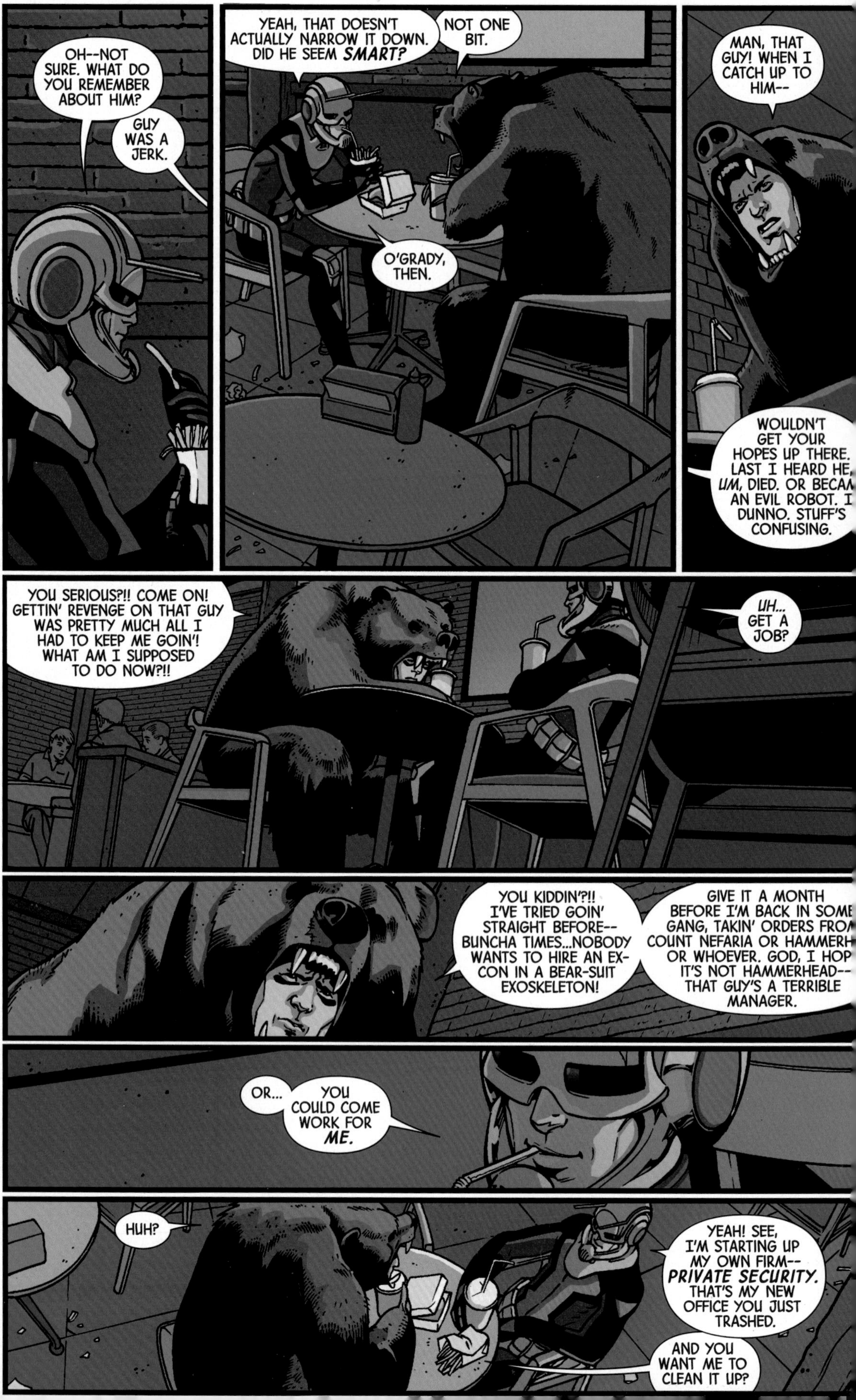
OH--NOT SURE. WHAT DO YOU REMEMBER ABOUT HIM?
GUY WAS A JERK.
YEAH, THAT DOESN'T ACTUALLY NARROW IT DOWN. DID HE SEEM SMART?
NOT ONE BIT.
O'GRADY, THEN.
MAN, THAT GUY! WHEN I CATCH UP TO HIM--
WOULDN'T GET YOUR HOPES UP THERE. LAST I HEARD HE, UM, DIED. OR BECAM AN EVIL ROBOT. I DUNNO. STUFF'S CONFUSING.
YOU SERIOUS?!! COME ON! GETTIN' REVENGE ON THAT GUY WAS PRETTY MUCH ALL I HAD TO KEEP ME GOIN'! WHAT AM I SUPPOSED TO DO NOW?!!
UH... GET A JOB?
YOU KIDDIN'?!! I'VE TRIED GOIN' STRAIGHT BEFORE-- BUNCHA TIMES...NOBODY WANTS TO HIRE AN EX-CON IN A BEAR-SUIT EXOSKELETON!
GIVE IT A MONTH BEFORE I'M BACK IN SOME GANG, TAKIN' ORDERS FROM COUNT NEFARIA OR HAMMERH OR WHOEVER. GOD, I HOP IT'S NOT HAMMERHEAD-- THAT GUY'S A TERRIBLE MANAGER.
OR...
YOU COULD COME WORK FOR ME.
HUH?
YEAH! SEE, I'M STARTING UP MY OWN FIRM-- PRIVATE SECURITY. THAT'S MY NEW OFFICE YOU JUST TRASHED.
AND YOU WANT ME TO CLEAN IT UP?

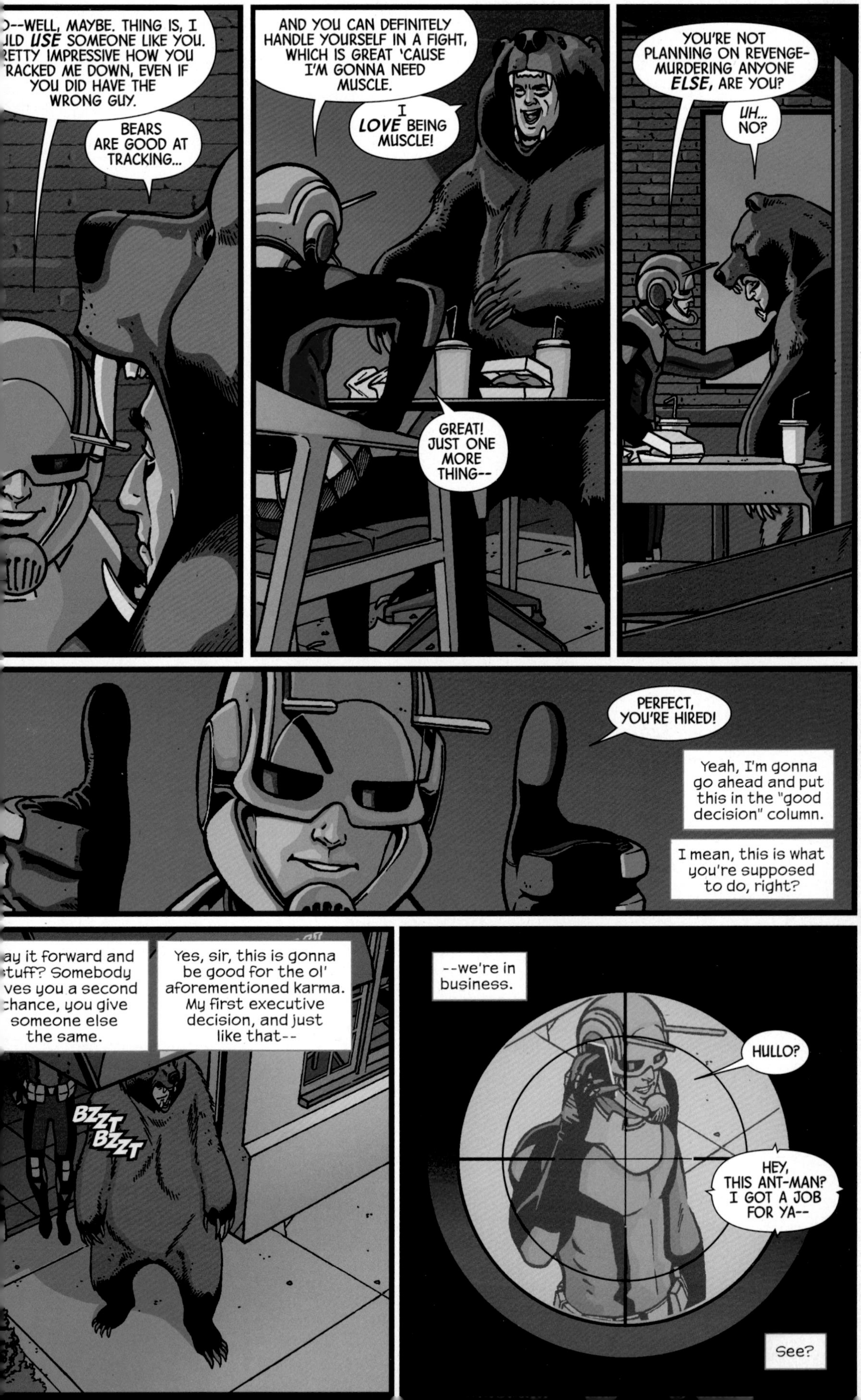
--WELL, MAYBE. THING IS, I
ULD USE SOMEONE LIKE YOU.
RETTY IMPRESSIVE HOW YOU
TRACKED ME DOWN, EVEN IF
YOU DID HAVE THE
WRONG GUY.
BEARS ARE GOOD AT TRACKING...
AND YOU CAN DEFINITELY HANDLE YOURSELF IN A FIGHT, WHICH IS GREAT 'CAUSE I'M GONNA NEED MUSCLE.
I LOVE BEING MUSCLE!
GREAT! JUST ONE MORE THING--
YOU'RE NOT PLANNING ON REVENGE-MURDERING ANYONE ELSE, ARE YOU?
UH... NO?
PERFECT, YOU'RE HIRED!
Yeah, I'm gonna go ahead and put this in the "good decision" column.
I mean, this is what you're supposed to do, right?
ay it forward and
tuff? Somebody
ves you a second
chance, you give
someone else
the same.
Yes, sir, this is gonna be good for the ol' aforementioned karma. My first executive decision, and just like that--
BZZT BZZT
--we're in business.
HULLO?
HEY, THIS ANT-MAN? I GOT A JOB FOR YA--
See?

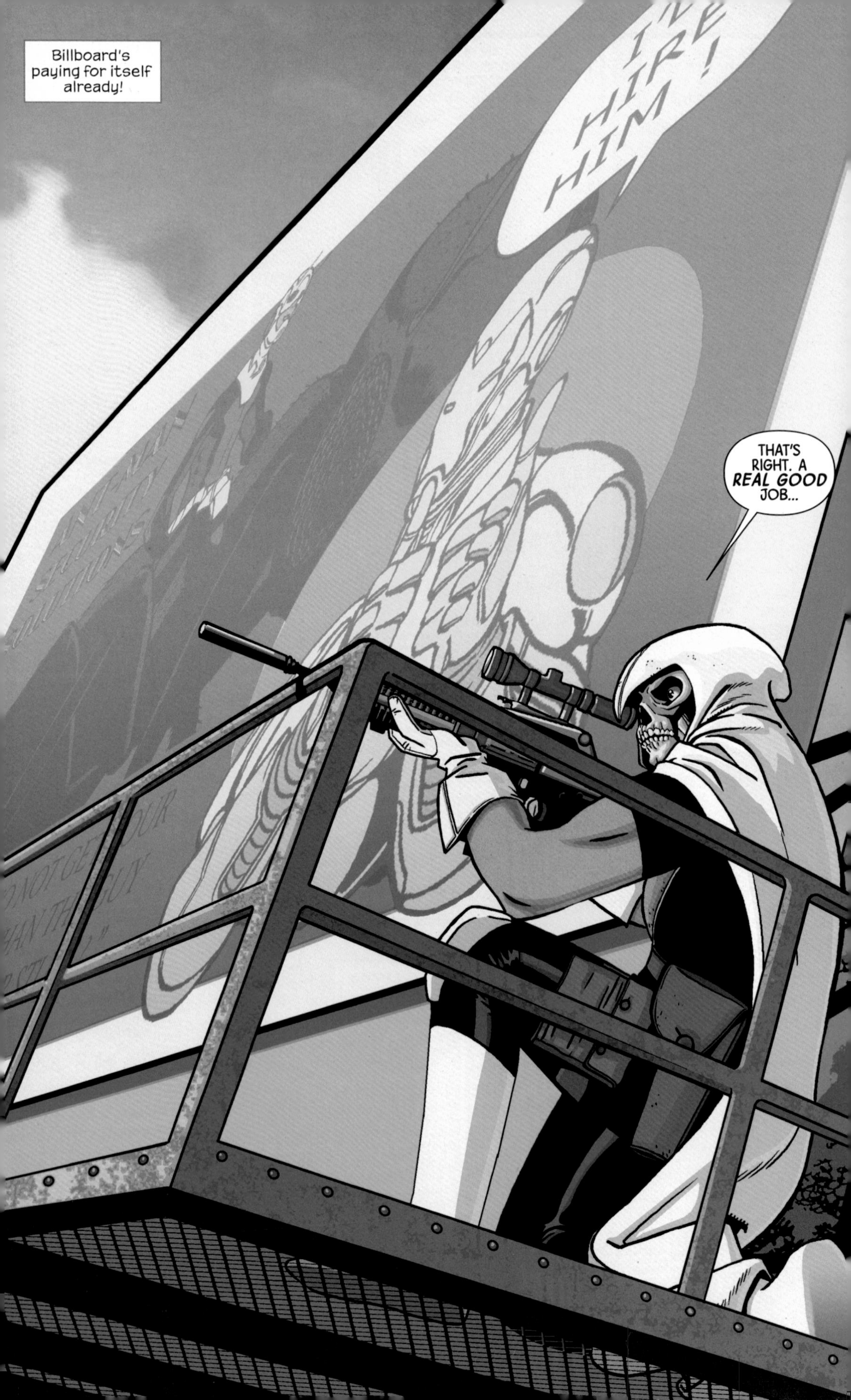
Billboard's paying for itself already!
HIRE HIM!
THAT'S RIGHT. A *REAL GOOD* JOB...

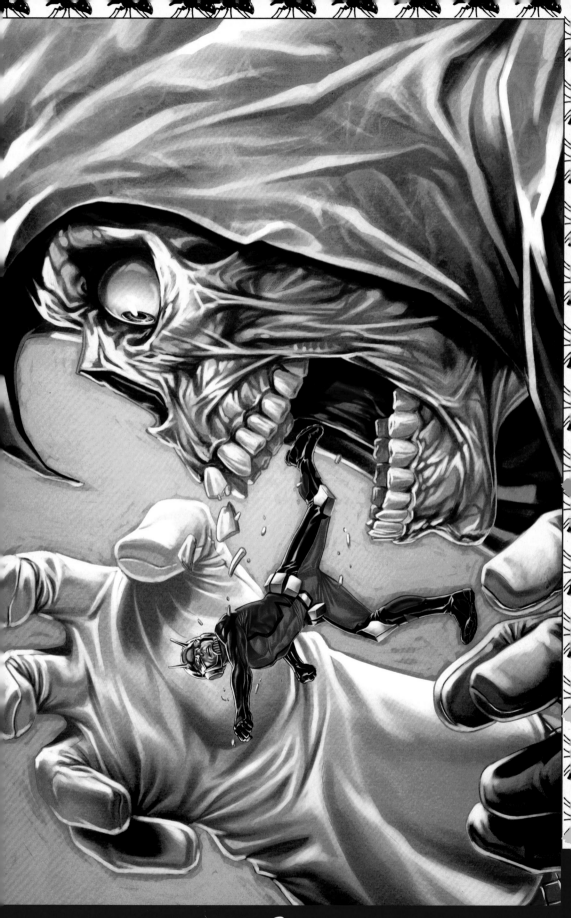

#3

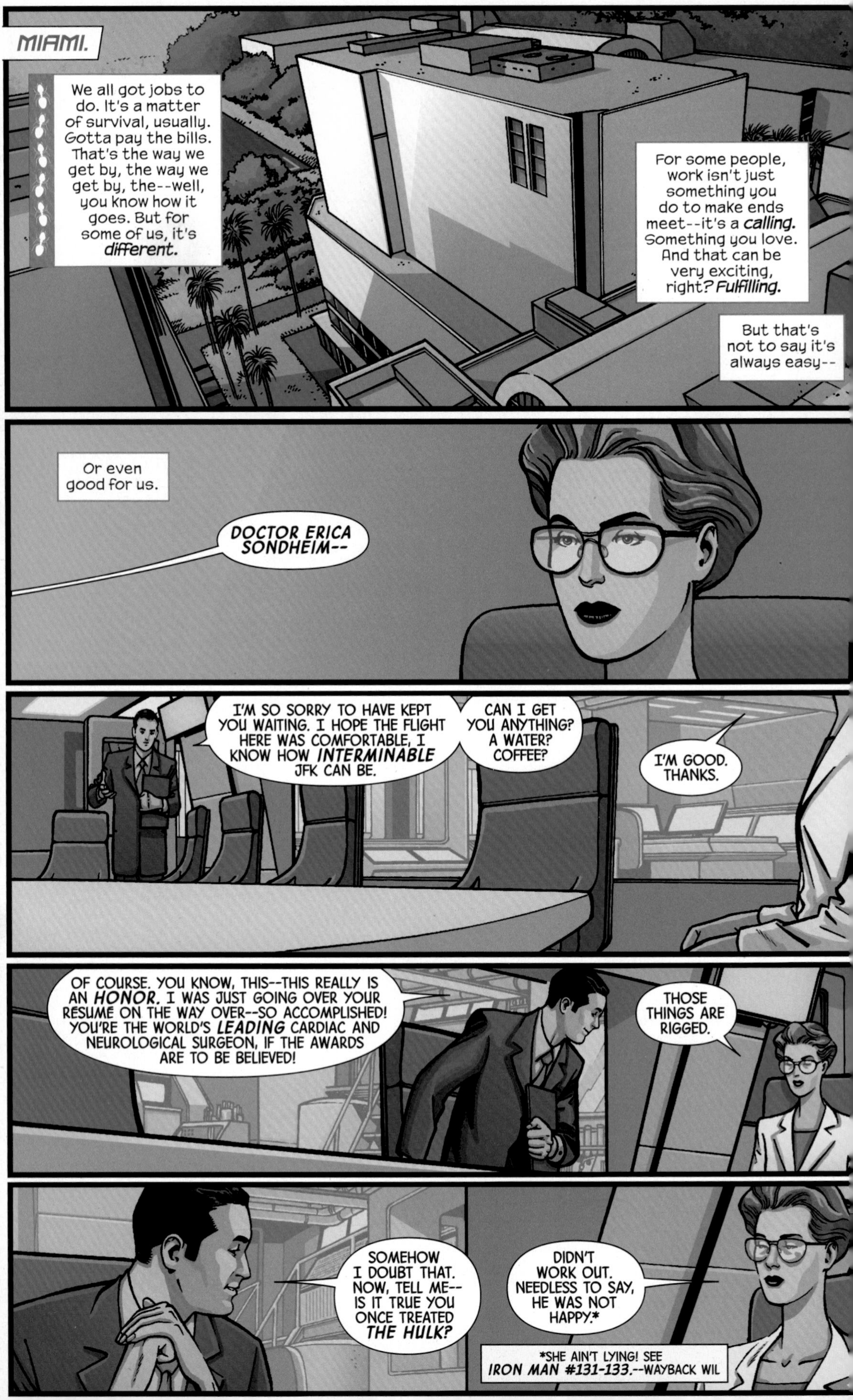

MIAMI.
We all got jobs to do. It's a matter of survival, usually. Gotta pay the bills. That's the way we get by, the way we get by, the--well, you know how it goes. But for some of us, it's *different.*
For some people, work isn't just something you do to make ends meet--it's a *calling.* Something you love. And that can be very exciting, right? *Fulfilling.*
But that's not to say it's always easy--
Or even good for us.
DOCTOR ERICA SONDHEIM--
I'M SO SORRY TO HAVE KEPT YOU WAITING. I HOPE THE FLIGHT HERE WAS COMFORTABLE, I KNOW HOW *INTERMINABLE* JFK CAN BE.
CAN I GET YOU ANYTHING? A WATER? COFFEE?
I'M GOOD. THANKS.
OF COURSE. YOU KNOW, THIS--THIS REALLY IS AN *HONOR.* I WAS JUST GOING OVER YOUR RESUMÉ ON THE WAY OVER--SO ACCOMPLISHED! YOU'RE THE WORLD'S *LEADING* CARDIAC AND NEUROLOGICAL SURGEON, IF THE AWARDS ARE TO BE BELIEVED!
THOSE THINGS ARE RIGGED.
SOMEHOW I DOUBT THAT. NOW, TELL ME-- IS IT TRUE YOU ONCE TREATED *THE HULK?*
DIDN'T WORK OUT. NEEDLESS TO SAY, HE WAS NOT HAPPY.*
*SHE AIN'T LYING! SEE *IRON MAN #131-133.*--WAYBACK WIL

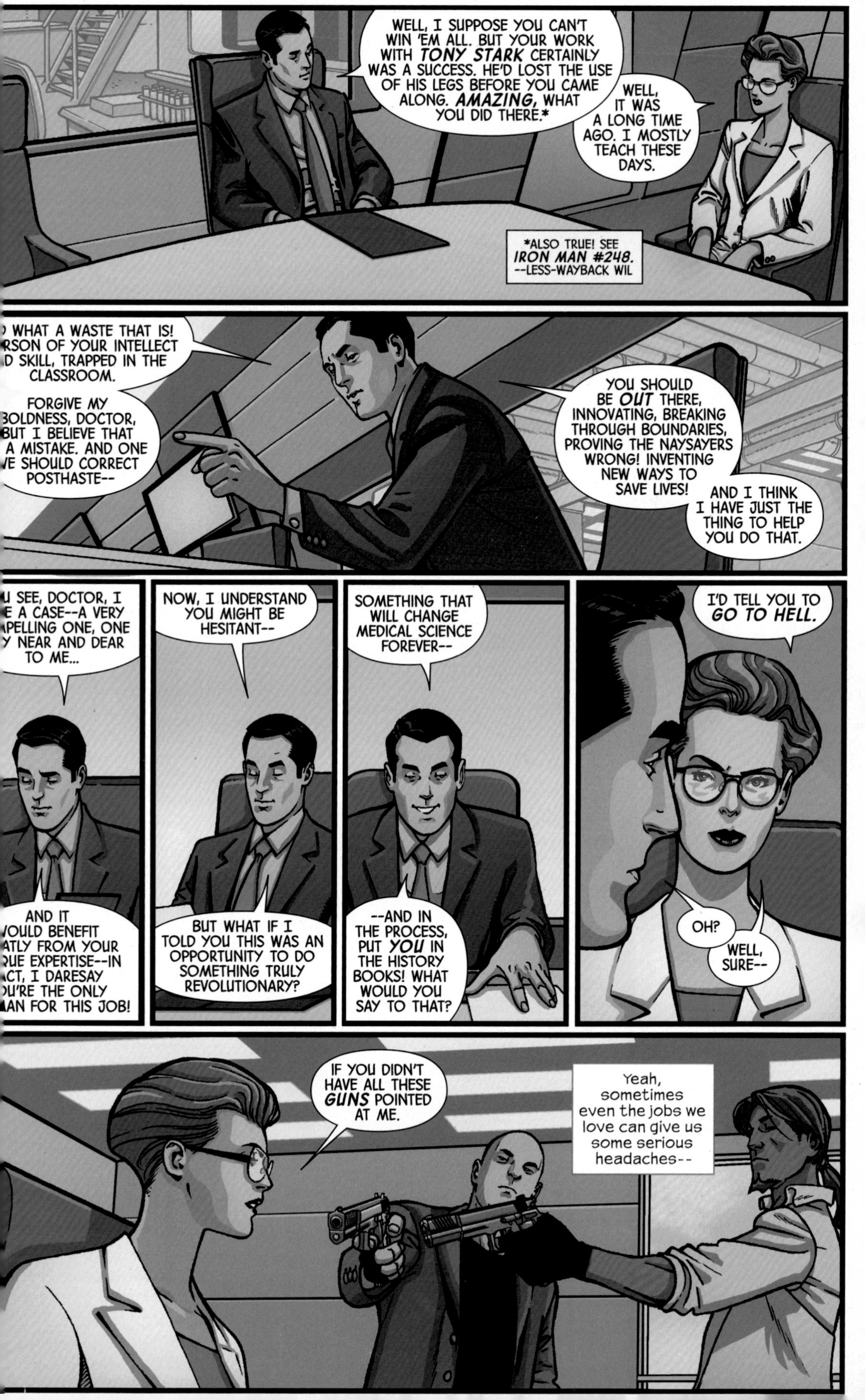

WELL, I SUPPOSE YOU CAN'T WIN 'EM ALL. BUT YOUR WORK WITH TONY STARK CERTAINLY WAS A SUCCESS. HE'D LOST THE USE OF HIS LEGS BEFORE YOU CAME ALONG. AMAZING, WHAT YOU DID THERE.*
WELL, IT WAS A LONG TIME AGO. I MOSTLY TEACH THESE DAYS.
*ALSO TRUE! SEE IRON MAN #248. --LESS-WAYBACK WIL
WHAT A WASTE THAT IS! RSON OF YOUR INTELLECT D SKILL, TRAPPED IN THE CLASSROOM.
FORGIVE MY BOLDNESS, DOCTOR, BUT I BELIEVE THAT A MISTAKE. AND ONE E SHOULD CORRECT POSTHASTE--
YOU SHOULD BE OUT THERE, INNOVATING, BREAKING THROUGH BOUNDARIES, PROVING THE NAYSAYERS WRONG! INVENTING NEW WAYS TO SAVE LIVES!
AND I THINK I HAVE JUST THE THING TO HELP YOU DO THAT.
SEE, DOCTOR, I E A CASE--A VERY PELLING ONE, ONE NEAR AND DEAR TO ME...
AND IT OULD BENEFIT ATLY FROM YOUR UE EXPERTISE--IN CT, I DARESAY U'RE THE ONLY AN FOR THIS JOB!
NOW, I UNDERSTAND YOU MIGHT BE HESITANT--
BUT WHAT IF I TOLD YOU THIS WAS AN OPPORTUNITY TO DO SOMETHING TRULY REVOLUTIONARY?
SOMETHING THAT WILL CHANGE MEDICAL SCIENCE FOREVER--
--AND IN THE PROCESS, PUT YOU IN THE HISTORY BOOKS! WHAT WOULD YOU SAY TO THAT?
OH?
WELL, SURE--
I'D TELL YOU TO GO TO HELL.
IF YOU DIDN'T HAVE ALL THESE GUNS POINTED AT ME.
Yeah, sometimes even the jobs we love can give us some serious headaches--

--as I'm finding out the hard way.

STUPID ANTS!

Fun Fact: Ants are great when it comes to acting as mini-drones or tunneling, or even complex formations-- but when it comes to installing motion detection systems?

They got a lot to learn.

I'M VERY DISAPPOINTED IN YOU, *TONY WILSON*. WE PRACTICED THIS.

It's the staying still that gets them. But maybe I should cut them some slack--

First day jitters are a real thing, after all.

That's right--it's really happening! *Ant-Man Security Solutions* has its first client, getting paid a sweet retainer to ensure no one can steal all these valuable...

Paperclips.

Hey, we all gotta start somewhere, right? And if my *Formicidae workforce* isn't off to the best start--

At least my *human* one is.

UH, HEY--BOSS? →NNN← HOW MUCH LONGER I GOTTA HOLD THIS DOOR?

Or, you know, *bear*-human. We're an equal opportunity employer! And did you hear him call me *boss*?

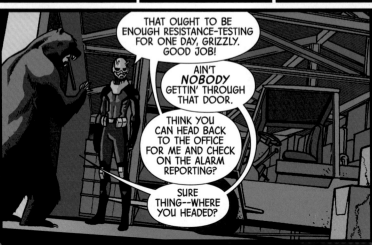

THAT OUGHT TO BE ENOUGH RESISTANCE-TESTING FOR ONE DAY, GRIZZLY. GOOD JOB!

AIN'T *NOBODY* GETTIN' THROUGH THAT DOOR.

THINK YOU CAN HEAD BACK TO THE OFFICE FOR ME AND CHECK ON THE ALARM REPORTING?

SURE THING--WHERE YOU HEADED?

LUNCH!

Which, sure, I get makes r sound a little lazy. But he I'm a CEO now! Gotta act t part! And anyhow, while we on the subject of jobs-

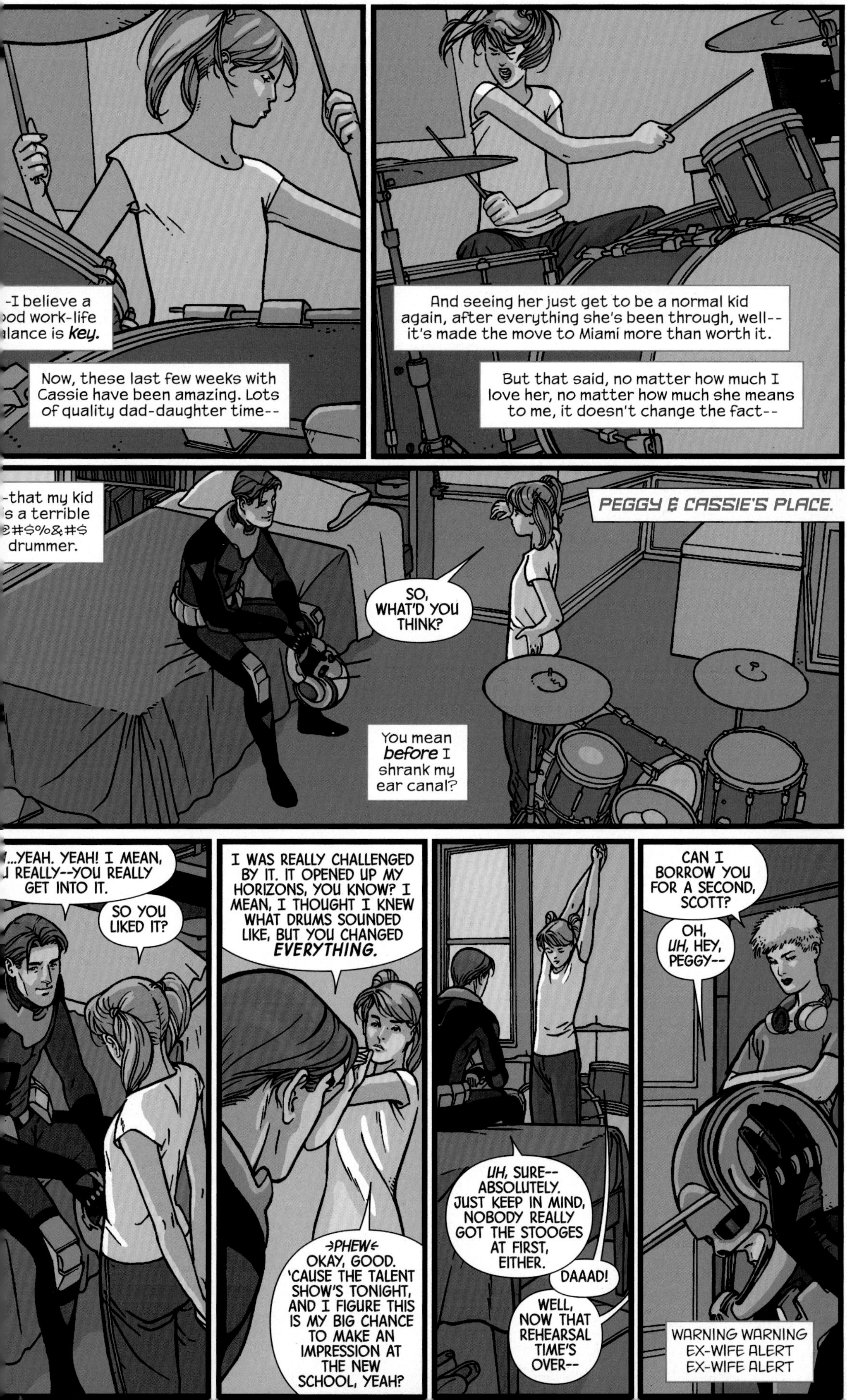

-I believe a
ood work-life
alance is key.
Now, these last few weeks with Cassie have been amazing. Lots of quality dad-daughter time--
And seeing her just get to be a normal kid again, after everything she's been through, well--it's made the move to Miami more than worth it.
But that said, no matter how much I love her, no matter how much she means to me, it doesn't change the fact--
-that my kid
s a terrible
@#$%&#$
drummer.
PEGGY & CASSIE'S PLACE.
SO, WHAT'D YOU THINK?
You mean before I shrank my ear canal?
...YEAH. YEAH! I MEAN,
J REALLY--YOU REALLY GET INTO IT.
SO YOU LIKED IT?
I WAS REALLY CHALLENGED BY IT. IT OPENED UP MY HORIZONS, YOU KNOW? I MEAN, I THOUGHT I KNEW WHAT DRUMS SOUNDED LIKE, BUT YOU CHANGED EVERYTHING.
PHEW
OKAY, GOOD. 'CAUSE THE TALENT SHOW'S TONIGHT, AND I FIGURE THIS IS MY BIG CHANCE TO MAKE AN IMPRESSION AT THE NEW SCHOOL, YEAH?
UH, SURE--ABSOLUTELY. JUST KEEP IN MIND, NOBODY REALLY GOT THE STOOGES AT FIRST, EITHER.
DAAAD!
WELL, NOW THAT REHEARSAL TIME'S OVER--
CAN I BORROW YOU FOR A SECOND, SCOTT?
OH, UH, HEY, PEGGY--
WARNING WARNING
EX-WIFE ALERT
EX-WIFE ALERT

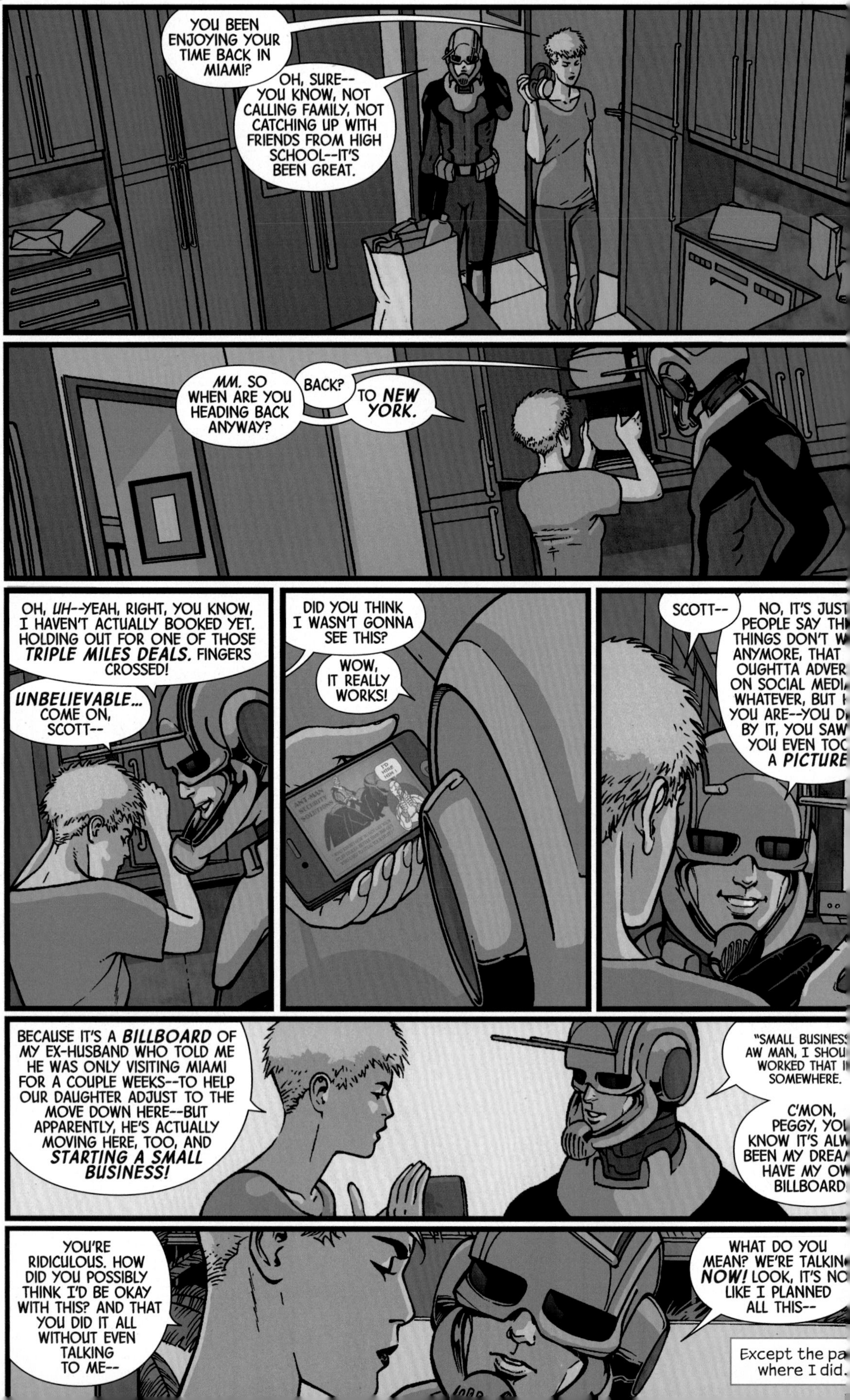

YOU BEEN ENJOYING YOUR TIME BACK IN MIAMI?
OH, SURE-- YOU KNOW, NOT CALLING FAMILY, NOT CATCHING UP WITH FRIENDS FROM HIGH SCHOOL--IT'S BEEN GREAT.
MM. SO WHEN ARE YOU HEADING BACK ANYWAY?
BACK?
TO NEW YORK.
OH, UH--YEAH, RIGHT, YOU KNOW, I HAVEN'T ACTUALLY BOOKED YET. HOLDING OUT FOR ONE OF THOSE TRIPLE MILES DEALS. FINGERS CROSSED!
UNBELIEVABLE... COME ON, SCOTT--
DID YOU THINK I WASN'T GONNA SEE THIS?
WOW, IT REALLY WORKS!
ANT-MAN SECURITY SOLUTIONS
I'D HIRE HIM!
SCOTT--
NO, IT'S JUST PEOPLE SAY TH THINGS DON'T W ANYMORE, THAT OUGHTTA ADVER ON SOCIAL MEDI WHATEVER, BUT YOU ARE--YOU D BY IT, YOU SAW YOU EVEN TOO A PICTURE
BECAUSE IT'S A BILLBOARD OF MY EX-HUSBAND WHO TOLD ME HE WAS ONLY VISITING MIAMI FOR A COUPLE WEEKS--TO HELP OUR DAUGHTER ADJUST TO THE MOVE DOWN HERE--BUT APPARENTLY, HE'S ACTUALLY MOVING HERE, TOO, AND STARTING A SMALL BUSINESS!
"SMALL BUSINES AW MAN, I SHOU WORKED THAT I SOMEWHERE.
C'MON, PEGGY, YO KNOW IT'S ALW BEEN MY DREA HAVE MY OW BILLBOARD
YOU'RE RIDICULOUS. HOW DID YOU POSSIBLY THINK I'D BE OKAY WITH THIS? AND THAT YOU DID IT ALL WITHOUT EVEN TALKING TO ME--
WHAT DO YOU MEAN? WE'RE TALKIN NOW! LOOK, IT'S NO LIKE I PLANNED ALL THIS--
Except the pa where I did.

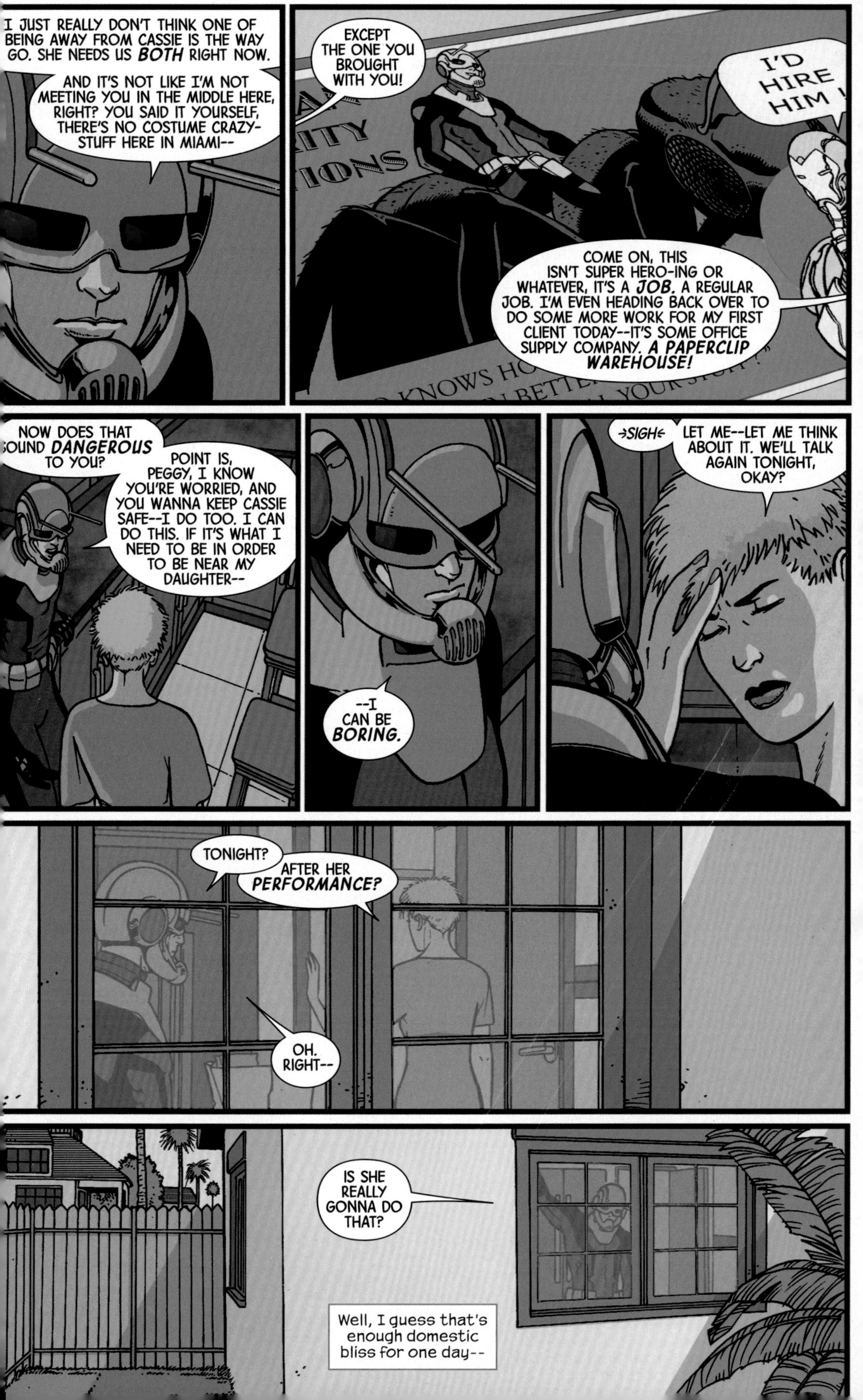
I JUST REALLY DON'T THINK ONE OF BEING AWAY FROM CASSIE IS THE WAY GO. SHE NEEDS US BOTH RIGHT NOW.
AND IT'S NOT LIKE I'M NOT MEETING YOU IN THE MIDDLE HERE, RIGHT? YOU SAID IT YOURSELF, THERE'S NO COSTUME CRAZY-STUFF HERE IN MIAMI--
EXCEPT THE ONE YOU BROUGHT WITH YOU!
I'D HIRE HIM
COME ON, THIS ISN'T SUPER HERO-ING OR WHATEVER, IT'S A JOB. A REGULAR JOB. I'M EVEN HEADING BACK OVER TO DO SOME MORE WORK FOR MY FIRST CLIENT TODAY--IT'S SOME OFFICE SUPPLY COMPANY. A PAPERCLIP WAREHOUSE!
NOW DOES THAT SOUND DANGEROUS TO YOU?
POINT IS, PEGGY, I KNOW YOU'RE WORRIED, AND YOU WANNA KEEP CASSIE SAFE--I DO TOO. I CAN DO THIS. IF IT'S WHAT I NEED TO BE IN ORDER TO BE NEAR MY DAUGHTER--
--I CAN BE BORING.
SIGH
LET ME--LET ME THINK ABOUT IT. WE'LL TALK AGAIN TONIGHT, OKAY?
TONIGHT?
AFTER HER PERFORMANCE?
OH. RIGHT--
IS SHE REALLY GONNA DO THAT?
Well, I guess that's enough domestic bliss for one day--

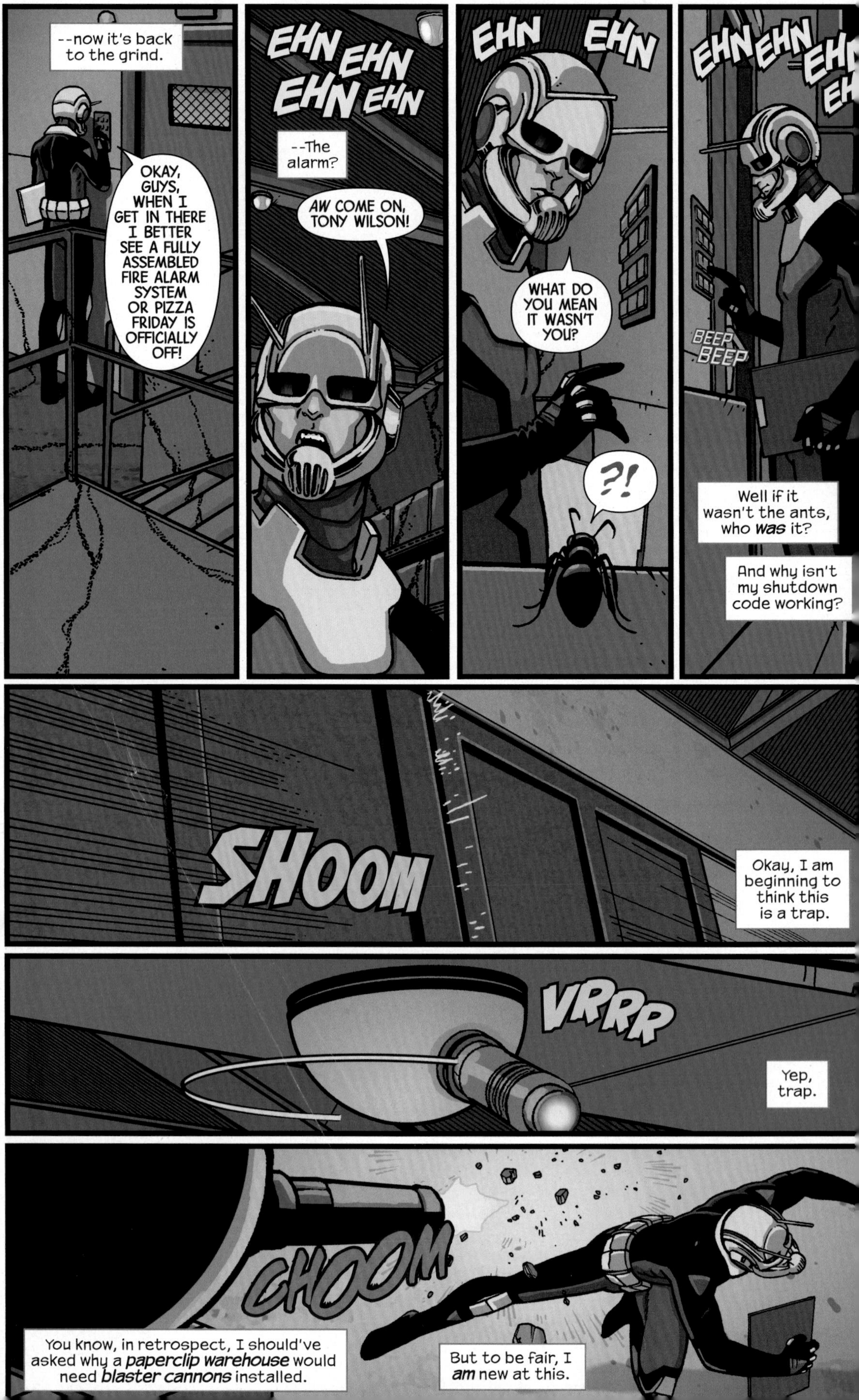

--now it's back to the grind.
OKAY, GUYS, WHEN I GET IN THERE I BETTER SEE A FULLY ASSEMBLED FIRE ALARM SYSTEM OR PIZZA FRIDAY IS OFFICIALLY OFF!
EHN EHN EHN EHN
--The alarm?
AW COME ON, TONY WILSON!
EHN EHN
WHAT DO YOU MEAN IT WASN'T YOU?
?!
EHN EHN EHN
BEEP BEEP
Well if it wasn't the ants, who was it?
And why isn't my shutdown code working?
SHOOM
Okay, I am beginning to think this is a trap.
VRRR
Yep, trap.
CHOOM
You know, in retrospect, I should've asked why a paperclip warehouse would need blaster cannons installed.
But to be fair, I am new at this.

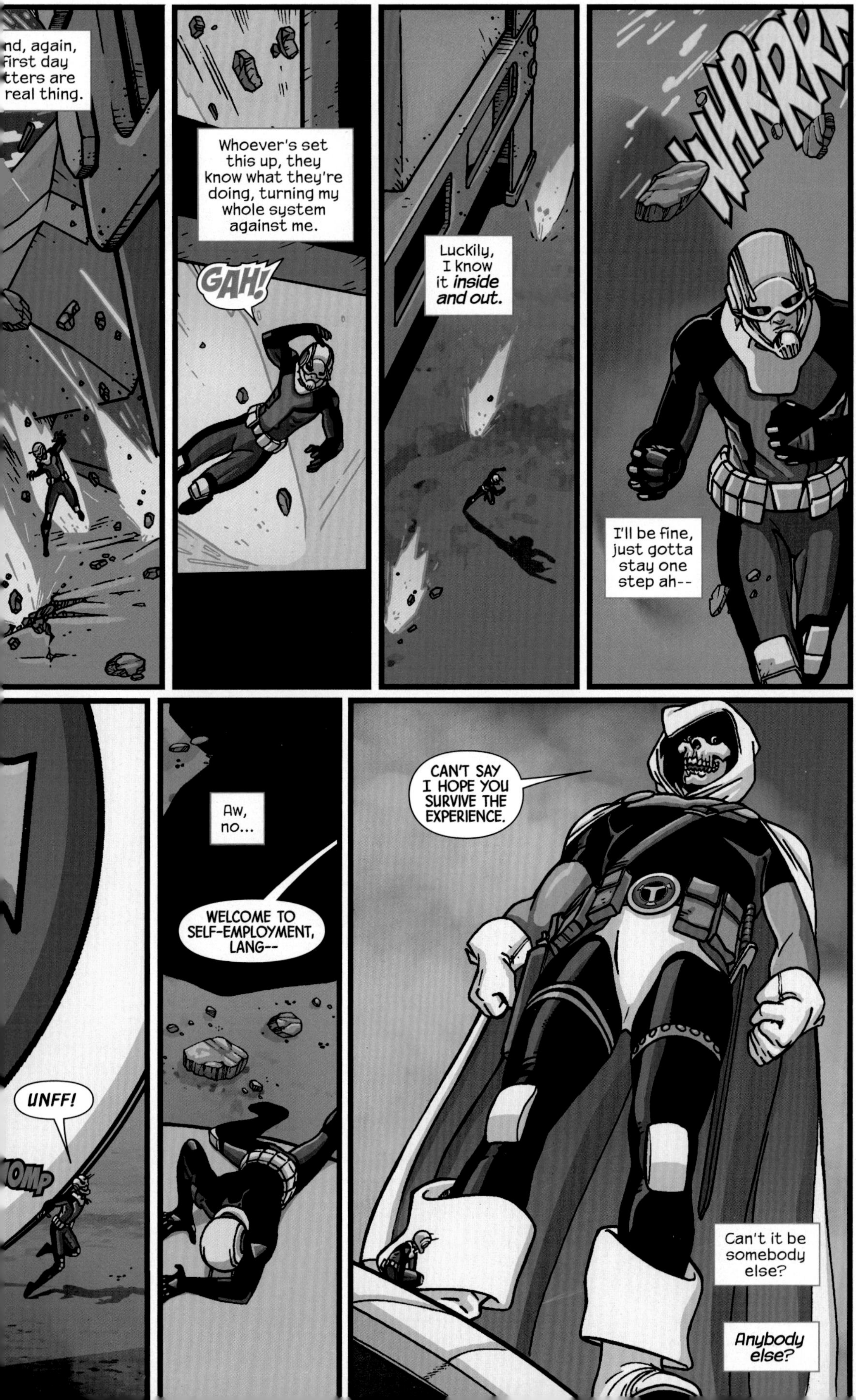
nd, again,
first day
tters are
real thing.
Whoever's set this up, they know what they're doing, turning my whole system against me.
GAH!
Luckily, I know it *inside and out.*
WHRRR
I'll be fine, just gotta stay one step ah--
UNFF!
OMP
Aw, no...
WELCOME TO SELF-EMPLOYMENT, LANG--
CAN'T SAY I HOPE YOU SURVIVE THE EXPERIENCE.
Can't it be somebody else?
Anybody else?

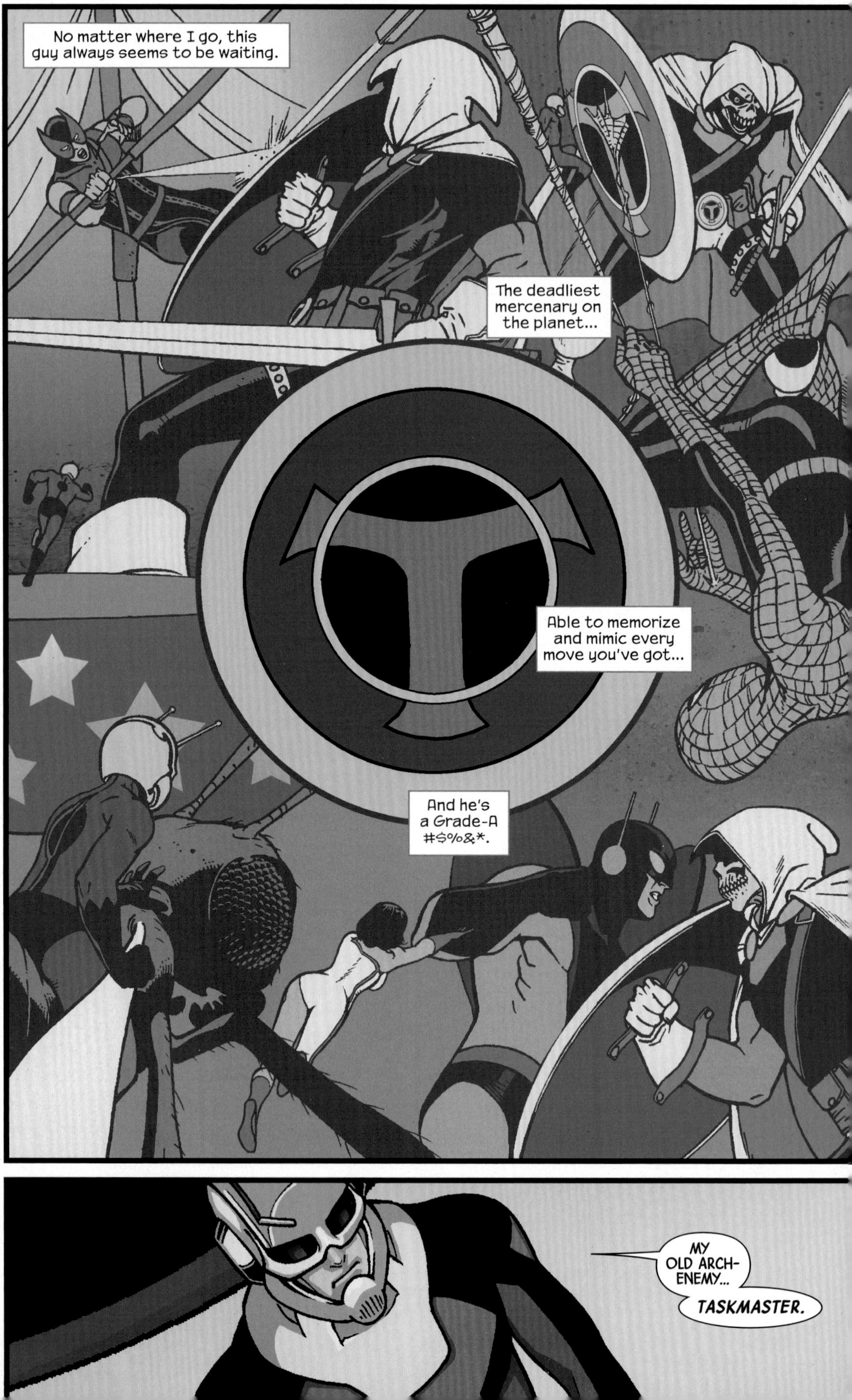
No matter where I go, this guy always seems to be waiting.
The deadliest mercenary on the planet...
Able to memorize and mimic every move you've got...
And he's a Grade-A #$%&*.
MY OLD ARCH-ENEMY... TASKMASTER.

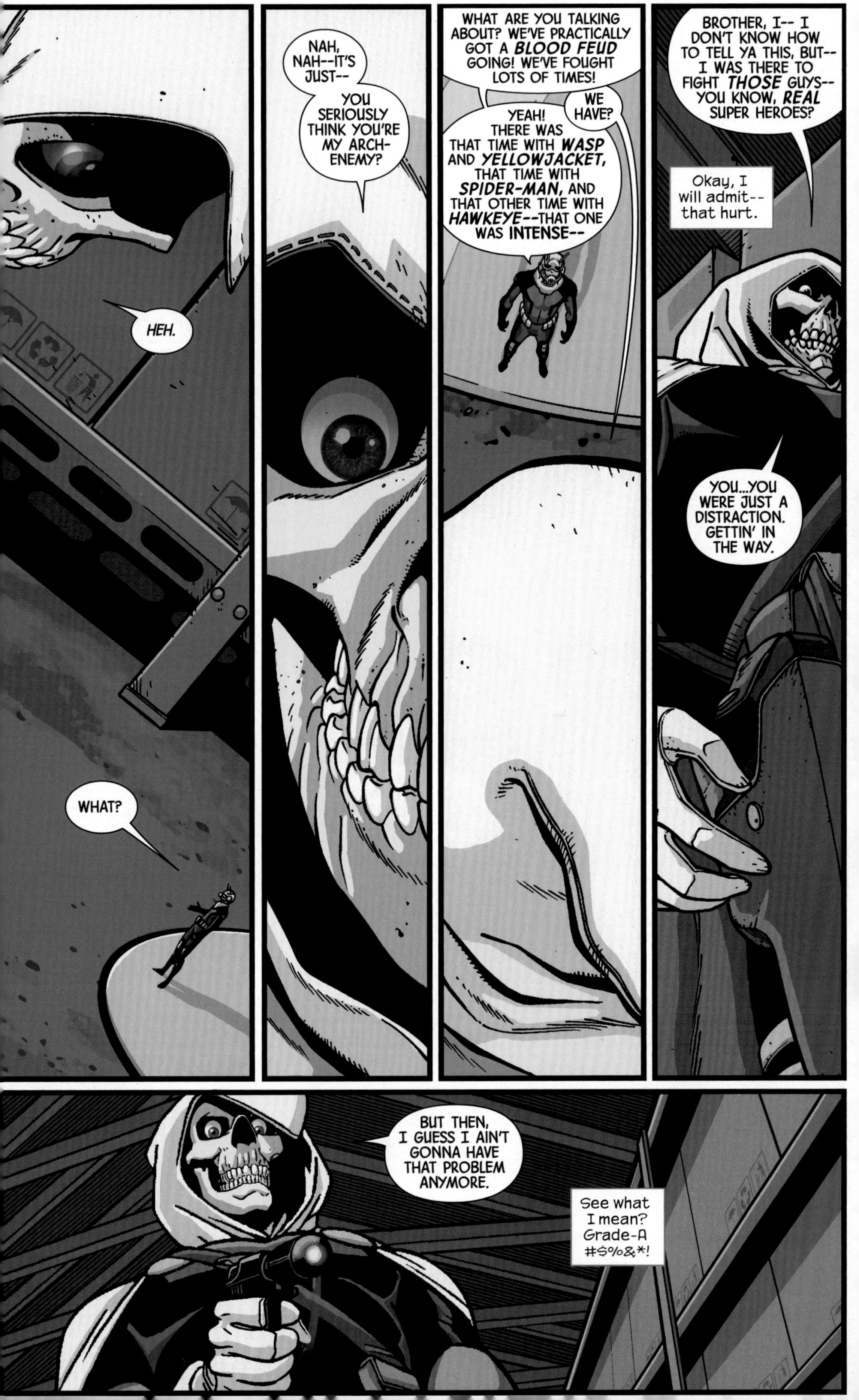
HEH.
WHAT?
NAH, NAH--IT'S JUST--
YOU SERIOUSLY THINK YOU'RE MY ARCH-ENEMY?
WHAT ARE YOU TALKING ABOUT? WE'VE PRACTICALLY GOT A BLOOD FEUD GOING! WE'VE FOUGHT LOTS OF TIMES!
WE HAVE?
YEAH! THERE WAS THAT TIME WITH WASP AND YELLOWJACKET, THAT TIME WITH SPIDER-MAN, AND THAT OTHER TIME WITH HAWKEYE--THAT ONE WAS INTENSE--
BROTHER, I-- I DON'T KNOW HOW TO TELL YA THIS, BUT-- I WAS THERE TO FIGHT THOSE GUYS-- YOU KNOW, REAL SUPER HEROES?
Okay, I will admit-- that hurt.
YOU...YOU WERE JUST A DISTRACTION. GETTIN' IN THE WAY.
BUT THEN, I GUESS I AIN'T GONNA HAVE THAT PROBLEM ANYMORE.
See what I mean? Grade-A #$%&*!

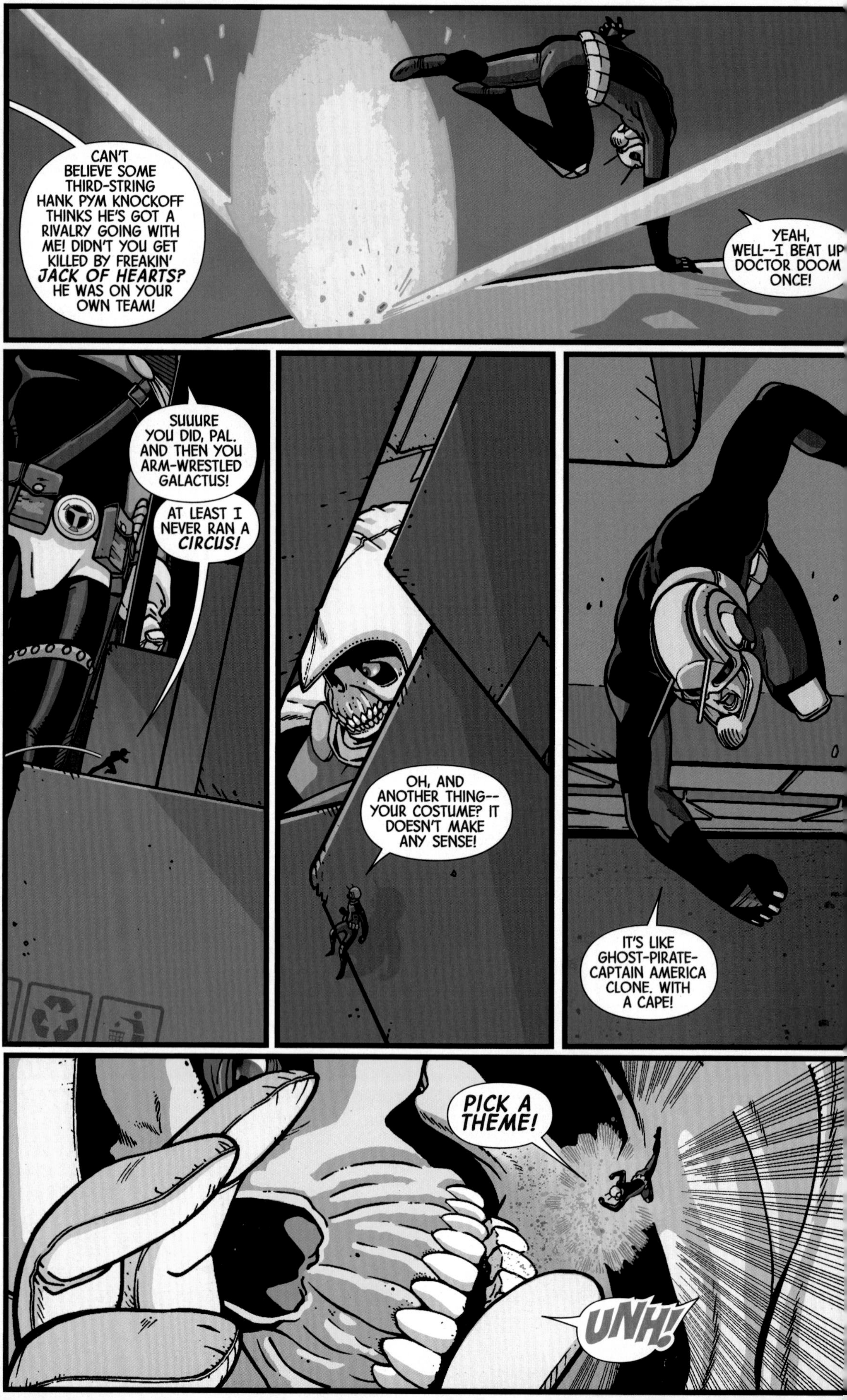

CAN'T BELIEVE SOME THIRD-STRING HANK PYM KNOCKOFF THINKS HE'S GOT A RIVALRY GOING WITH ME! DIDN'T YOU GET KILLED BY FREAKIN' *JACK OF HEARTS?* HE WAS ON YOUR OWN TEAM!
YEAH, WELL--I BEAT UP DOCTOR DOOM ONCE!
SUUURE YOU DID, PAL. AND THEN YOU ARM-WRESTLED GALACTUS!
AT LEAST I NEVER RAN A *CIRCUS!*
OH, AND ANOTHER THING-- YOUR COSTUME? IT DOESN'T MAKE ANY SENSE!
IT'S LIKE GHOST-PIRATE-CAPTAIN AMERICA CLONE. WITH A CAPE!
PICK A THEME!
UNH!

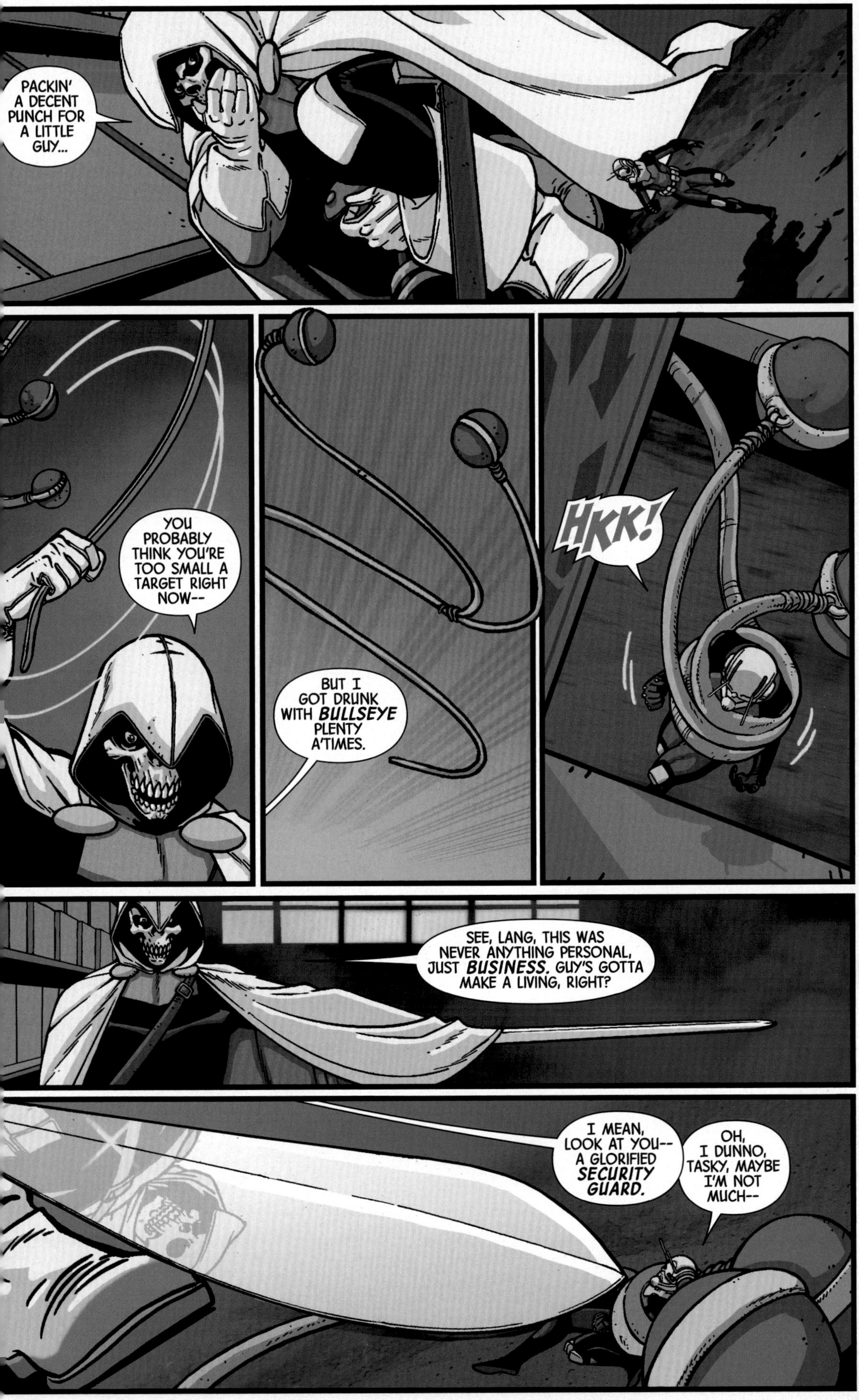
PACKIN' A DECENT PUNCH FOR A LITTLE GUY...
YOU PROBABLY THINK YOU'RE TOO SMALL A TARGET RIGHT NOW--
BUT I GOT DRUNK WITH BULLSEYE PLENTY A'TIMES.
HKK!
SEE, LANG, THIS WAS NEVER ANYTHING PERSONAL, JUST BUSINESS. GUY'S GOTTA MAKE A LIVING, RIGHT?
I MEAN, LOOK AT YOU-- A GLORIFIED SECURITY GUARD.
OH, I DUNNO, TASKY, MAYBE I'M NOT MUCH--

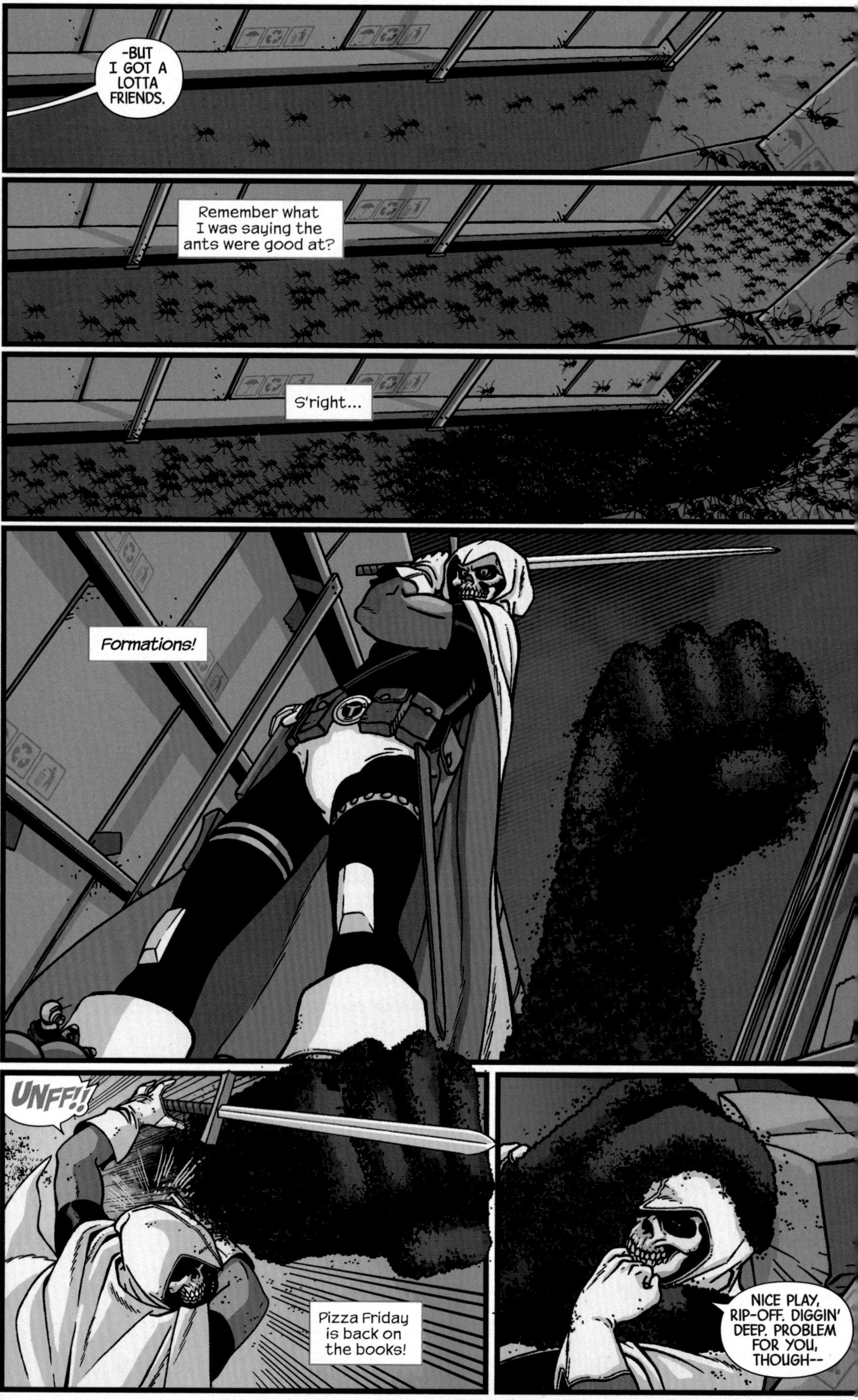
-BUT I GOT A LOTTA FRIENDS.
Remember what I was saying the ants were good at?
S'right...
Formations!
UNFF!!
Pizza Friday is back on the books!
NICE PLAY, RIP-OFF. DIGGIN' DEEP. PROBLEM FOR YOU, THOUGH--

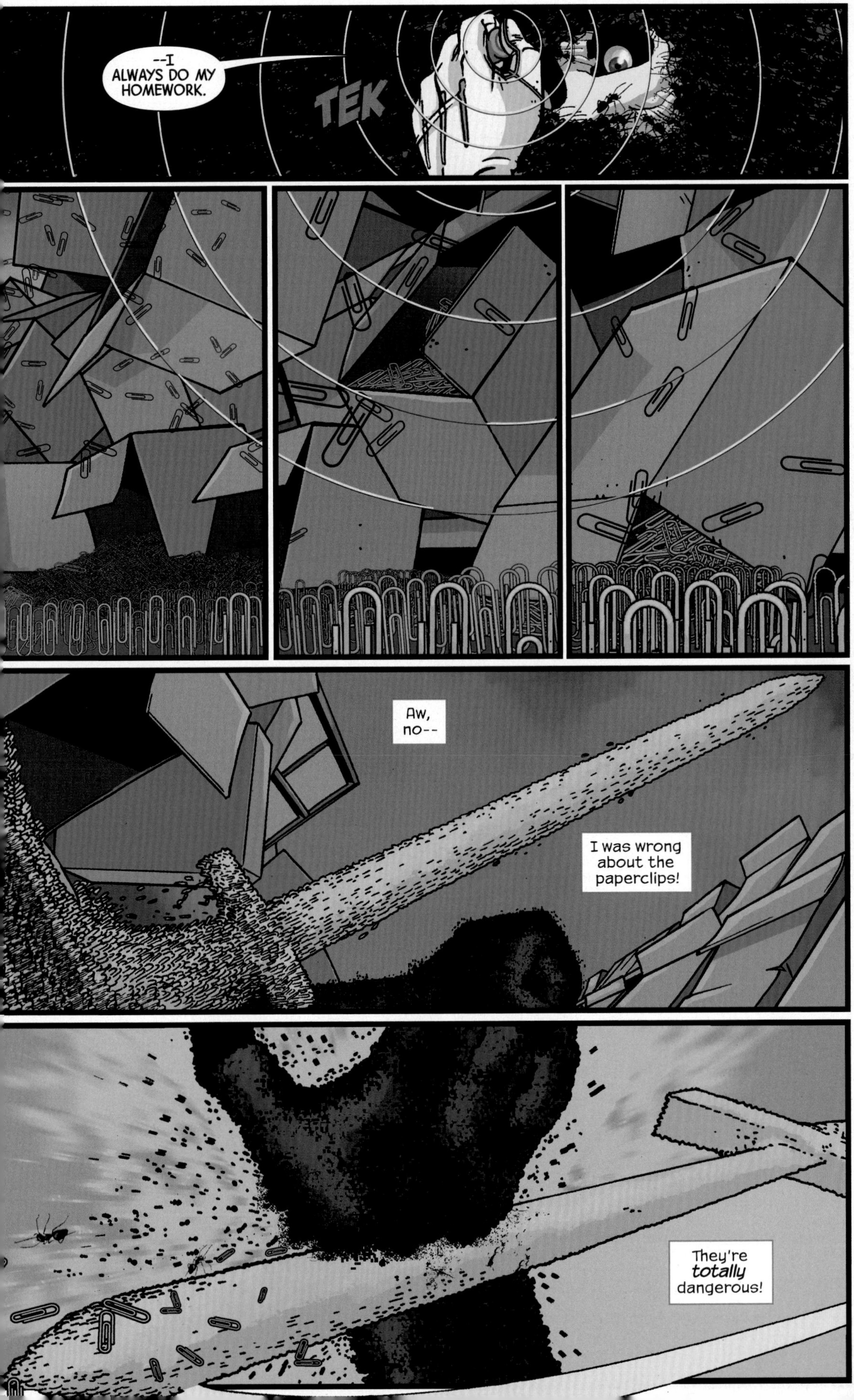
--I ALWAYS DO MY HOMEWORK.
TEK
Aw, no--
I was wrong about the paperclips!
They're *totally* dangerous!

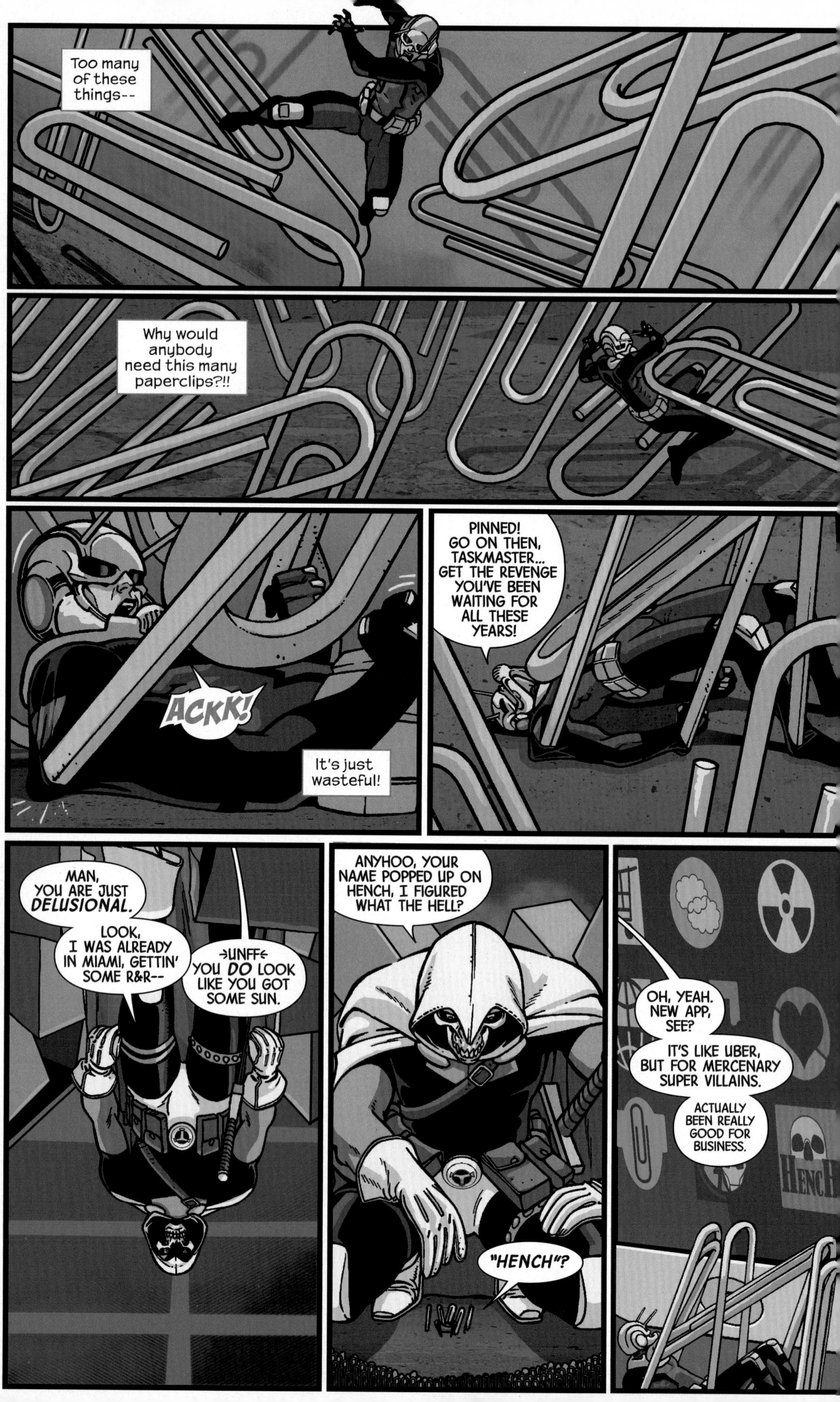
Too many of these things--
Why would anybody need this many paperclips?!!
ACKK!
It's just wasteful!
PINNED! GO ON THEN, TASKMASTER... GET THE REVENGE YOU'VE BEEN WAITING FOR ALL THESE YEARS!
MAN, YOU ARE JUST DELUSIONAL.
LOOK, I WAS ALREADY IN MIAMI, GETTIN' SOME R&R--
UNFF
YOU DO LOOK LIKE YOU GOT SOME SUN.
ANYHOO, YOUR NAME POPPED UP ON HENCH, I FIGURED WHAT THE HELL?
"HENCH"?
OH, YEAH. NEW APP, SEE?
IT'S LIKE UBER, BUT FOR MERCENARY SUPER VILLAINS.
ACTUALLY BEEN REALLY GOOD FOR BUSINESS.
HENCH

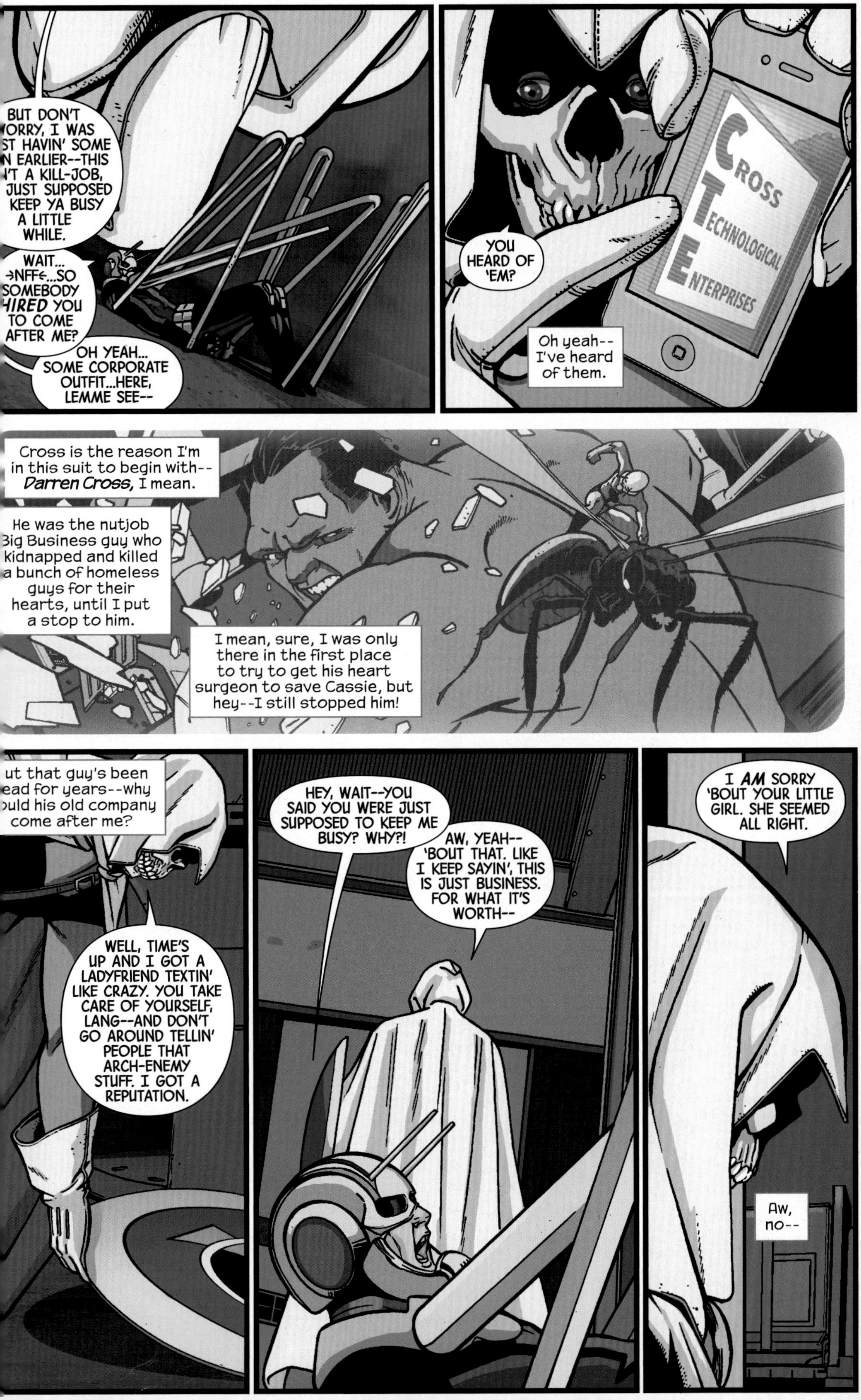

BUT DON'T ORRY, I WAS ST HAVIN' SOME N EARLIER--THIS 'T A KILL-JOB, JUST SUPPOSED KEEP YA BUSY A LITTLE WHILE.
WAIT... ➔NFF⬅...SO SOMEBODY HIRED YOU TO COME AFTER ME?
OH YEAH... SOME CORPORATE OUTFIT...HERE, LEMME SEE--
CROSS TECHNOLOGICAL ENTERPRISES
YOU HEARD OF 'EM?
Oh yeah-- I've heard of them.
Cross is the reason I'm in this suit to begin with-- Darren Cross, I mean.
He was the nutjob Big Business guy who kidnapped and killed a bunch of homeless guys for their hearts, until I put a stop to him.
I mean, sure, I was only there in the first place to try to get his heart surgeon to save Cassie, but hey--I still stopped him!
ut that guy's been ead for years--why ould his old company come after me?
WELL, TIME'S UP AND I GOT A LADYFRIEND TEXTIN' LIKE CRAZY. YOU TAKE CARE OF YOURSELF, LANG--AND DON'T GO AROUND TELLIN' PEOPLE THAT ARCH-ENEMY STUFF. I GOT A REPUTATION.
HEY, WAIT--YOU SAID YOU WERE JUST SUPPOSED TO KEEP ME BUSY? WHY?!
AW, YEAH-- 'BOUT THAT. LIKE I KEEP SAYIN', THIS IS JUST BUSINESS. FOR WHAT IT'S WORTH--
I AM SORRY 'BOUT YOUR LITTLE GIRL. SHE SEEMED ALL RIGHT.
Aw, no--

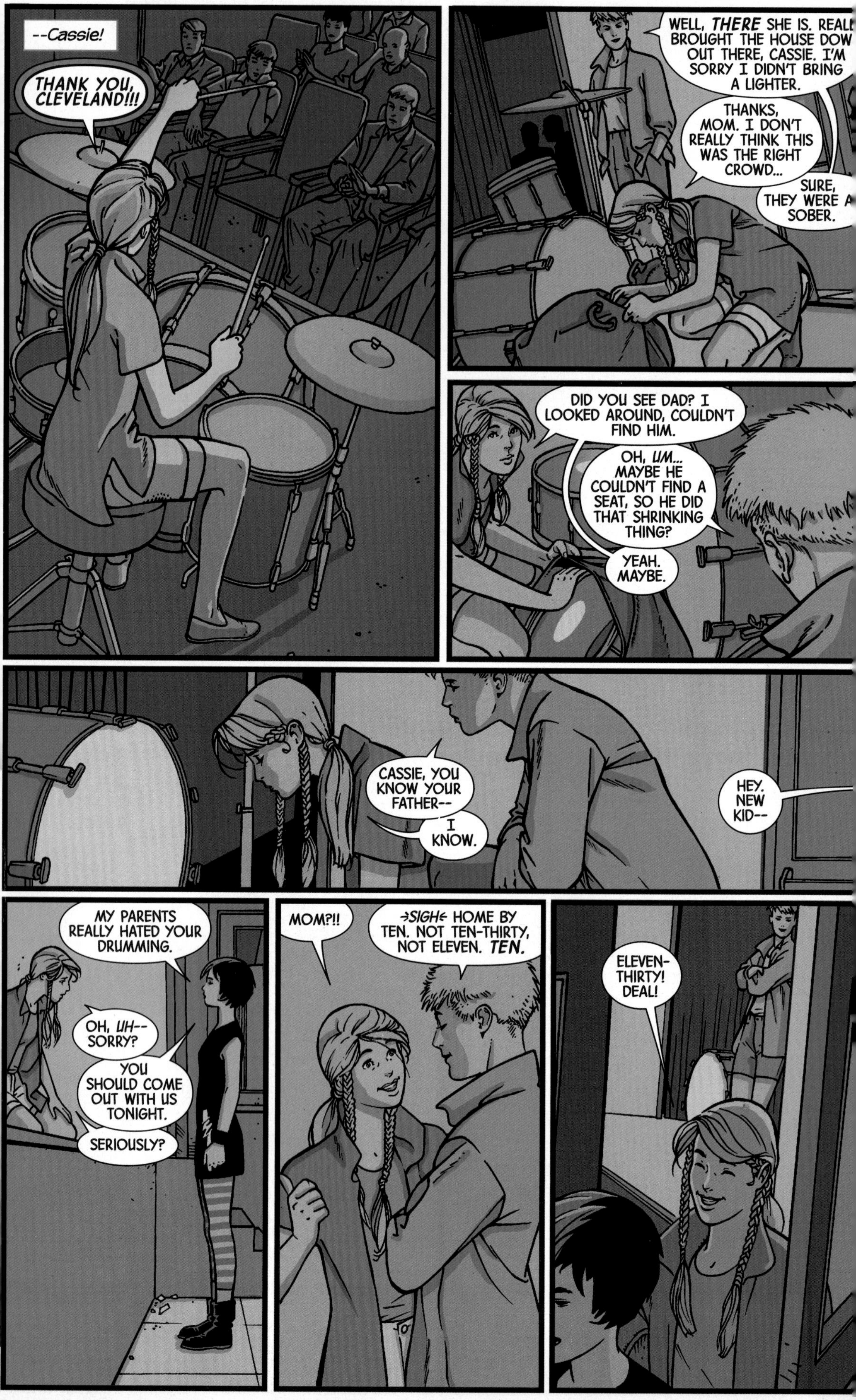
--Cassie!
THANK YOU, CLEVELAND!!!
WELL, *THERE* SHE IS. REALL BROUGHT THE HOUSE DOW OUT THERE, CASSIE. I'M SORRY I DIDN'T BRING A LIGHTER.
THANKS, MOM. I DON'T REALLY THINK THIS WAS THE RIGHT CROWD...
SURE, THEY WERE A SOBER.
DID YOU SEE DAD? I LOOKED AROUND, COULDN'T FIND HIM.
OH, *UM*... MAYBE HE COULDN'T FIND A SEAT, SO HE DID THAT SHRINKING THING?
YEAH. MAYBE.
CASSIE, YOU KNOW YOUR FATHER--
I KNOW.
HEY. NEW KID--
MY PARENTS REALLY HATED YOUR DRUMMING.
OH, *UH*-- SORRY?
YOU SHOULD COME OUT WITH US TONIGHT.
SERIOUSLY?
MOM?!!
→*SIGH*← HOME BY TEN. NOT TEN-THIRTY, NOT ELEVEN. *TEN.*
ELEVEN-THIRTY! DEAL!

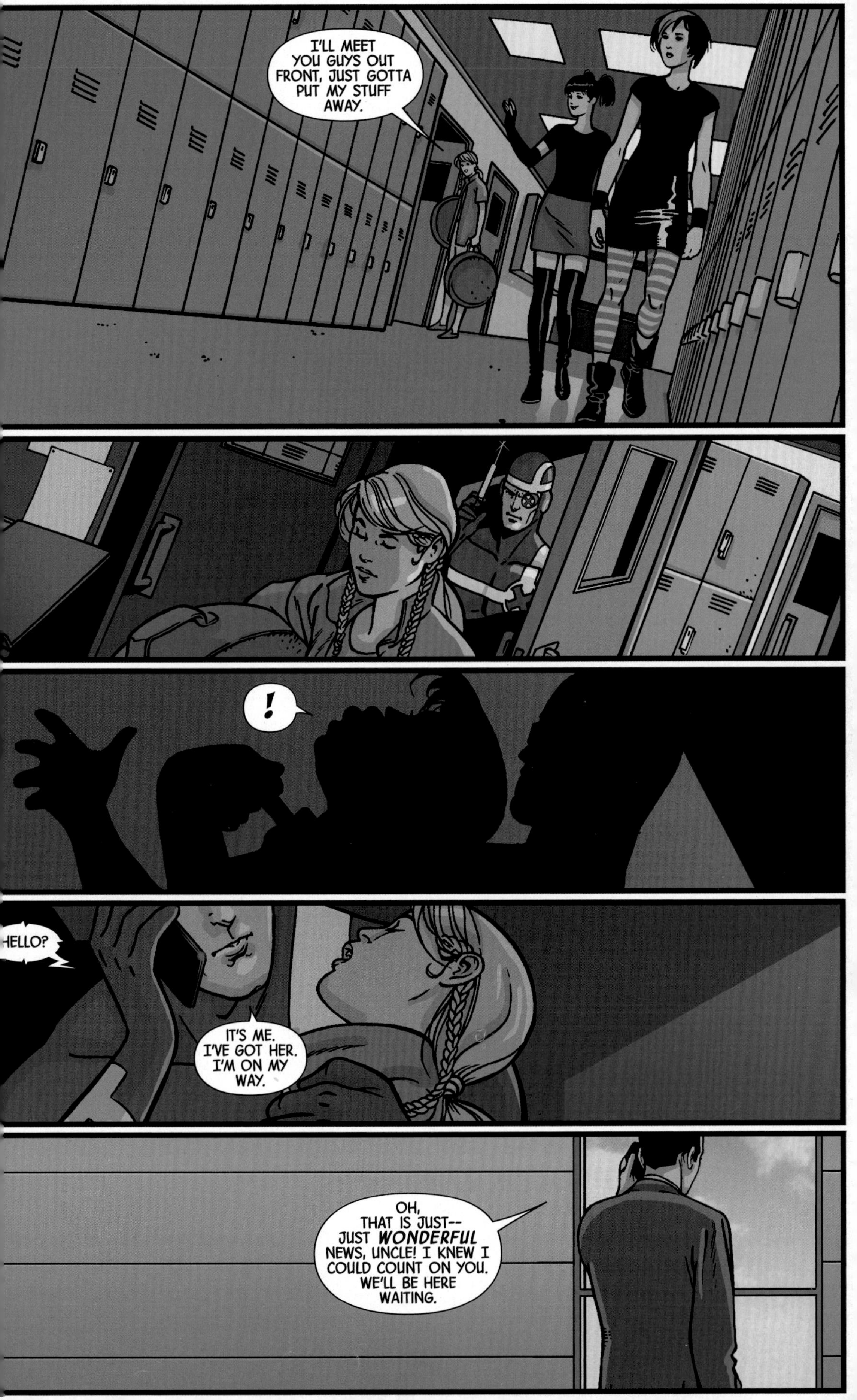
I'LL MEET YOU GUYS OUT FRONT, JUST GOTTA PUT MY STUFF AWAY.
!
HELLO?
IT'S ME. I'VE GOT HER. I'M ON MY WAY.
OH, THAT IS JUST-- JUST WONDERFUL NEWS, UNCLE! I KNEW I COULD COUNT ON YOU. WE'LL BE HERE WAITING.

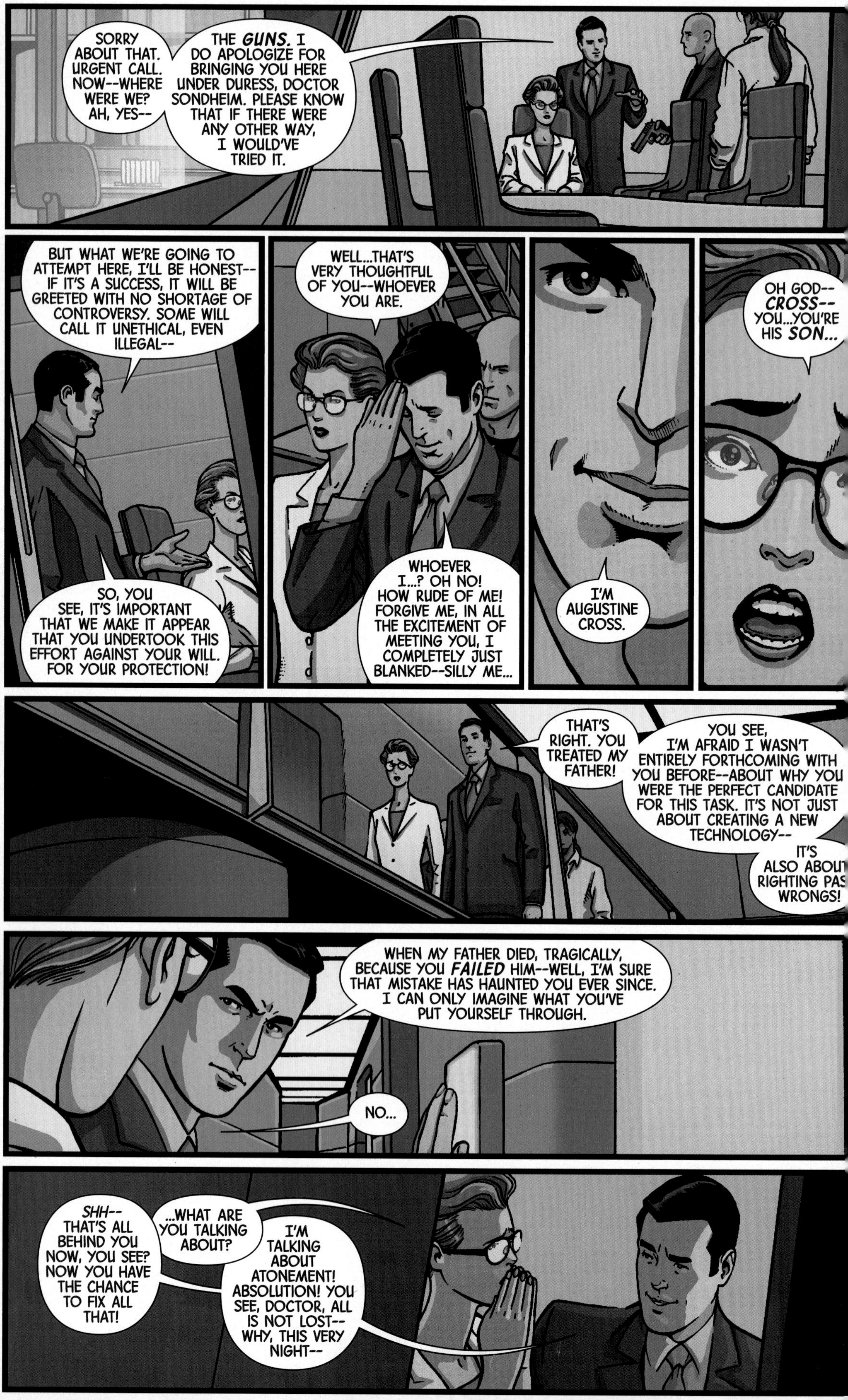
SORRY ABOUT THAT. URGENT CALL. NOW--WHERE WERE WE? AH, YES--
THE GUNS. I DO APOLOGIZE FOR BRINGING YOU HERE UNDER DURESS, DOCTOR SONDHEIM. PLEASE KNOW THAT IF THERE WERE ANY OTHER WAY, I WOULD'VE TRIED IT.
BUT WHAT WE'RE GOING TO ATTEMPT HERE, I'LL BE HONEST--IF IT'S A SUCCESS, IT WILL BE GREETED WITH NO SHORTAGE OF CONTROVERSY. SOME WILL CALL IT UNETHICAL, EVEN ILLEGAL--
SO, YOU SEE, IT'S IMPORTANT THAT WE MAKE IT APPEAR THAT YOU UNDERTOOK THIS EFFORT AGAINST YOUR WILL. FOR YOUR PROTECTION!
WELL...THAT'S VERY THOUGHTFUL OF YOU--WHOEVER YOU ARE.
WHOEVER I...? OH NO! HOW RUDE OF ME! FORGIVE ME, IN ALL THE EXCITEMENT OF MEETING YOU, I COMPLETELY JUST BLANKED--SILLY ME...
I'M AUGUSTINE CROSS.
OH GOD--CROSS--YOU...YOU'RE HIS SON...
THAT'S RIGHT. YOU TREATED MY FATHER!
YOU SEE, I'M AFRAID I WASN'T ENTIRELY FORTHCOMING WITH YOU BEFORE--ABOUT WHY YOU WERE THE PERFECT CANDIDATE FOR THIS TASK. IT'S NOT JUST ABOUT CREATING A NEW TECHNOLOGY--
IT'S ALSO ABOUT RIGHTING PAS WRONGS!
WHEN MY FATHER DIED, TRAGICALLY, BECAUSE YOU FAILED HIM--WELL, I'M SURE THAT MISTAKE HAS HAUNTED YOU EVER SINCE. I CAN ONLY IMAGINE WHAT YOU'VE PUT YOURSELF THROUGH.
NO...
...WHAT ARE YOU TALKING ABOUT?
SHH--THAT'S ALL BEHIND YOU NOW, YOU SEE? NOW YOU HAVE THE CHANCE TO FIX ALL THAT!
I'M TALKING ABOUT ATONEMENT! ABSOLUTION! YOU SEE, DOCTOR, ALL IS NOT LOST--WHY, THIS VERY NIGHT--

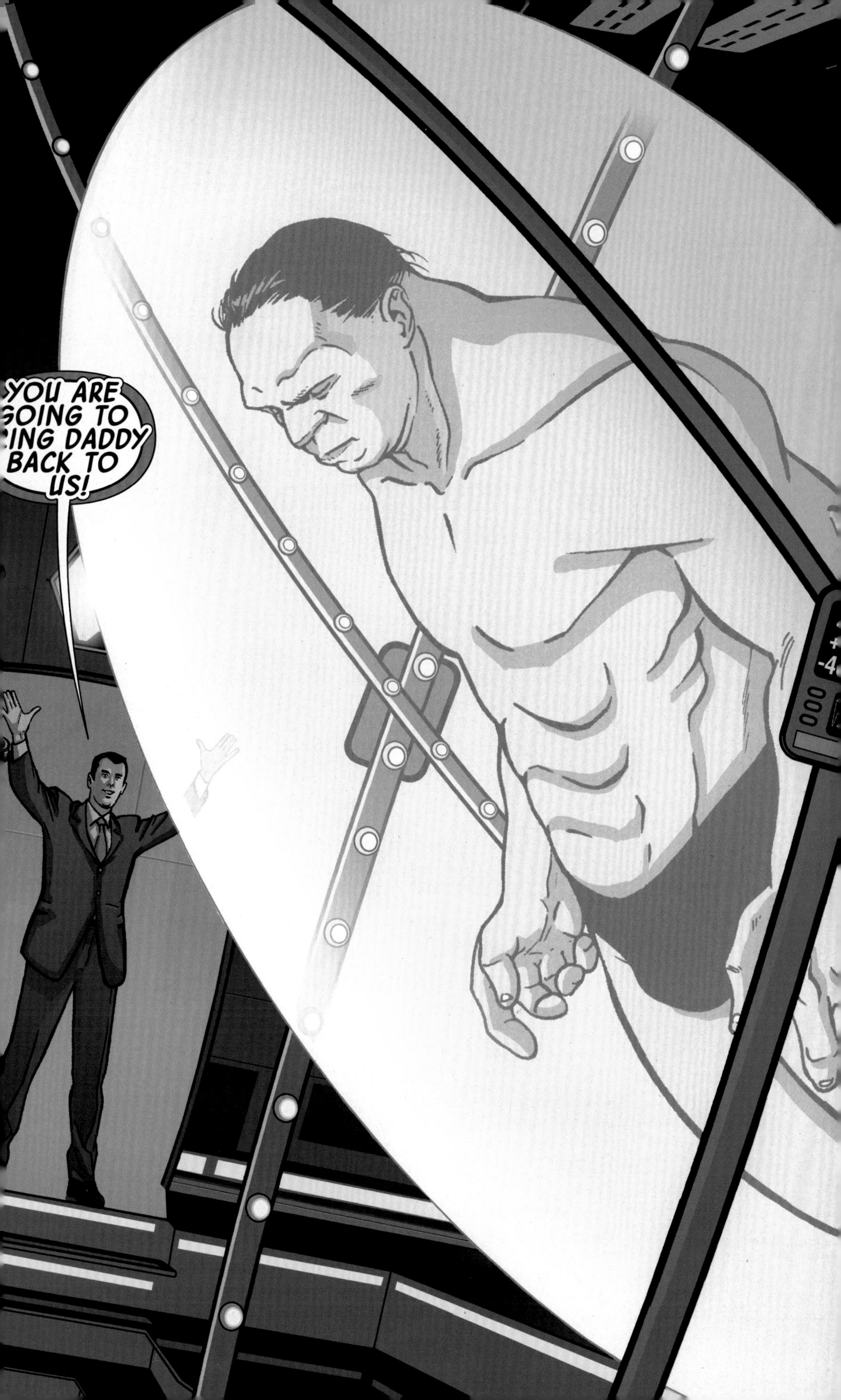
YOU ARE GOING TO ING DADDY BACK TO US!

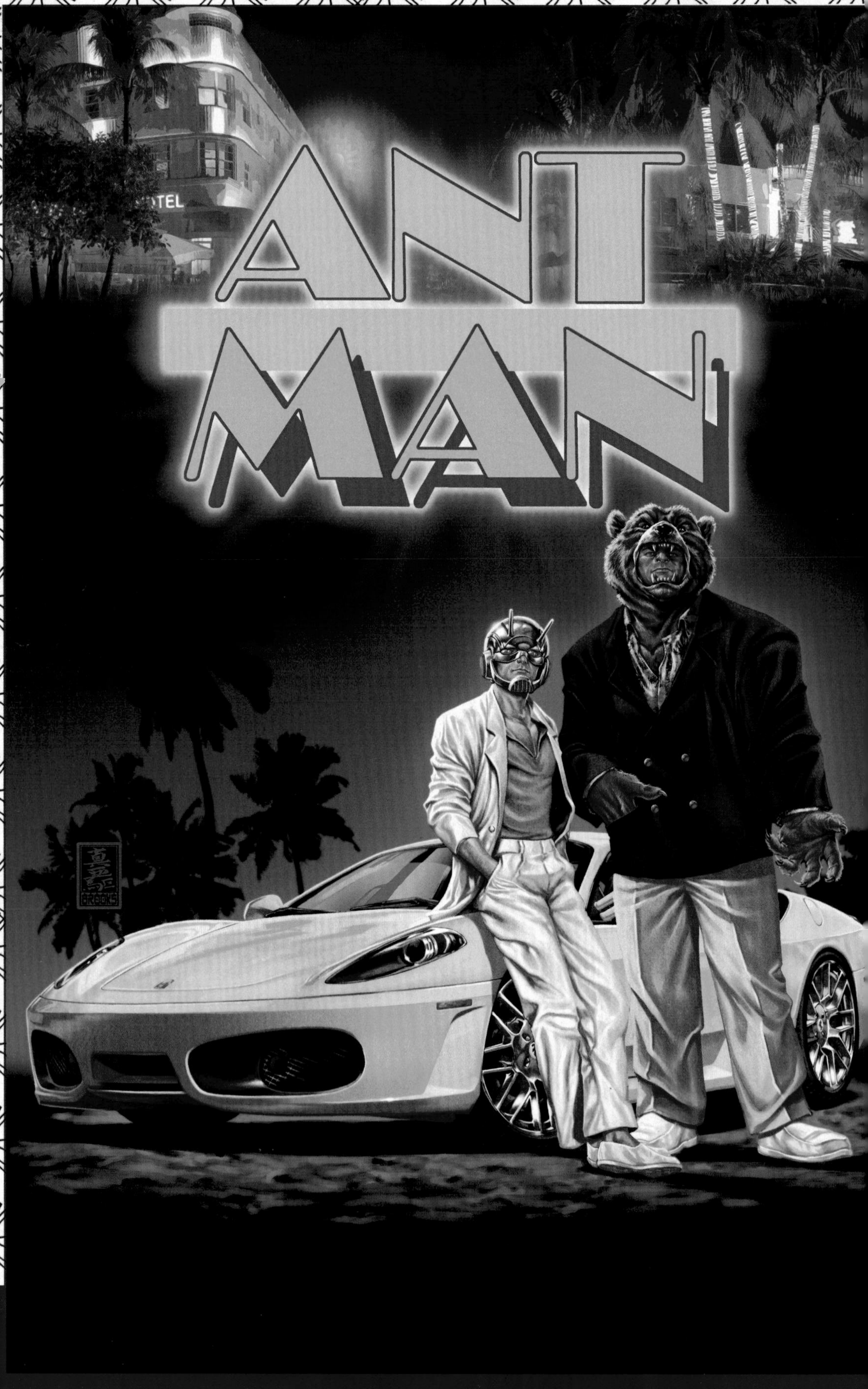
ANT
MAN
BROOKS

#4

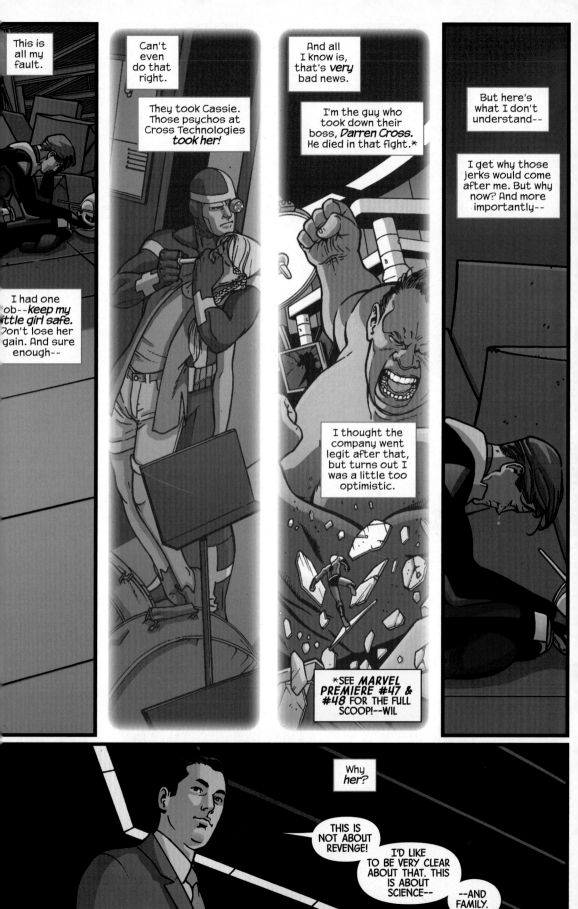

This is all my fault.

I had one job--*keep my little girl safe. Don't lose her again.* And sure enough--

Can't even do that right.

They took Cassie. Those psychos at Cross Technologies *took her!*

And all I know is, that's *very* bad news.

I'm the guy who took down their boss, *Darren Cross.* He died in that fight.*

I thought the company went legit after that, but turns out I was a little too optimistic.

*SEE *MARVEL PREMIERE #47* & *#48* FOR THE FULL SCOOP!--WIL

But here's what I don't understand--

I get why those jerks would come after me. But why now? And more importantly--

Why *her?*

THIS IS NOT ABOUT REVENGE!

I'D LIKE TO BE VERY CLEAR ABOUT THAT. THIS IS ABOUT SCIENCE--

--AND FAMILY.

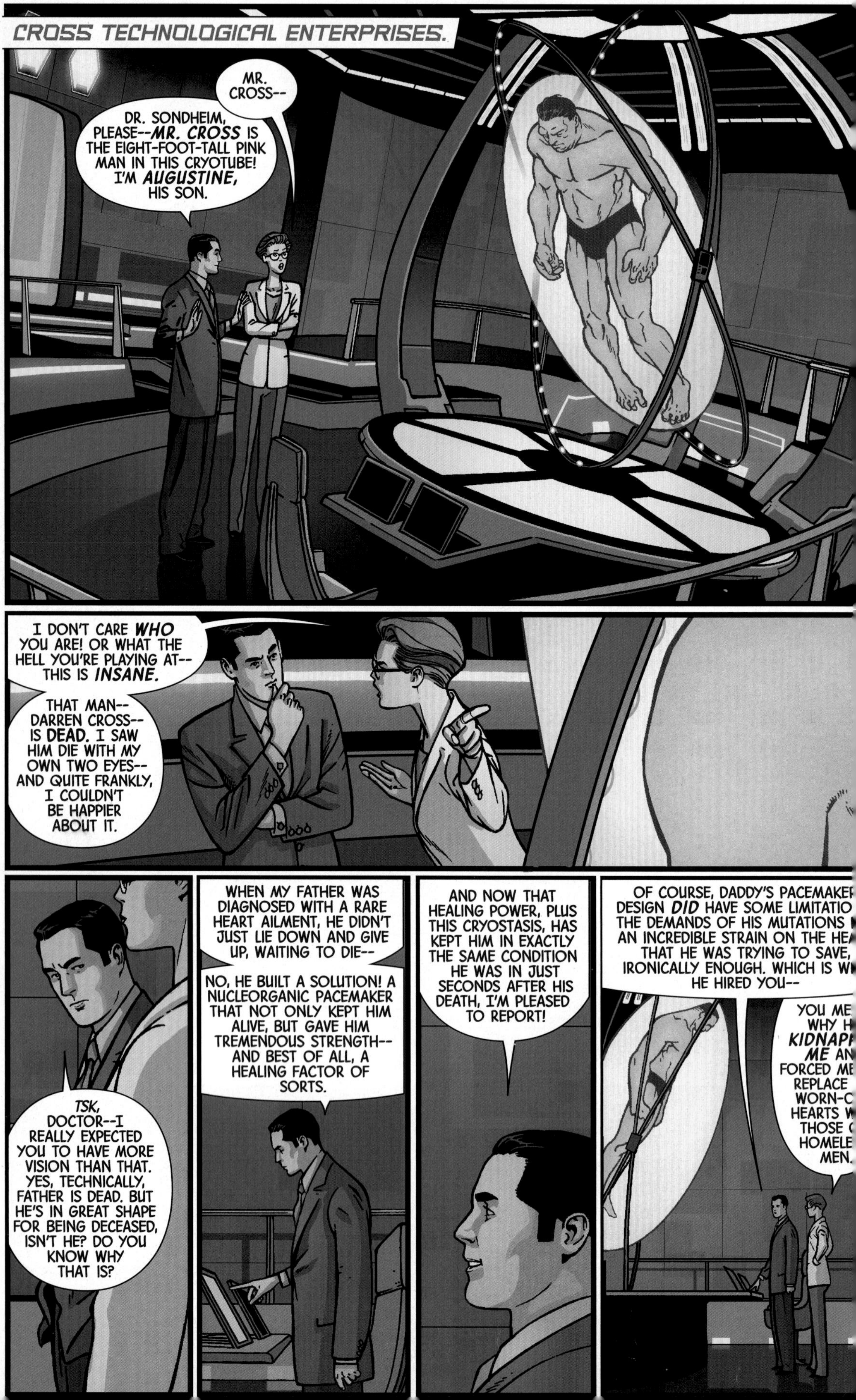
CROSS TECHNOLOGICAL ENTERPRISES.
MR. CROSS--
DR. SONDHEIM, PLEASE--MR. CROSS IS THE EIGHT-FOOT-TALL PINK MAN IN THIS CRYOTUBE! I'M AUGUSTINE, HIS SON.
I DON'T CARE WHO YOU ARE! OR WHAT THE HELL YOU'RE PLAYING AT-- THIS IS INSANE.
THAT MAN-- DARREN CROSS-- IS DEAD. I SAW HIM DIE WITH MY OWN TWO EYES-- AND QUITE FRANKLY, I COULDN'T BE HAPPIER ABOUT IT.
TSK, DOCTOR--I REALLY EXPECTED YOU TO HAVE MORE VISION THAN THAT. YES, TECHNICALLY, FATHER IS DEAD. BUT HE'S IN GREAT SHAPE FOR BEING DECEASED, ISN'T HE? DO YOU KNOW WHY THAT IS?
WHEN MY FATHER WAS DIAGNOSED WITH A RARE HEART AILMENT, HE DIDN'T JUST LIE DOWN AND GIVE UP, WAITING TO DIE--
NO, HE BUILT A SOLUTION! A NUCLEORGANIC PACEMAKER THAT NOT ONLY KEPT HIM ALIVE, BUT GAVE HIM TREMENDOUS STRENGTH-- AND BEST OF ALL, A HEALING FACTOR OF SORTS.
AND NOW THAT HEALING POWER, PLUS THIS CRYOSTASIS, HAS KEPT HIM IN EXACTLY THE SAME CONDITION HE WAS IN JUST SECONDS AFTER HIS DEATH, I'M PLEASED TO REPORT!
OF COURSE, DADDY'S PACEMAKER DESIGN DID HAVE SOME LIMITATIO THE DEMANDS OF HIS MUTATIONS AN INCREDIBLE STRAIN ON THE HE THAT HE WAS TRYING TO SAVE, IRONICALLY ENOUGH. WHICH IS W HE HIRED YOU--
YOU ME WHY H KIDNAPP ME AN FORCED ME REPLACE WORN-C HEARTS W THOSE HOMELE MEN.

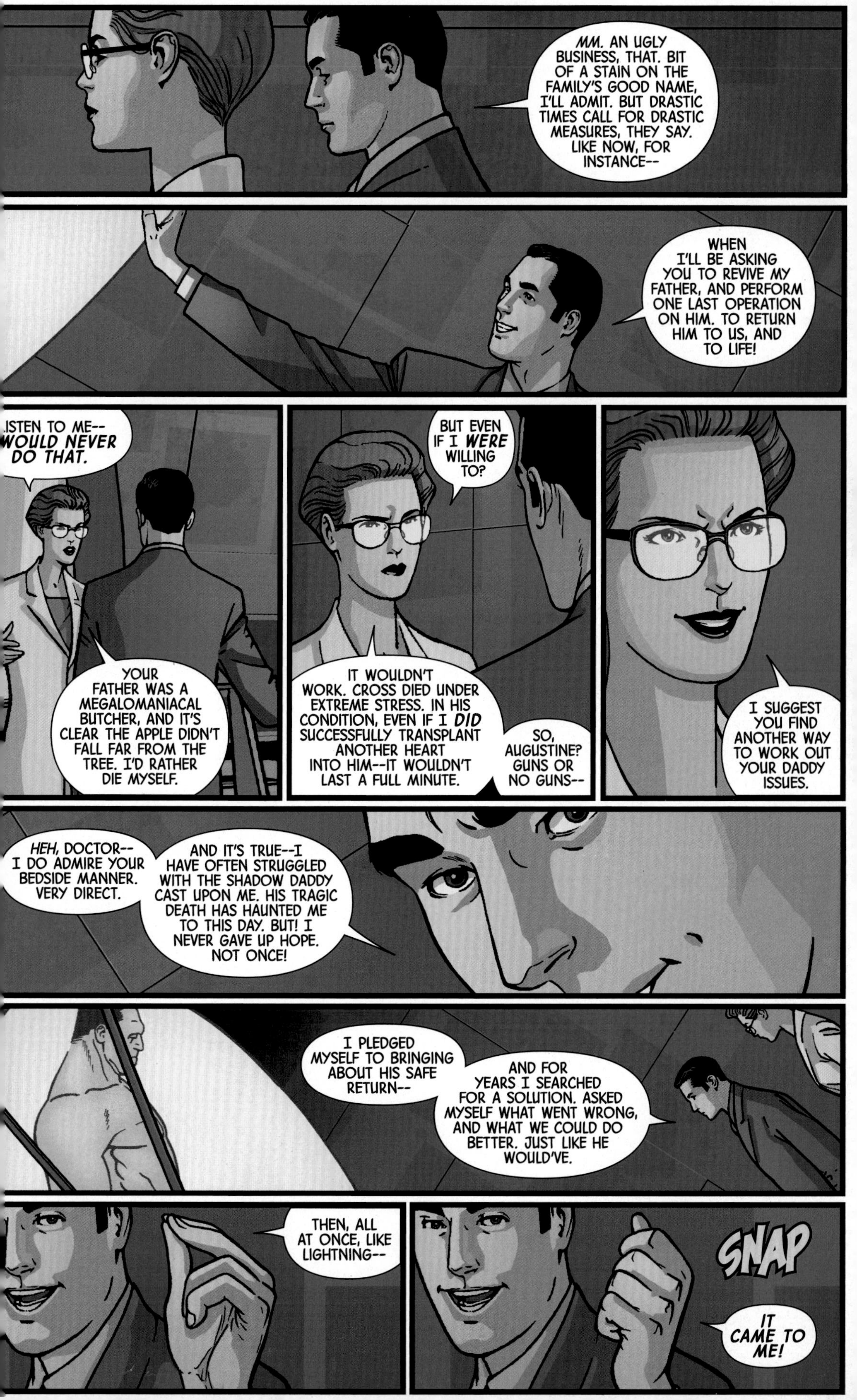
MM. AN UGLY BUSINESS, THAT. BIT OF A STAIN ON THE FAMILY'S GOOD NAME, I'LL ADMIT. BUT DRASTIC TIMES CALL FOR DRASTIC MEASURES, THEY SAY. LIKE NOW, FOR INSTANCE--
WHEN I'LL BE ASKING YOU TO REVIVE MY FATHER, AND PERFORM ONE LAST OPERATION ON HIM. TO RETURN HIM TO US, AND TO LIFE!
ISTEN TO ME-- WOULD NEVER DO THAT.
YOUR FATHER WAS A MEGALOMANIACAL BUTCHER, AND IT'S CLEAR THE APPLE DIDN'T FALL FAR FROM THE TREE. I'D RATHER DIE MYSELF.
BUT EVEN IF I WERE WILLING TO?
IT WOULDN'T WORK. CROSS DIED UNDER EXTREME STRESS. IN HIS CONDITION, EVEN IF I DID SUCCESSFULLY TRANSPLANT ANOTHER HEART INTO HIM--IT WOULDN'T LAST A FULL MINUTE.
SO, AUGUSTINE? GUNS OR NO GUNS--
I SUGGEST YOU FIND ANOTHER WAY TO WORK OUT YOUR DADDY ISSUES.
HEH, DOCTOR-- I DO ADMIRE YOUR BEDSIDE MANNER. VERY DIRECT.
AND IT'S TRUE--I HAVE OFTEN STRUGGLED WITH THE SHADOW DADDY CAST UPON ME. HIS TRAGIC DEATH HAS HAUNTED ME TO THIS DAY. BUT! I NEVER GAVE UP HOPE. NOT ONCE!
I PLEDGED MYSELF TO BRINGING ABOUT HIS SAFE RETURN--
AND FOR YEARS I SEARCHED FOR A SOLUTION. ASKED MYSELF WHAT WENT WRONG, AND WHAT WE COULD DO BETTER. JUST LIKE HE WOULD'VE.
THEN, ALL AT ONCE, LIKE LIGHTNING--
SNAP
IT CAME TO ME!

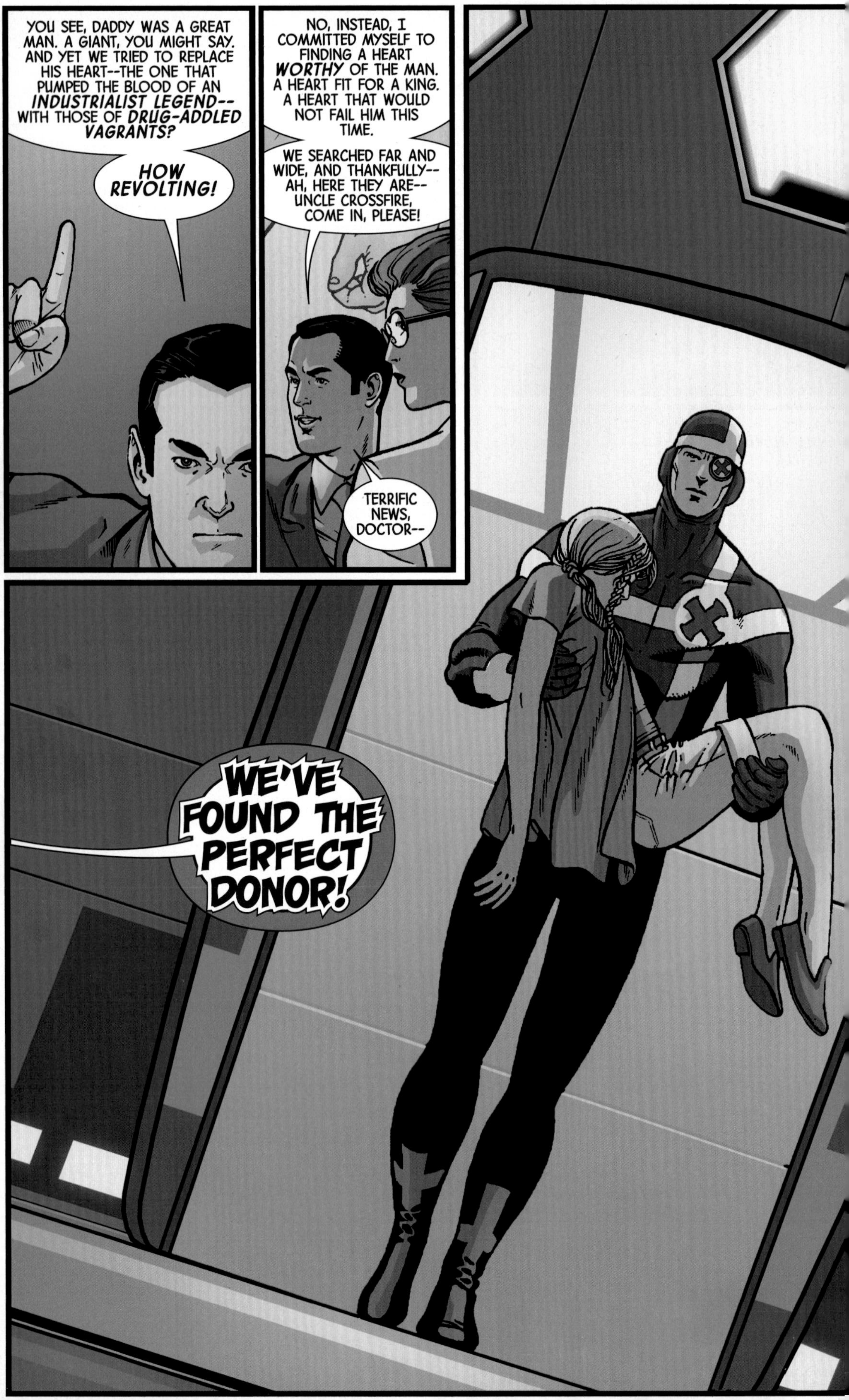
YOU SEE, DADDY WAS A GREAT MAN. A GIANT, YOU MIGHT SAY. AND YET WE TRIED TO REPLACE HIS HEART--THE ONE THAT PUMPED THE BLOOD OF AN INDUSTRIALIST LEGEND--WITH THOSE OF DRUG-ADDLED VAGRANTS?
HOW REVOLTING!
NO, INSTEAD, I COMMITTED MYSELF TO FINDING A HEART WORTHY OF THE MAN. A HEART FIT FOR A KING. A HEART THAT WOULD NOT FAIL HIM THIS TIME.
WE SEARCHED FAR AND WIDE, AND THANKFULLY--AH, HERE THEY ARE--UNCLE CROSSFIRE, COME IN, PLEASE!
TERRIFIC NEWS, DOCTOR--
WE'VE FOUND THE PERFECT DONOR!

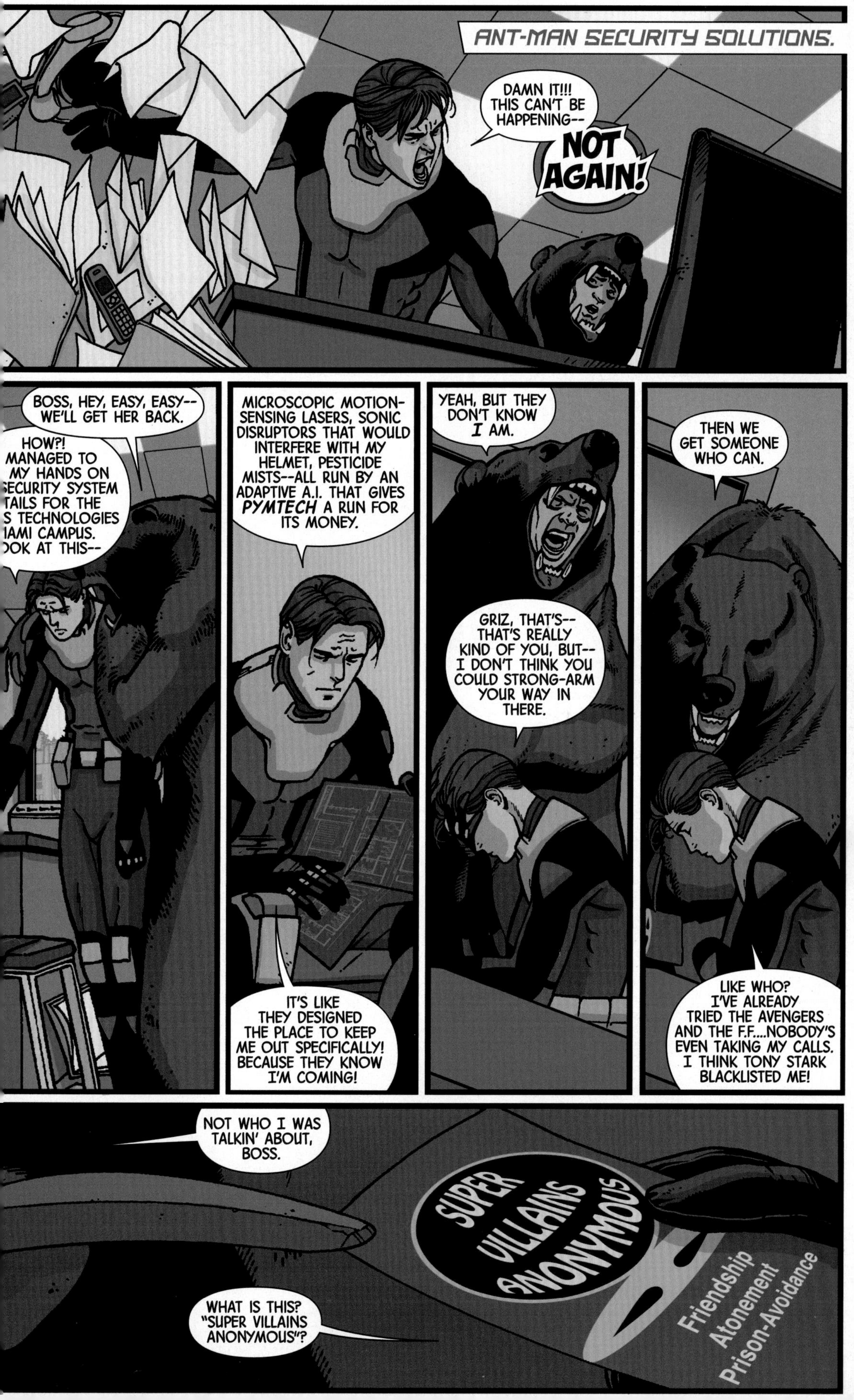
ANT-MAN SECURITY SOLUTIONS.
DAMN IT!!! THIS CAN'T BE HAPPENING--
NOT AGAIN!
BOSS, HEY, EASY, EASY-- WE'LL GET HER BACK.
HOW?! MANAGED TO MY HANDS ON SECURITY SYSTEM TAILS FOR THE S TECHNOLOGIES IAMI CAMPUS. OOK AT THIS--
MICROSCOPIC MOTION-SENSING LASERS, SONIC DISRUPTORS THAT WOULD INTERFERE WITH MY HELMET, PESTICIDE MISTS--ALL RUN BY AN ADAPTIVE A.I. THAT GIVES PYMTECH A RUN FOR ITS MONEY.
IT'S LIKE THEY DESIGNED THE PLACE TO KEEP ME OUT SPECIFICALLY! BECAUSE THEY KNOW I'M COMING!
GRIZ, THAT'S-- THAT'S REALLY KIND OF YOU, BUT-- I DON'T THINK YOU COULD STRONG-ARM YOUR WAY IN THERE.
YEAH, BUT THEY DON'T KNOW I AM.
THEN WE GET SOMEONE WHO CAN.
LIKE WHO? I'VE ALREADY TRIED THE AVENGERS AND THE F.F....NOBODY'S EVEN TAKING MY CALLS. I THINK TONY STARK BLACKLISTED ME!
NOT WHO I WAS TALKIN' ABOUT, BOSS.
SUPER VILLAINS ANONYMOUS
Friendship
Atonement
Prison-Avoidance
WHAT IS THIS? "SUPER VILLAINS ANONYMOUS"?

IT'S MY SUPPORT GROUP. YOU KNOW, SO I DON'T REVENGE-MURDER NO MORE.

I WAS ACTUALLY THINKING ABOUT ASKING YOU TO COME TO A MEETING--

WHY? I WAS NEVER A SUPER VILLAIN...

THOUGHT YOU SAID YOU'D BEEN TO PRISON?

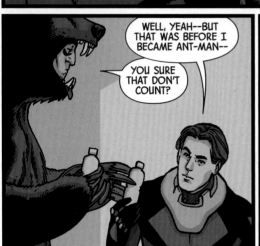

WELL, YEAH--BUT THAT WAS BEFORE I BECAME ANT-MAN--

YOU SURE THAT DON'T COUNT?

ANYHOW, WE GOT A GOOD GROUP DOWN HERE, LOTTA FORMER NEW YORK GUYS. WE PLAY VOLLEYBALL ON SATURDAYS.

VOLLEYBALL?

BOSS, JUST TRUST ME, OKAY? WE LOOK OUT FOR EACH OTHER IN THE PROGRAM. I SAY I NEED HELP, I'LL GET IT. AND BELIEVE ME--

27th Street

"THIS GUY CAN HELP."

YOU THINK YOU CAN TAKE ME ON, THOR?!

YOU'LL RUE THE DAY YOU MESSED WITH THE MALEVOLENT

MACHINESMITH!

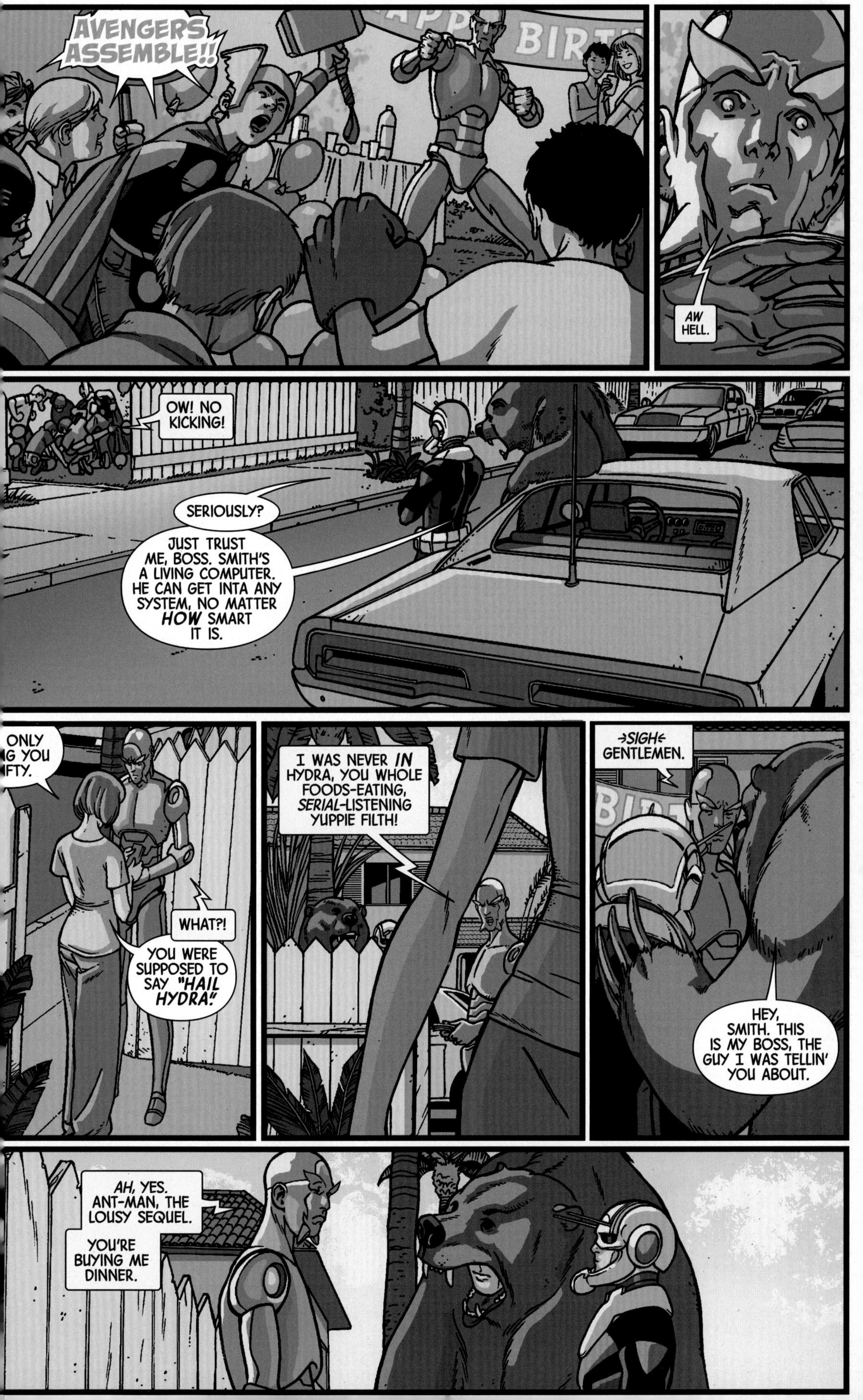

AVENGERS ASSEMBLE!!
AW HELL.
OW! NO KICKING!
SERIOUSLY?
JUST TRUST ME, BOSS. SMITH'S A LIVING COMPUTER. HE CAN GET INTA ANY SYSTEM, NO MATTER HOW SMART IT IS.
ONLY G YOU FTY.
WHAT?!
YOU WERE SUPPOSED TO SAY "HAIL HYDRA!"
I WAS NEVER IN HYDRA, YOU WHOLE FOODS-EATING, SERIAL-LISTENING YUPPIE FILTH!
SIGH GENTLEMEN.
HEY, SMITH. THIS IS MY BOSS, THE GUY I WAS TELLIN' YOU ABOUT.
AH, YES. ANT-MAN, THE LOUSY SEQUEL.
YOU'RE BUYING ME DINNER.

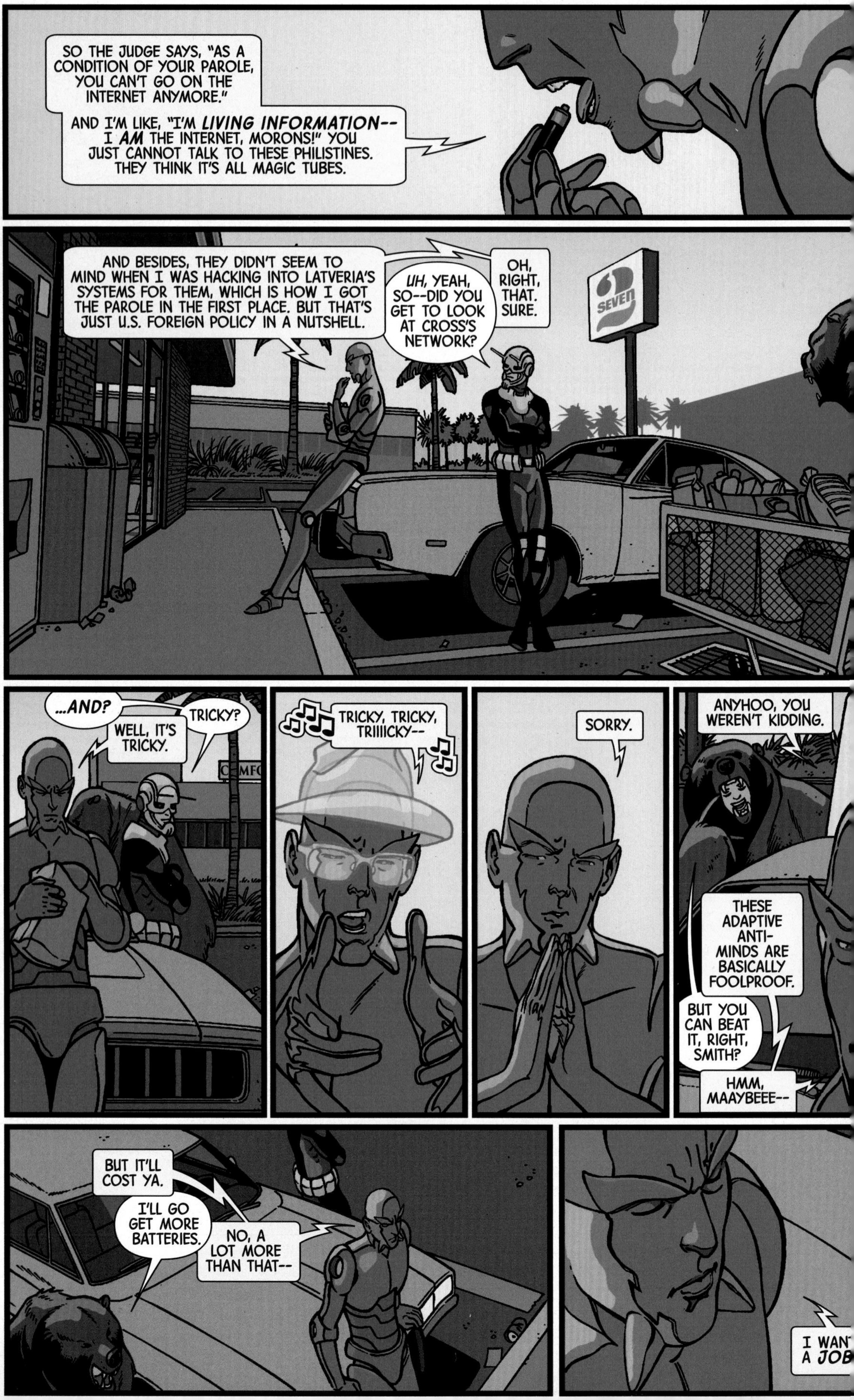

SO THE JUDGE SAYS, "AS A CONDITION OF YOUR PAROLE, YOU CAN'T GO ON THE INTERNET ANYMORE."
AND I'M LIKE, "I'M *LIVING INFORMATION*-- I ***AM*** THE INTERNET, MORONS!" YOU JUST CANNOT TALK TO THESE PHILISTINES. THEY THINK IT'S ALL MAGIC TUBES.
AND BESIDES, THEY DIDN'T SEEM TO MIND WHEN I WAS HACKING INTO LATVERIA'S SYSTEMS FOR THEM, WHICH IS HOW I GOT THE PAROLE IN THE FIRST PLACE. BUT THAT'S JUST U.S. FOREIGN POLICY IN A NUTSHELL.
OH, RIGHT, THAT. SURE.
UH, YEAH, SO--DID YOU GET TO LOOK AT CROSS'S NETWORK?
SEVEN
WELL, IT'S TRICKY.
...AND?
TRICKY?
TRICKY, TRICKY, TRIIIICKY--
SORRY.
ANYHOO, YOU WEREN'T KIDDING.
THESE ADAPTIVE ANTI-MINDS ARE BASICALLY FOOLPROOF.
BUT YOU CAN BEAT IT, RIGHT, SMITH?
HMM, MAAYBEEE--
BUT IT'LL COST YA.
I'LL GO GET MORE BATTERIES.
NO, A LOT MORE THAN THAT--
I WAN
A *JOB*

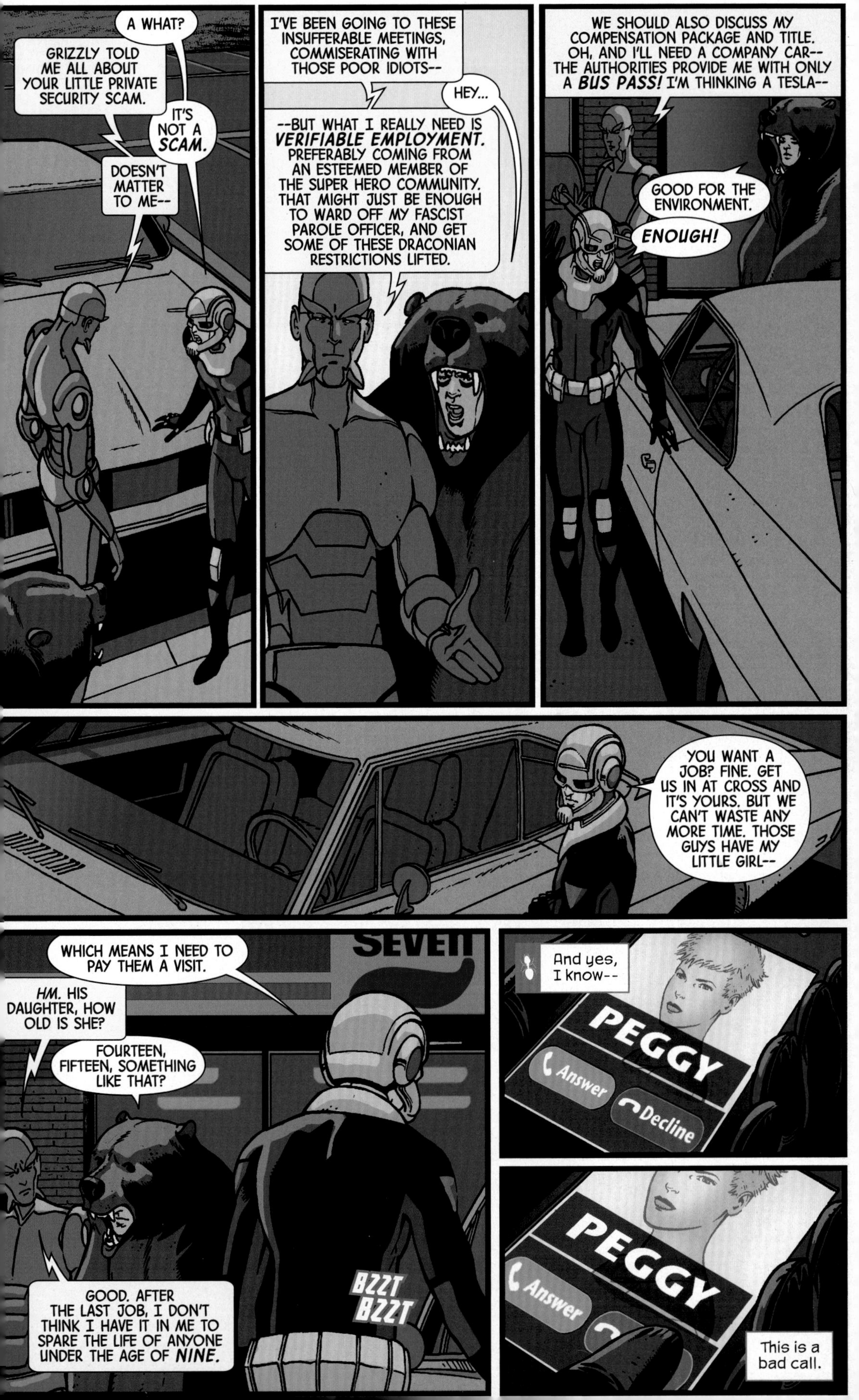
A WHAT?
GRIZZLY TOLD ME ALL ABOUT YOUR LITTLE PRIVATE SECURITY SCAM.
IT'S NOT A SCAM.
DOESN'T MATTER TO ME--
I'VE BEEN GOING TO THESE INSUFFERABLE MEETINGS, COMMISERATING WITH THOSE POOR IDIOTS--
HEY...
--BUT WHAT I REALLY NEED IS VERIFIABLE EMPLOYMENT. PREFERABLY COMING FROM AN ESTEEMED MEMBER OF THE SUPER HERO COMMUNITY. THAT MIGHT JUST BE ENOUGH TO WARD OFF MY FASCIST PAROLE OFFICER, AND GET SOME OF THESE DRACONIAN RESTRICTIONS LIFTED.
WE SHOULD ALSO DISCUSS MY COMPENSATION PACKAGE AND TITLE. OH, AND I'LL NEED A COMPANY CAR-- THE AUTHORITIES PROVIDE ME WITH ONLY A BUS PASS! I'M THINKING A TESLA--
GOOD FOR THE ENVIRONMENT.
ENOUGH!
YOU WANT A JOB? FINE. GET US IN AT CROSS AND IT'S YOURS. BUT WE CAN'T WASTE ANY MORE TIME. THOSE GUYS HAVE MY LITTLE GIRL--
SEVEN
WHICH MEANS I NEED TO PAY THEM A VISIT.
HM. HIS DAUGHTER, HOW OLD IS SHE?
FOURTEEN, FIFTEEN, SOMETHING LIKE THAT?
GOOD. AFTER THE LAST JOB, I DON'T THINK I HAVE IT IN ME TO SPARE THE LIFE OF ANYONE UNDER THE AGE OF NINE.
BZZT BZZT
And yes, I know--
PEGGY
Answer
Decline
PEGGY
Answer
This is a bad call.

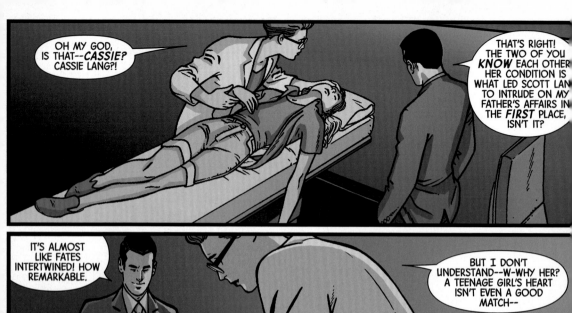

OH MY GOD, IS THAT--*CASSIE?* CASSIE LANG?!

THAT'S RIGHT! THE TWO OF YOU *KNOW* EACH OTHER. HER CONDITION IS WHAT LED SCOTT LANG TO INTRUDE ON MY FATHER'S AFFAIRS IN THE *FIRST* PLACE, ISN'T IT?

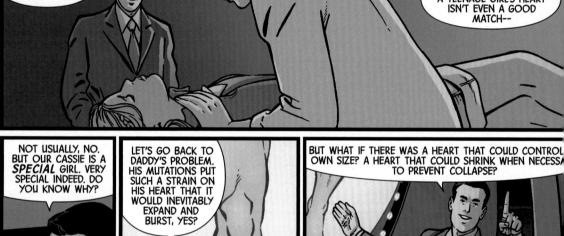

IT'S ALMOST LIKE FATES INTERTWINED! HOW REMARKABLE.

BUT I DON'T UNDERSTAND--W-WHY HER? A TEENAGE GIRL'S HEART ISN'T EVEN A GOOD MATCH--

NOT USUALLY, NO. BUT OUR CASSIE IS A *SPECIAL* GIRL. VERY SPECIAL INDEED. DO YOU KNOW WHY?

LET'S GO BACK TO DADDY'S PROBLEM. HIS MUTATIONS PUT SUCH A STRAIN ON HIS HEART THAT IT WOULD INEVITABLY EXPAND AND BURST, YES?

BUT WHAT IF THERE WAS A HEART THAT COULD CONTROL OWN SIZE? A HEART THAT COULD SHRINK WHEN NECESSA TO PREVENT COLLAPSE?

THAT'S RIGHT--A HEART IMBUED WITH *PYM PARTICLES!*

GO TO HELL! DO YOU REALLY THINK I WOULD KILL A YOUNG GIRL TO BRING THAT MURDEROUS BASTARD BACK TO LIFE?! IF *THAT'S* YOUR PLAN, GO AHEAD AND SHOOT ME NOW--

WHICH BRINGS ME TO MY OFFER.

...OU REFUSE, I WILL SHOOT ...OU. WELL, HAVE ONE OF ...Y MEN SHOOT YOU. I DETEST GUNS. ...ROUBLE IS, THEY'LL KILL ...U, BUT NOT UNTIL AFTER ...EY'VE KILLED CASSIE HERE. ...HEY'LL WANT YOU TO SEE THAT.

...D--WHAT'S ...HAT THEY ...Y IN THOSE ...OMERCIALS? ...WAIT, THAT'S ...OT ALL--"

ABE?

YES, YOUR SON. BEAUTIFUL BOY. NAMED FOR HIS LATE FATHER, WASN'T HE? WOULD BE SUCH A SHAME TO HAVE TO SAY GOODBYE TO HIM AS WELL.

SEEMS TO ME YOU CAN EITHER LOSE A FAMILY--

OR, YOU CAN BRING ONE BACK TOGETHER!

WHAT SAY YOU, DOCTOR? WE'VE GOT A STATE-OF-THE-ART LAB WAITING. IT HAS EVERYTHING YOU NEED--

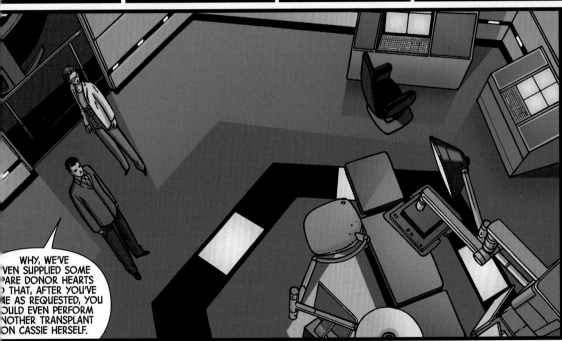

WHY, WE'VE ...VEN SUPPLIED SOME ...PARE DONOR HEARTS ...O THAT, AFTER YOU'VE ...NE AS REQUESTED, YOU ...OULD EVEN PERFORM ...NOTHER TRANSPLANT ...ON CASSIE HERSELF.

WE'VE GOT NO ILL-WILL TOWARDS THE GIRL, AFTER ALL-- I TOLD YOU, THIS IS NOT ABOUT REVENGE!

SO YOU CAN EITHER MAKE SURE EVERYONE HAS A HAPPY ENDING--

OR, YOU CAN DIE WITH THE BLOOD OF TWO CHILDREN ON YOUR HANDS. ENTIRELY YOUR CHOICE.

YOU JUST LET ME KNOW WHEN YOU'VE DECIDED.

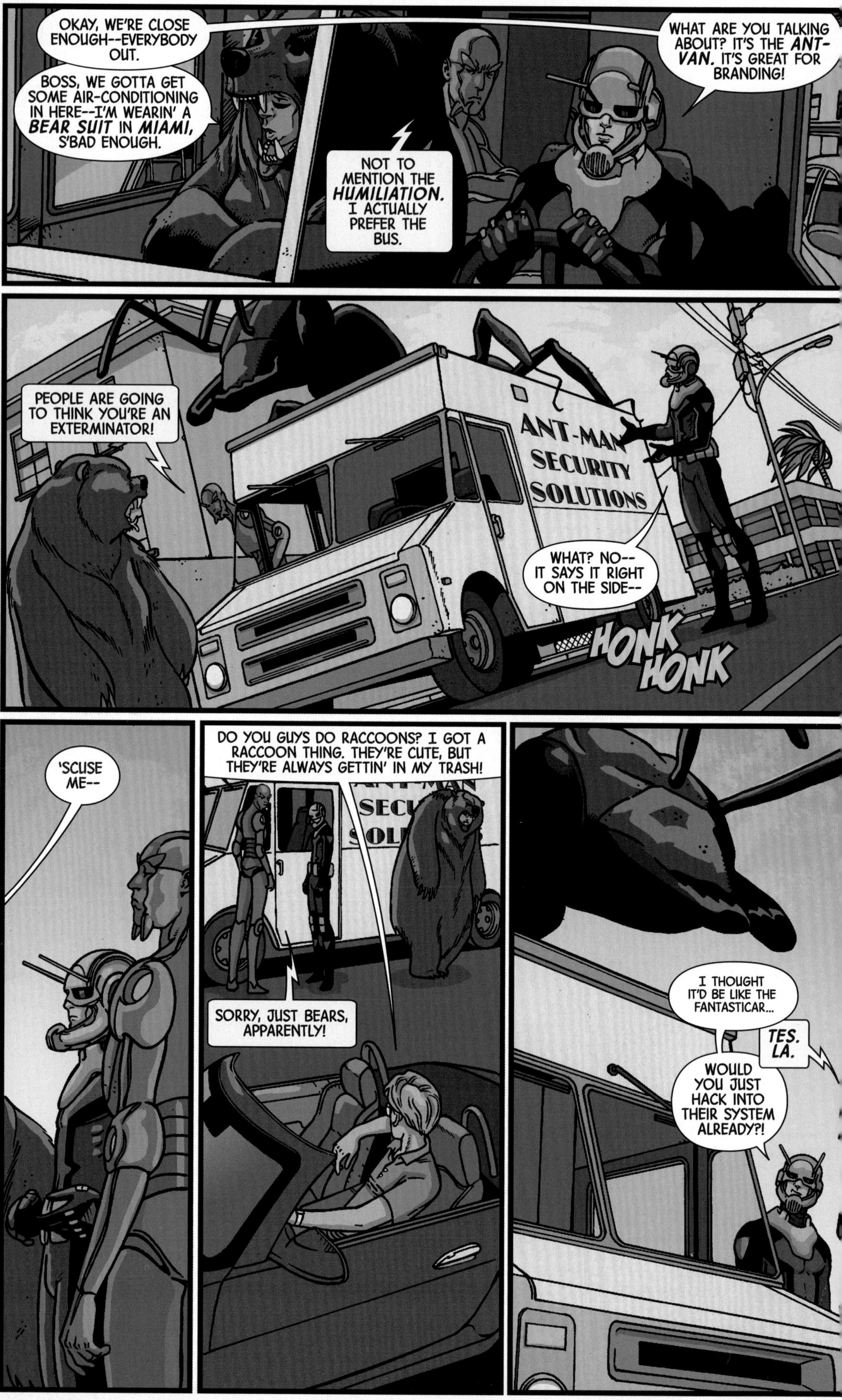

OKAY, WE'RE CLOSE ENOUGH--EVERYBODY OUT.
BOSS, WE GOTTA GET SOME AIR-CONDITIONING IN HERE--I'M WEARIN' A BEAR SUIT IN MIAMI, S'BAD ENOUGH.
NOT TO MENTION THE HUMILIATION. I ACTUALLY PREFER THE BUS.
WHAT ARE YOU TALKING ABOUT? IT'S THE ANT-VAN. IT'S GREAT FOR BRANDING!
PEOPLE ARE GOING TO THINK YOU'RE AN EXTERMINATOR!
ANT-MAN SECURITY SOLUTIONS
WHAT? NO--IT SAYS IT RIGHT ON THE SIDE--
HONK HONK
'SCUSE ME--
DO YOU GUYS DO RACCOONS? I GOT A RACCOON THING. THEY'RE CUTE, BUT THEY'RE ALWAYS GETTIN' IN MY TRASH!
SORRY, JUST BEARS, APPARENTLY!
I THOUGHT IT'D BE LIKE THE FANTASTICAR...
TES. LA.
WOULD YOU JUST HACK INTO THEIR SYSTEM ALREADY?!

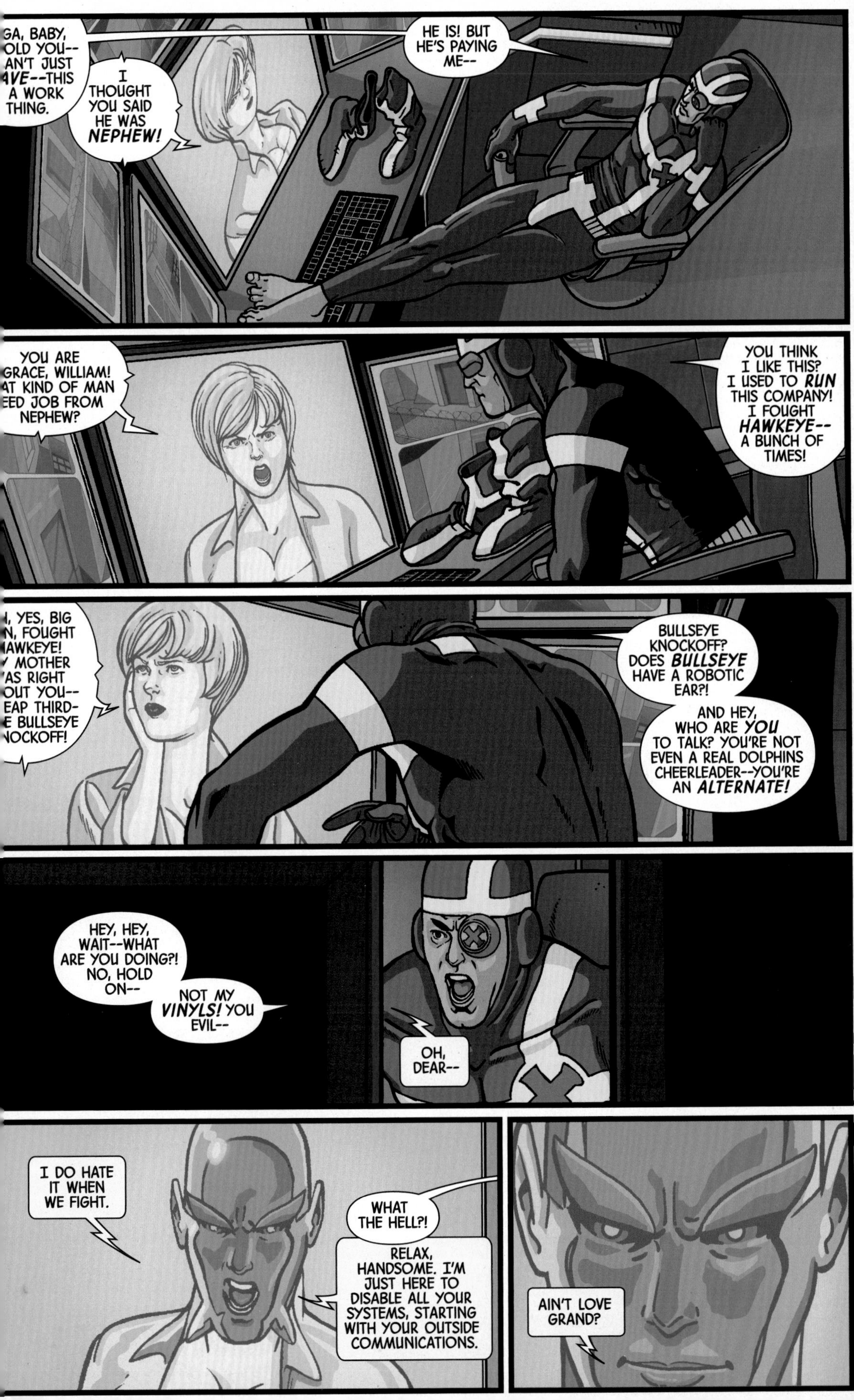
GA, BABY, OLD YOU-- AN'T JUST AVE--THIS A WORK THING.
HE IS! BUT HE'S PAYING ME--
I THOUGHT YOU SAID HE WAS NEPHEW!
YOU ARE GRACE, WILLIAM! AT KIND OF MAN EED JOB FROM NEPHEW?
YOU THINK I LIKE THIS? I USED TO RUN THIS COMPANY! I FOUGHT HAWKEYE-- A BUNCH OF TIMES!
, YES, BIG N, FOUGHT AWKEYE! MOTHER AS RIGHT OUT YOU-- EAP THIRD- E BULLSEYE NOCKOFF!
BULLSEYE KNOCKOFF? DOES BULLSEYE HAVE A ROBOTIC EAR?!
AND HEY, WHO ARE YOU TO TALK? YOU'RE NOT EVEN A REAL DOLPHINS CHEERLEADER--YOU'RE AN ALTERNATE!
HEY, HEY, WAIT--WHAT ARE YOU DOING?! NO, HOLD ON--
NOT MY VINYLS! YOU EVIL--
OH, DEAR--
I DO HATE IT WHEN WE FIGHT.
WHAT THE HELL?!
RELAX, HANDSOME. I'M JUST HERE TO DISABLE ALL YOUR SYSTEMS, STARTING WITH YOUR OUTSIDE COMMUNICATIONS.
AIN'T LOVE GRAND?

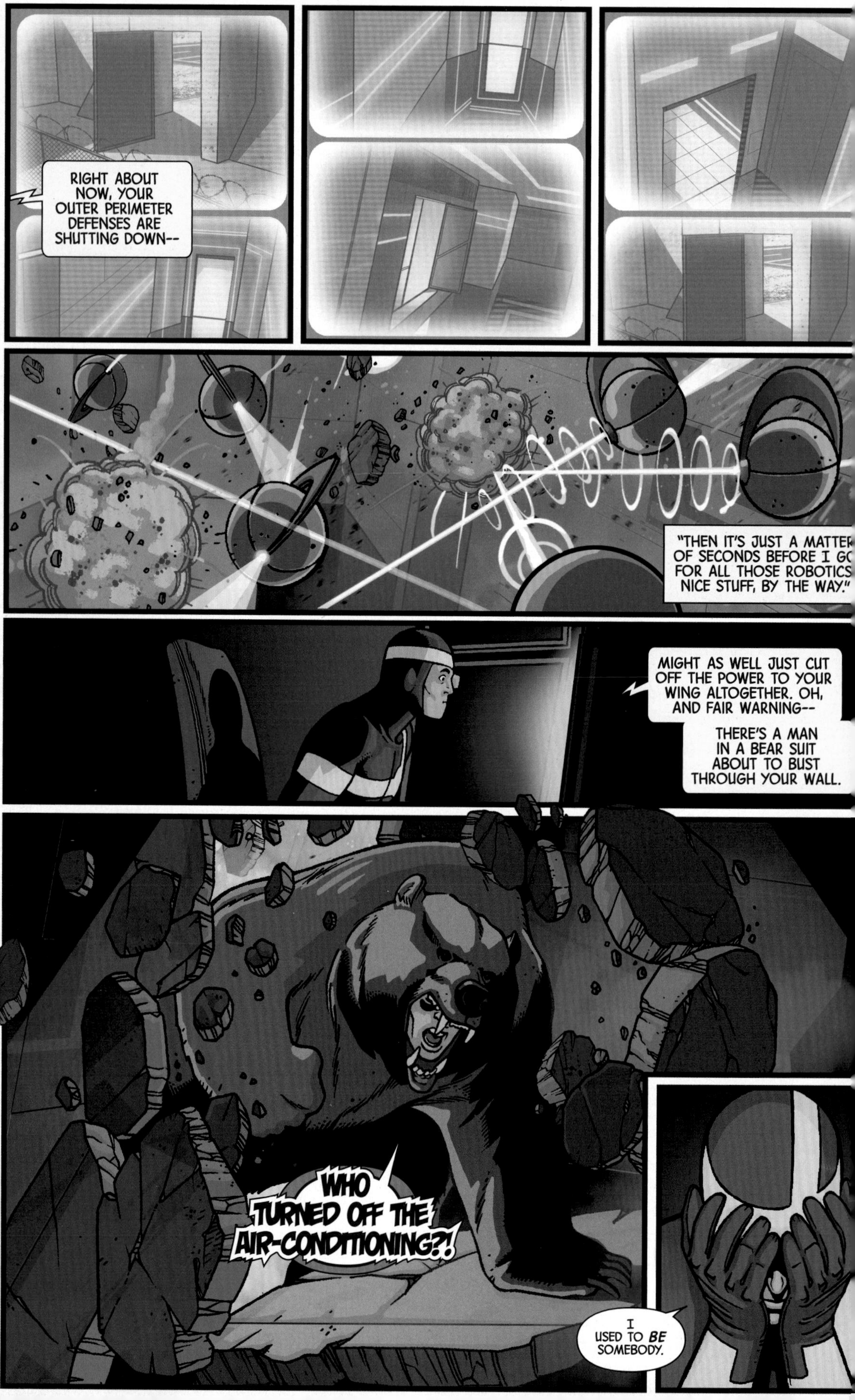

RIGHT ABOUT NOW, YOUR OUTER PERIMETER DEFENSES ARE SHUTTING DOWN--
"THEN IT'S JUST A MATTER OF SECONDS BEFORE I GO FOR ALL THOSE ROBOTICS. NICE STUFF, BY THE WAY."
MIGHT AS WELL JUST CUT OFF THE POWER TO YOUR WING ALTOGETHER. OH, AND FAIR WARNING--
THERE'S A MAN IN A BEAR SUIT ABOUT TO BUST THROUGH YOUR WALL.
WHO TURNED OFF THE AIR-CONDITIONING?!
I USED TO BE SOMEBODY.

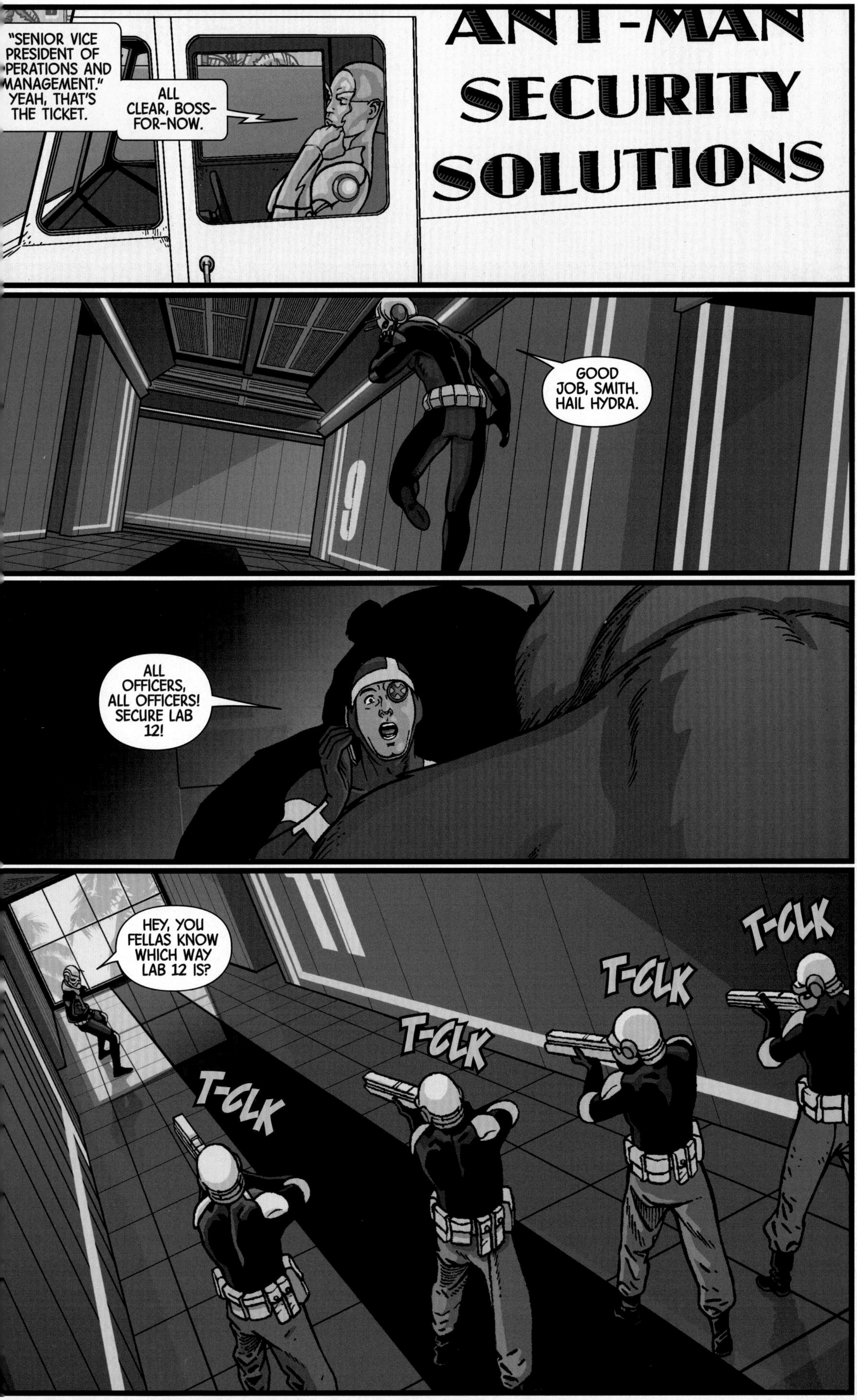

"SENIOR VICE PRESIDENT OF OPERATIONS AND MANAGEMENT." YEAH, THAT'S THE TICKET.
ALL CLEAR, BOSS-FOR-NOW.
ANT-MAN SECURITY SOLUTIONS
GOOD JOB, SMITH. HAIL HYDRA.
9
ALL OFFICERS, ALL OFFICERS! SECURE LAB 12!
11
HEY, YOU FELLAS KNOW WHICH WAY LAB 12 IS?
T-CLK
T-CLK
T-CLK
T-CLK

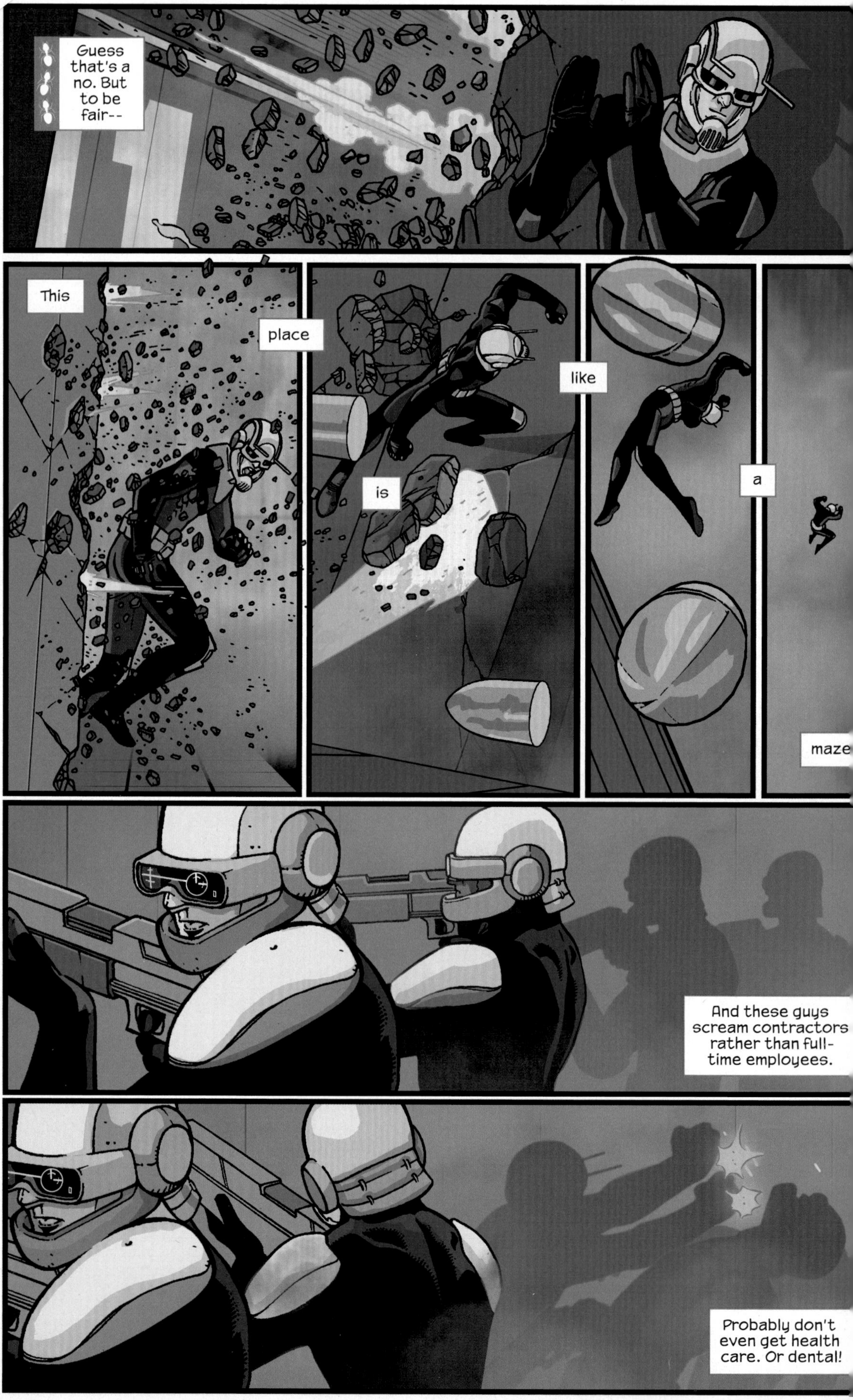

Guess that's a no. But to be fair--
This
place
is
like
a
maze
And these guys scream contractors rather than full-time employees.
Probably don't even get health care. Or dental!

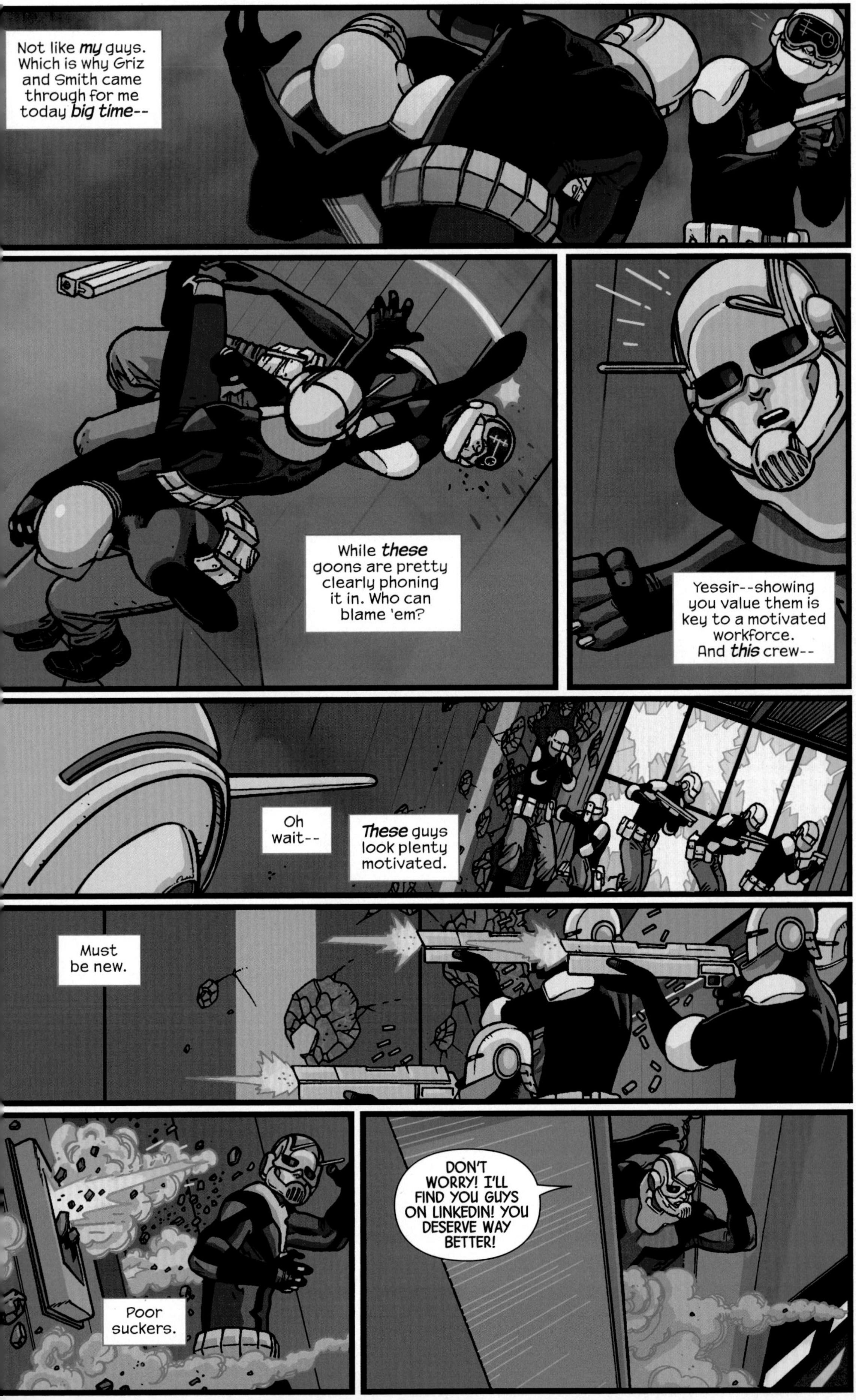
Not like *my* guys. Which is why Griz and Smith came through for me today *big time*--
While *these* goons are pretty clearly phoning it in. Who can blame 'em?
Yessir--showing you value them is key to a motivated workforce. And *this* crew--
Oh wait--
These guys look plenty motivated.
Must be new.
Poor suckers.
DON'T WORRY! I'LL FIND YOU GUYS ON LINKEDIN! YOU DESERVE WAY BETTER!

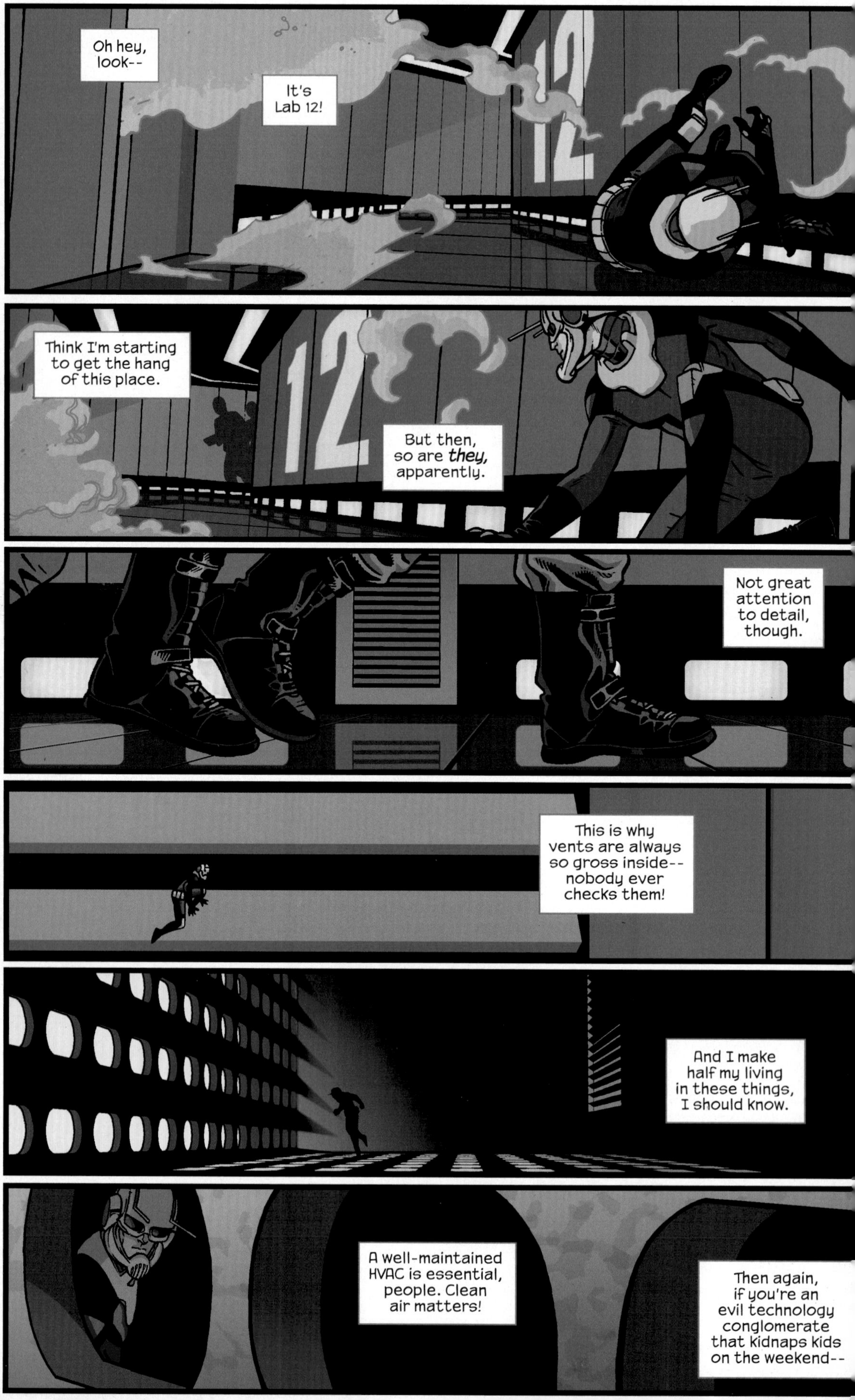
Oh hey, look--
It's Lab 12!
Think I'm starting to get the hang of this place.
But then, so are *they,* apparently.
Not great attention to detail, though.
This is why vents are always so gross inside-- nobody ever checks them!
And I make half my living in these things, I should know.
A well-maintained HVAC is essential, people. Clean air matters!
Then again, if you're an evil technology conglomerate that kidnaps kids on the weekend--

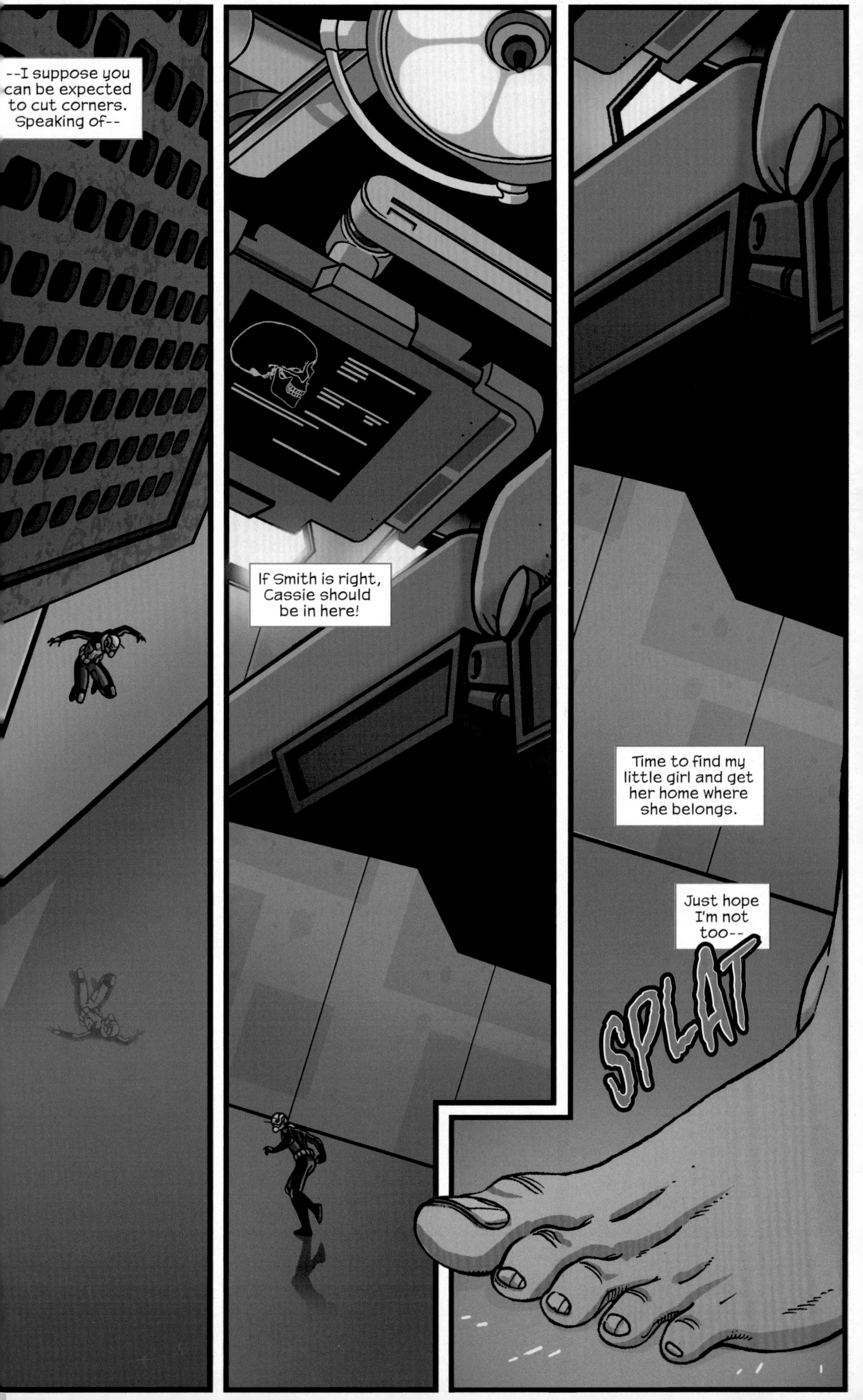
--I suppose you can be expected to cut corners. Speaking of--
If Smith is right, Cassie should be in here!
Time to find my little girl and get her home where she belongs.
Just hope I'm not too--
SPLAT

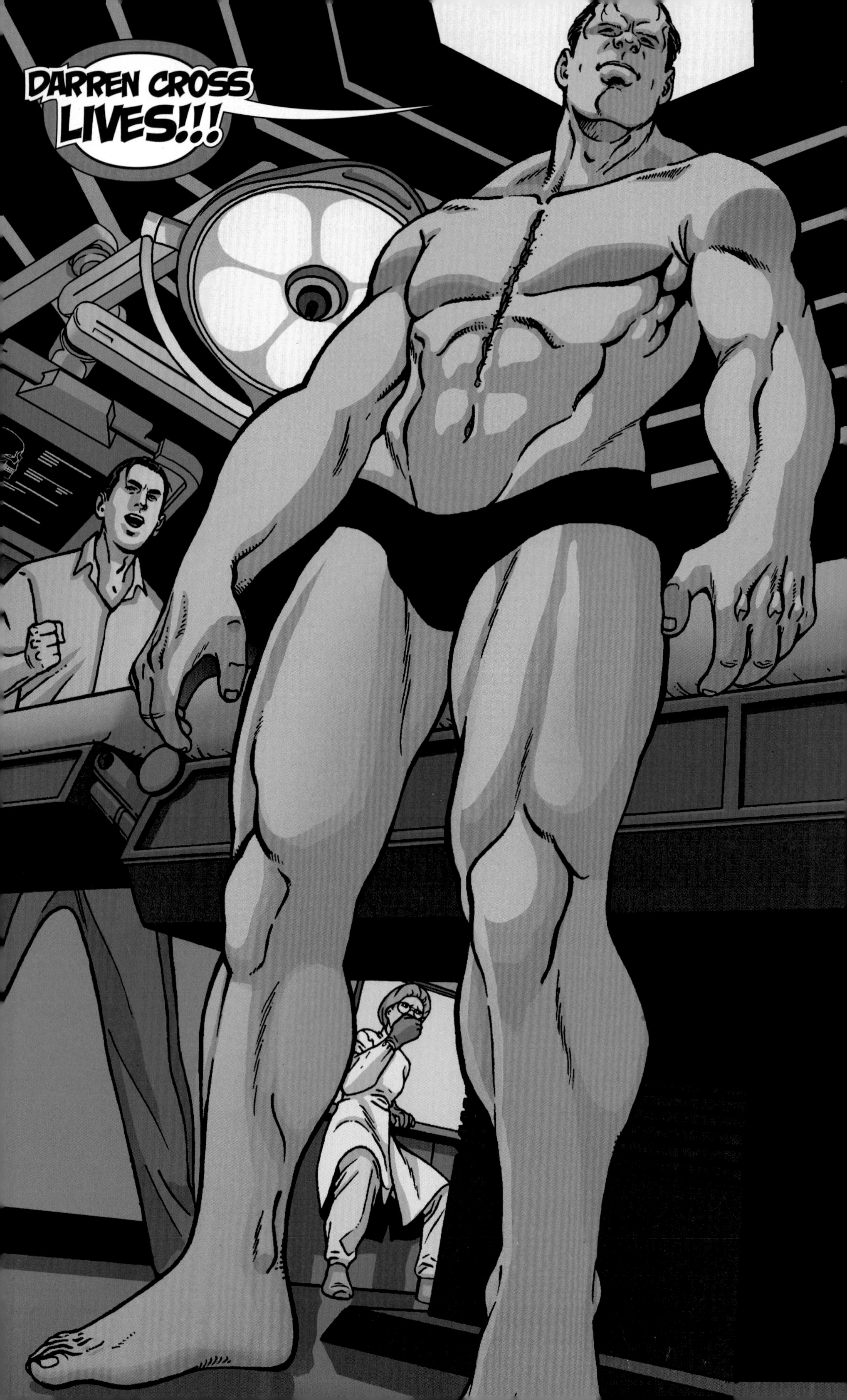
DARREN CROSS LIVES!!!

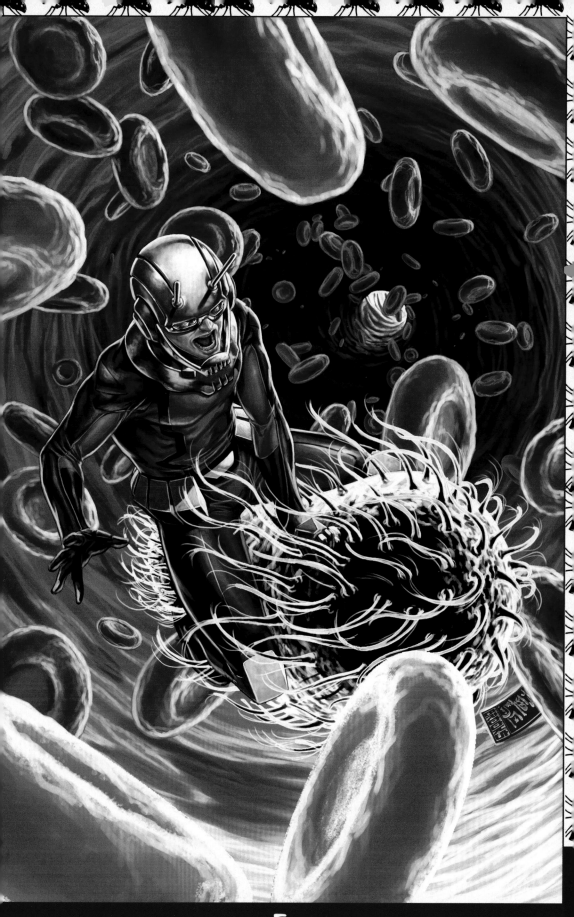

#5

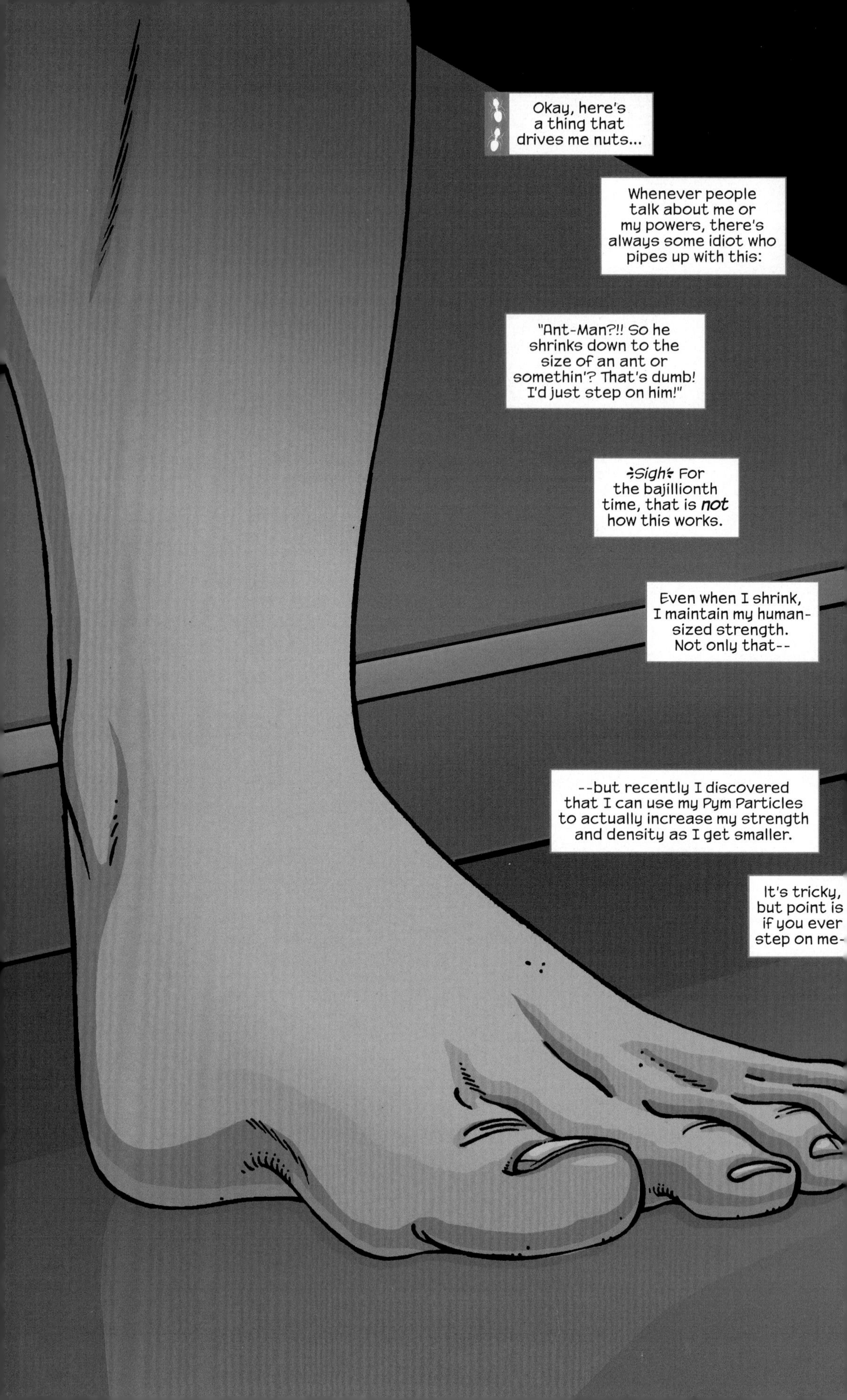

Okay, here's a thing that drives me nuts...
Whenever people talk about me or my powers, there's always some idiot who pipes up with this:
"Ant-Man?!! So he shrinks down to the size of an ant or somethin'? That's dumb! I'd just step on him!"
Sigh For the bajillionth time, that is **not** how this works.
Even when I shrink, I maintain my human-sized strength. Not only that--
--but recently I discovered that I can use my Pym Particles to actually increase my strength and density as I get smaller.
It's tricky, but point is if you ever step on me-

--*this* is what happens.

AH!

Darren Cross.

Darren Cross is alive!

This guy is the entire reason I got to be Ant-Man in the first place--

Scumbag tech industrialist who killed homeless dudes and took their hearts to keep himself alive.

'Til we fought and he died of a massive coronary. But, as always, it apparently didn't stick!

Is it hypocritical of me to hate the revolving door of death?

Either way, before I can even ask how this could possibly get worse--

I get the answer.

DOCTOR SONDHEIM?!!

STAY BACK--

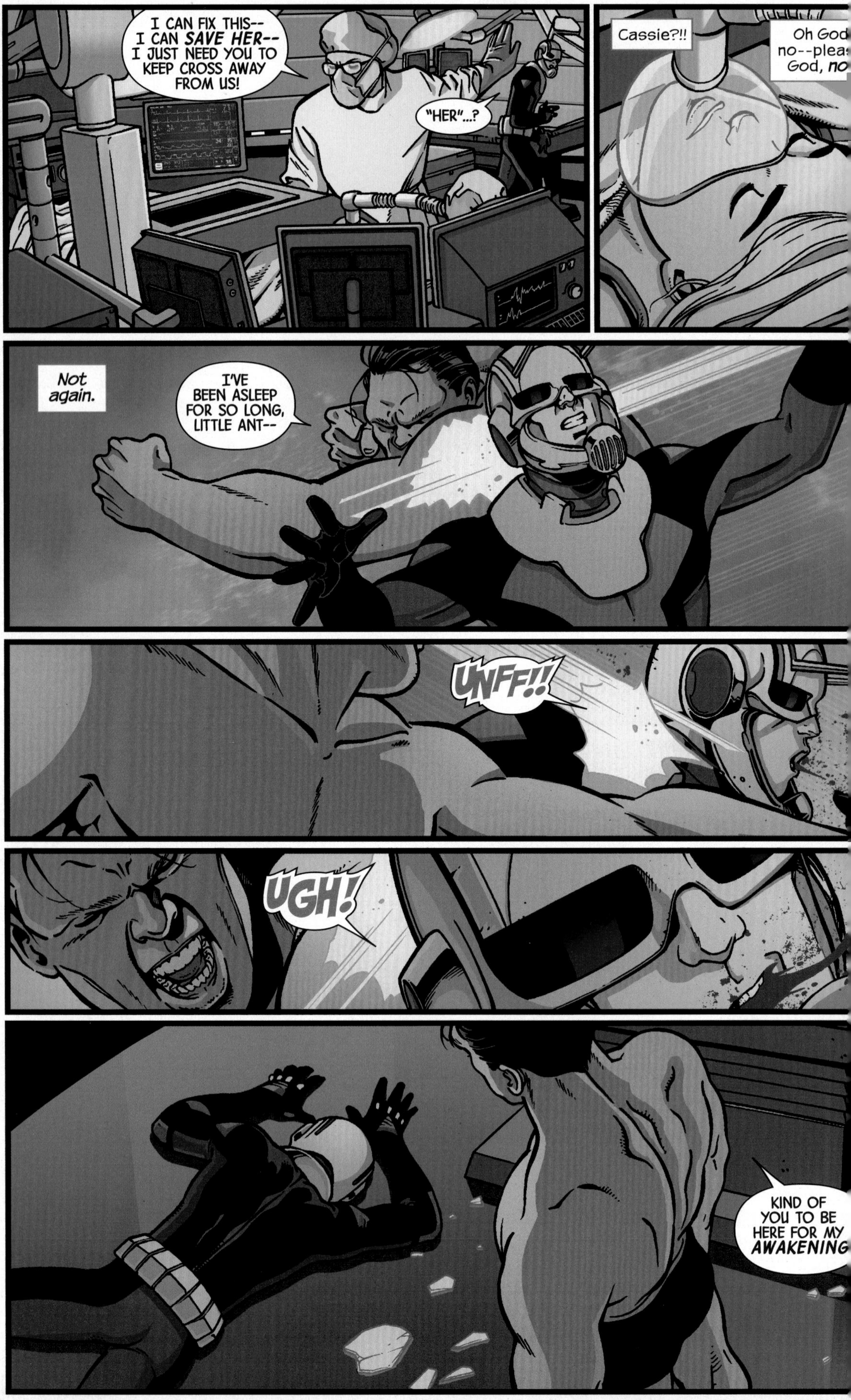
I CAN FIX THIS-- I CAN SAVE HER-- I JUST NEED YOU TO KEEP CROSS AWAY FROM US!
"HER"...?
Cassie?!!
Oh God no--pleas God, no
Not again.
I'VE BEEN ASLEEP FOR SO LONG, LITTLE ANT--
UNFF!!
UGH!
KIND OF YOU TO BE HERE FOR MY AWAKENING

...uy is too strong... ...aught me ...f-guard...

I FEEL REFRESHED!

REBORN!

I'm sorry, Cassie--

I tried.

REVENGEFUL!

AND NOW I'LL--

DADDY!

I'M SO HAPPY YOU'RE BACK!

...?

I KNEW IT WOULD WORK! I JUST KNEW IT!

HRR...

THE WHOLE THING WAS MY IDEA--KIDNAPPING ANT-MAN'S DAUGHTER, GIVING YOU HER HEART-- I THOUGHT OF IT ALL ON MY OWN! ARE YOU PROUD OF ME, DAD? ARE YOU?

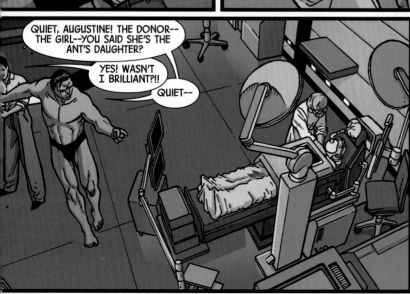

QUIET, AUGUSTINE! THE DONOR-- THE GIRL--YOU SAID SHE'S THE ANT'S DAUGHTER?

YES! WASN'T I BRILLIANT?!!

QUIET--

I THOUGHT I'D KILL YOU NOW, BUG--BUT APPARENTLY THERE'S SOMETHING YOU SHOULD SEE--

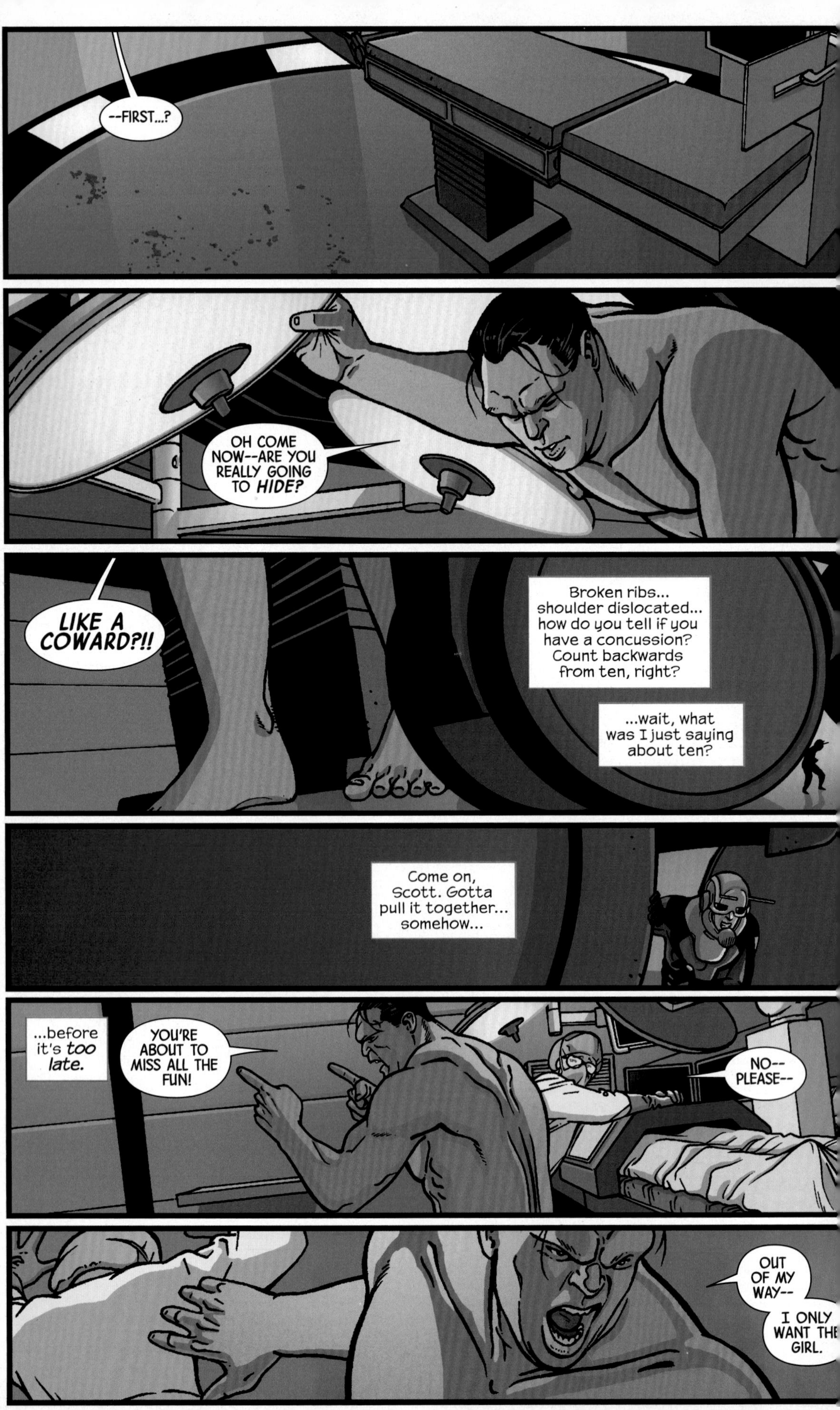
--FIRST...?
OH COME NOW--ARE YOU REALLY GOING TO HIDE?
LIKE A COWARD?!!
Broken ribs... shoulder dislocated... how do you tell if you have a concussion? Count backwards from ten, right?
...wait, what was I just saying about ten?
Come on, Scott. Gotta pull it together... somehow...
...before it's too late.
YOU'RE ABOUT TO MISS ALL THE FUN!
NO-- PLEASE--
OUT OF MY WAY--
I ONLY WANT THE GIRL.

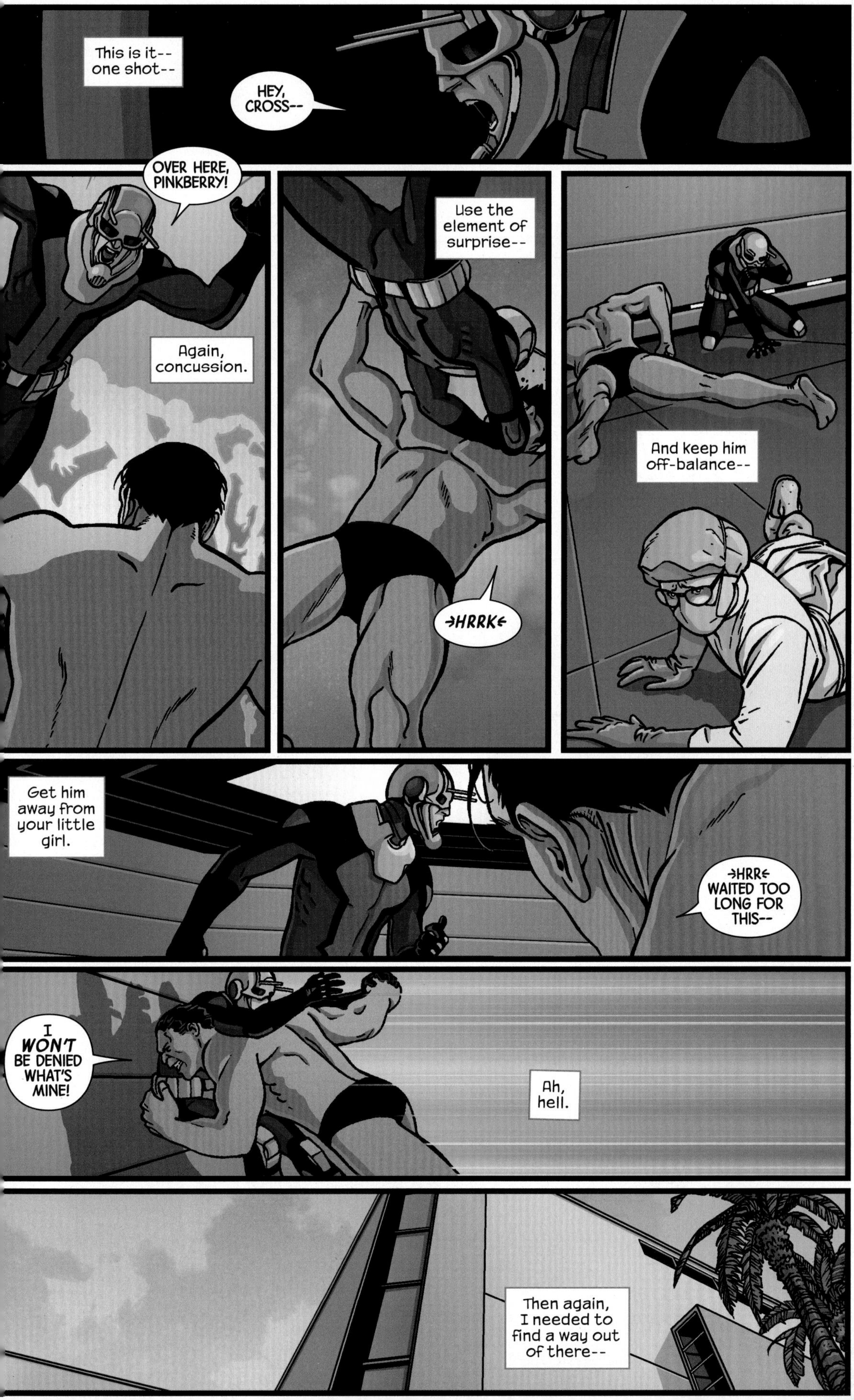
This is it--
one shot--
HEY, CROSS--
OVER HERE, PINKBERRY!
Again, concussion.
Use the element of surprise--
→HRRK←
And keep him off-balance--
Get him away from your little girl.
→HRR← WAITED TOO LONG FOR THIS--
I WON'T BE DENIED WHAT'S MINE!
Ah, hell.
Then again, I needed to find a way out of there--

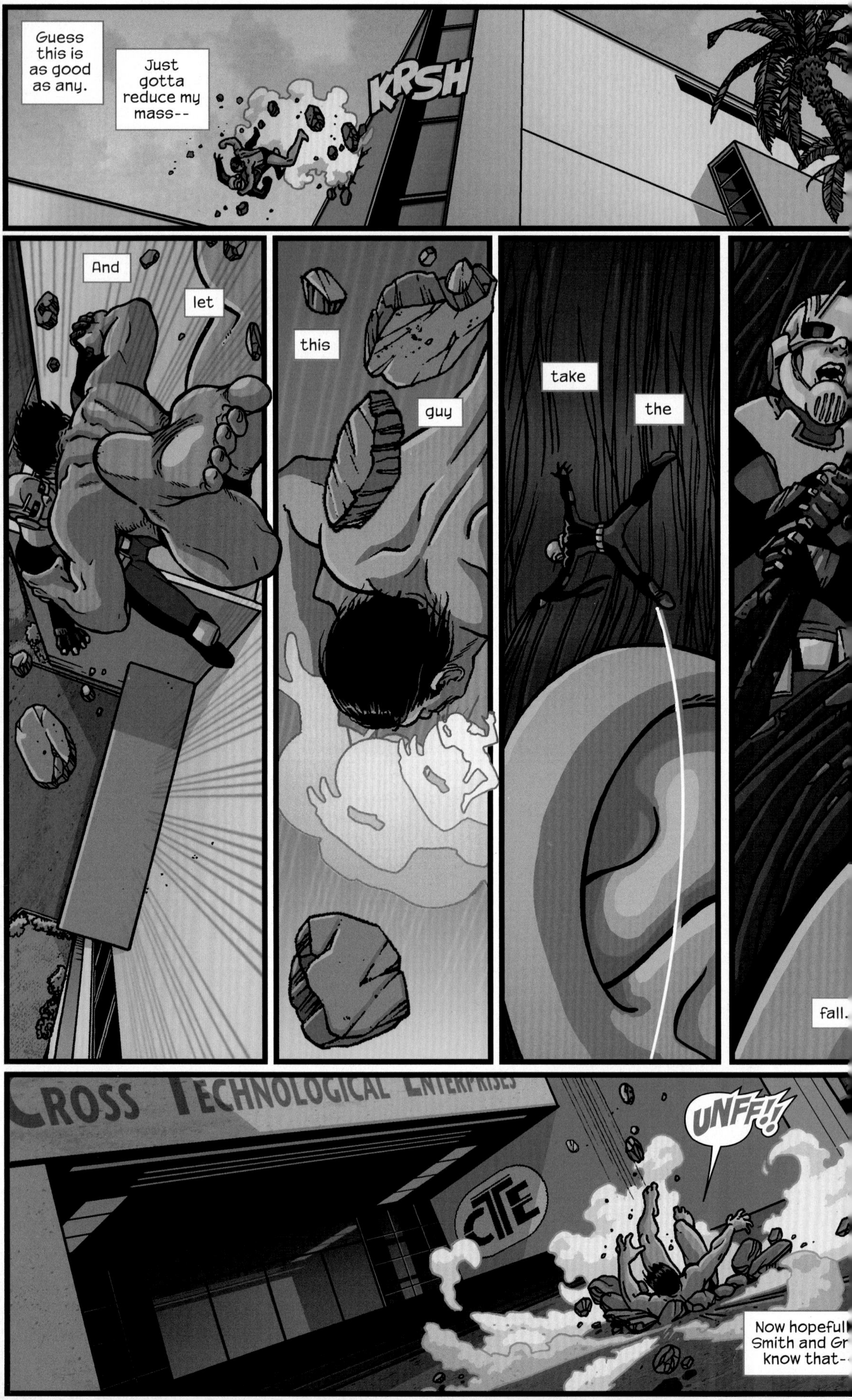
Guess this is as good as any.
Just gotta reduce my mass--
KRSH
And
let
this
guy
take
the
fall.
CROSS TECHNOLOGICAL ENTERPRISES
CTE
UNFF!!
Now hopefull
Smith and Gr
know that--

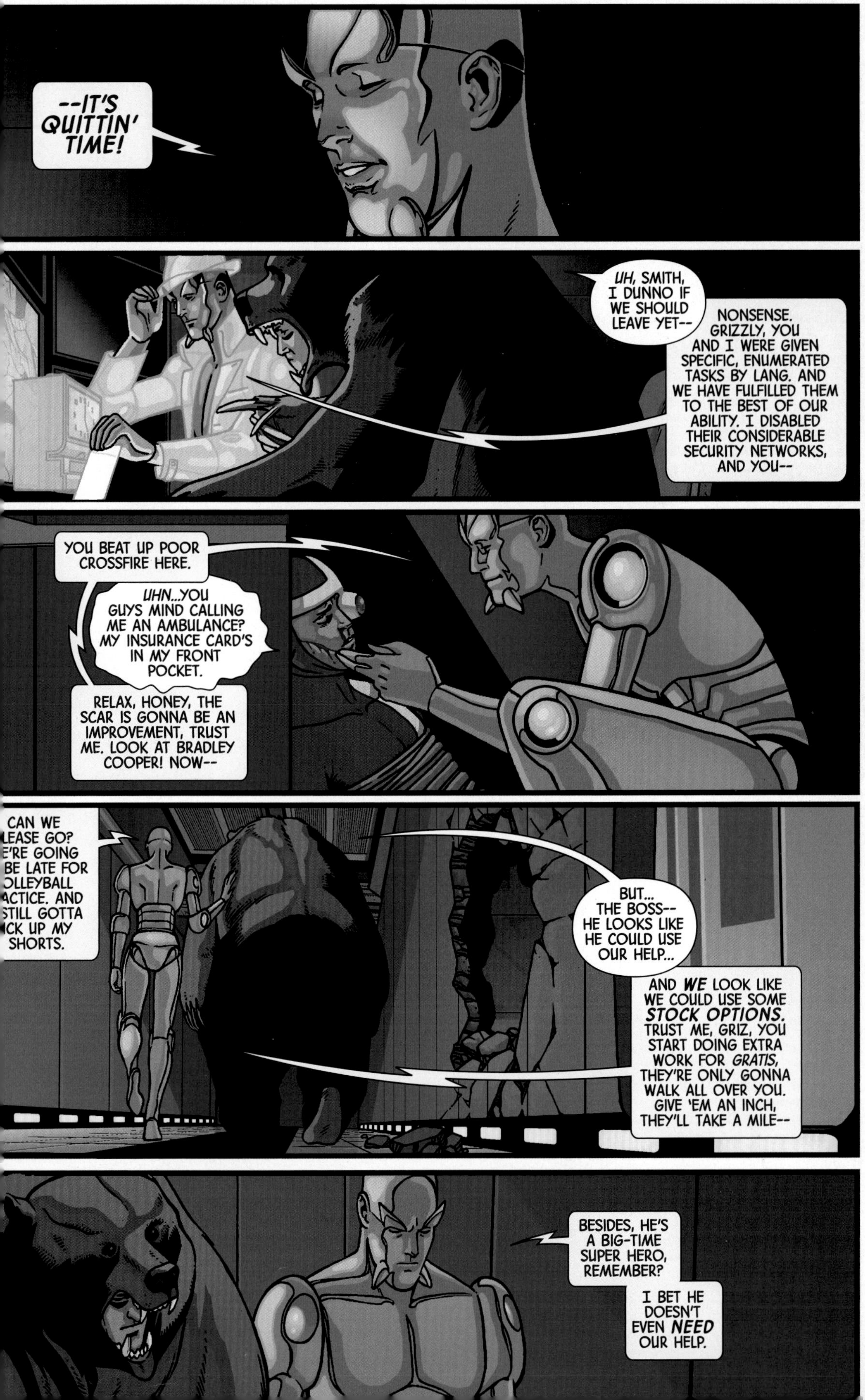
--IT'S QUITTIN' TIME!
UH, SMITH, I DUNNO IF WE SHOULD LEAVE YET--
NONSENSE. GRIZZLY, YOU AND I WERE GIVEN SPECIFIC, ENUMERATED TASKS BY LANG. AND WE HAVE FULFILLED THEM TO THE BEST OF OUR ABILITY. I DISABLED THEIR CONSIDERABLE SECURITY NETWORKS, AND YOU--
YOU BEAT UP POOR CROSSFIRE HERE.
UHN...YOU GUYS MIND CALLING ME AN AMBULANCE? MY INSURANCE CARD'S IN MY FRONT POCKET.
RELAX, HONEY, THE SCAR IS GONNA BE AN IMPROVEMENT, TRUST ME. LOOK AT BRADLEY COOPER! NOW--
CAN WE LEASE GO? E'RE GOING BE LATE FOR OLLEYBALL ACTICE. AND STILL GOTTA CK UP MY SHORTS.
BUT... THE BOSS-- HE LOOKS LIKE HE COULD USE OUR HELP...
AND WE LOOK LIKE WE COULD USE SOME STOCK OPTIONS. TRUST ME, GRIZ, YOU START DOING EXTRA WORK FOR GRATIS, THEY'RE ONLY GONNA WALK ALL OVER YOU. GIVE 'EM AN INCH, THEY'LL TAKE A MILE--
BESIDES, HE'S A BIG-TIME SUPER HERO, REMEMBER?
I BET HE DOESN'T EVEN NEED OUR HELP.

--I could really use some help!

JUST YOU AND ME, INSECT--

That's what *he* thinks.

Even if my workforce seems to'v skipped ou on me--

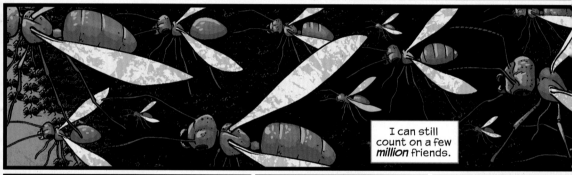

I can still count on a few *million* friends.

WHAT IS THIS? ANTS?!!

HEH. "A CENTER FOR *ANTS?!!*"

OH, SORRY--YOU WERE DEAD FOR THAT REFERENCE. GOTTA WATCH OUT FOR THAT KINDA STUFF--

DON'T LET ANYBODY SPOIL *HOUSE OF CARDS* FOR YOU.

YOU--!

There we go-- that oughta--

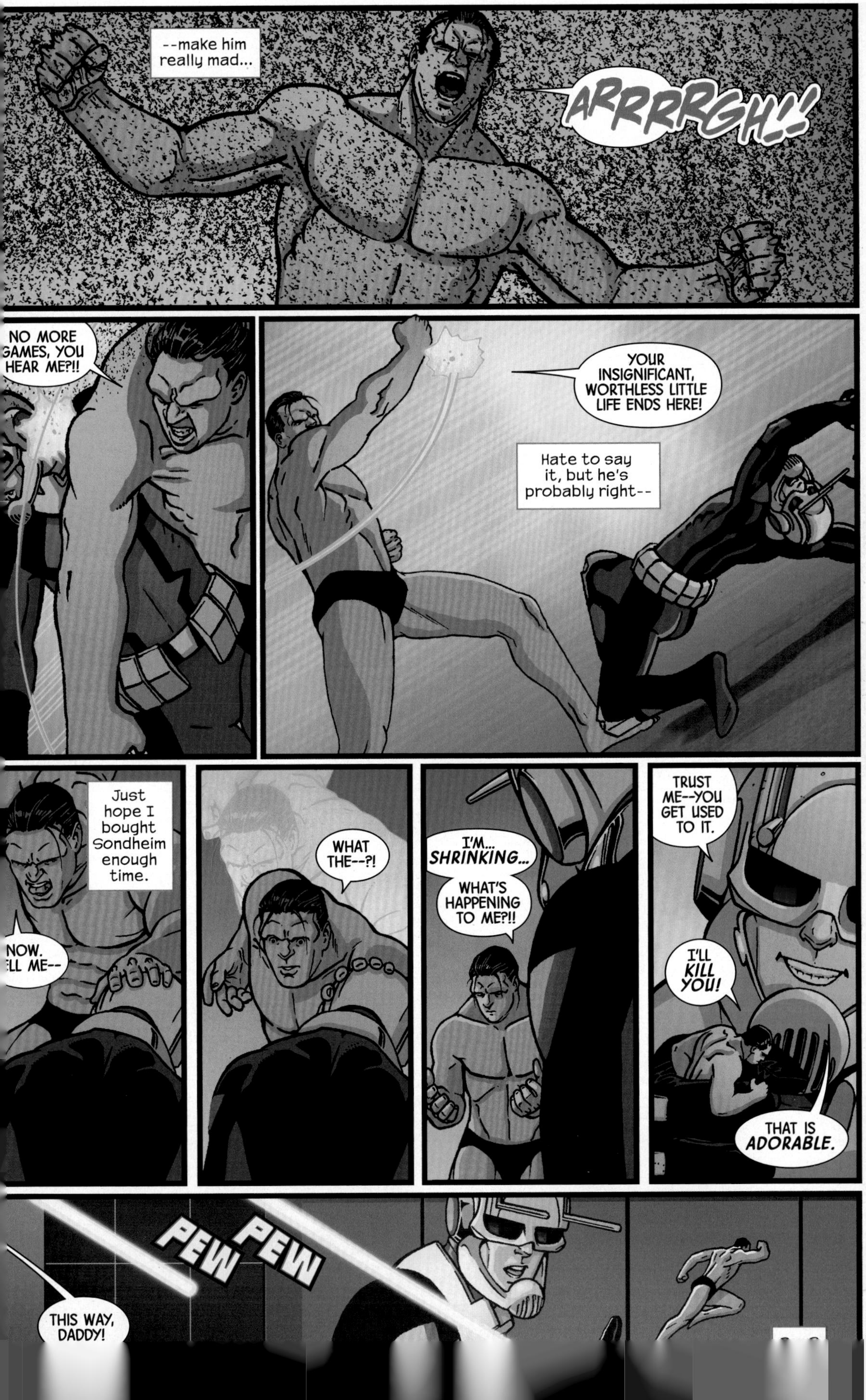

--make him really mad...
ARRRRGH!!
NO MORE GAMES, YOU HEAR ME?!!
YOUR INSIGNIFICANT, WORTHLESS LITTLE LIFE ENDS HERE!
Hate to say it, but he's probably right--
Just hope I bought Sondheim enough time.
NOW. ELL ME--
WHAT THE--?!
I'M... SHRINKING...
WHAT'S HAPPENING TO ME?!!
TRUST ME--YOU GET USED TO IT.
I'LL KILL YOU!
THAT IS ADORABLE.
PEW PEW
THIS WAY, DADDY!

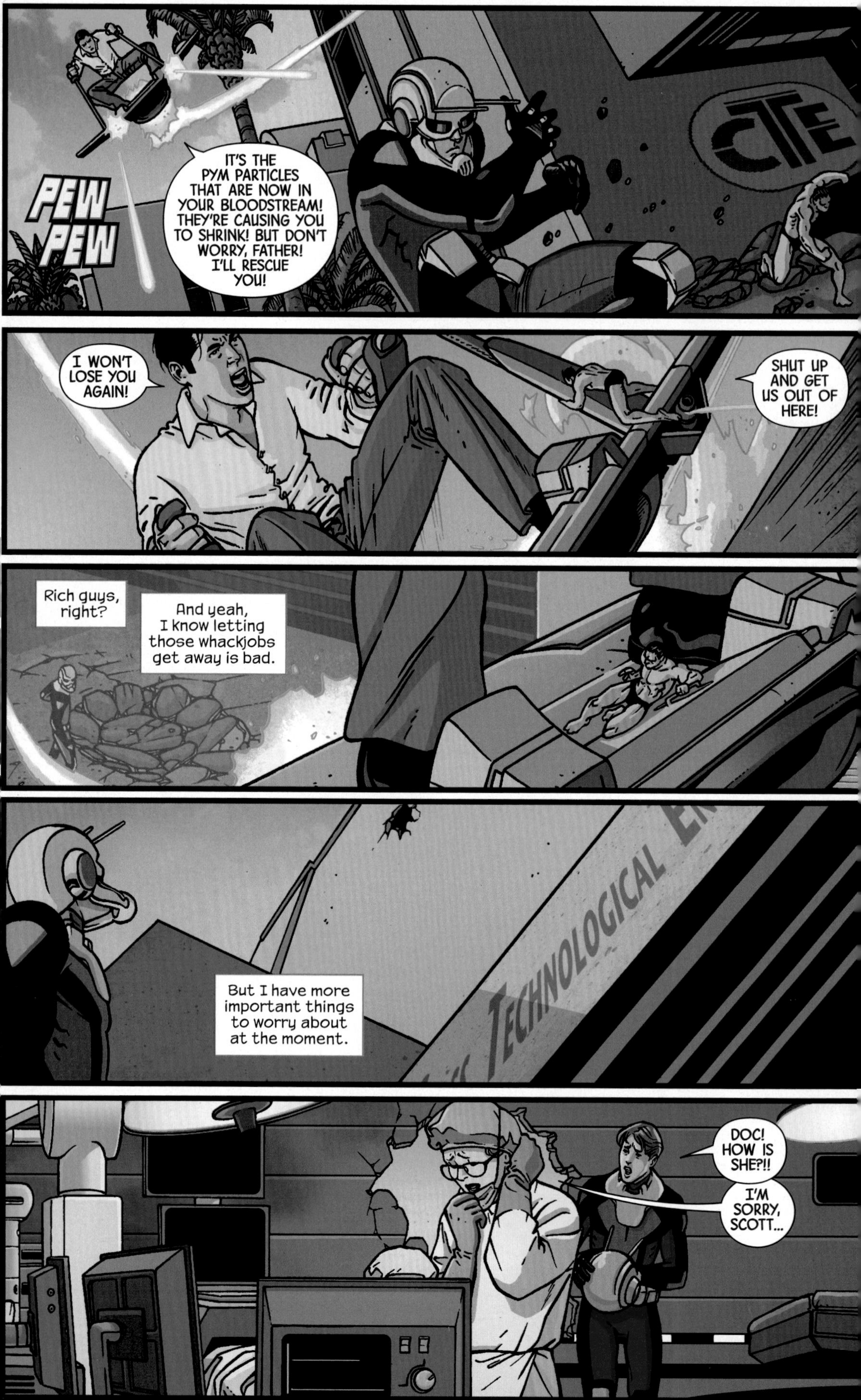

IT'S THE PYM PARTICLES THAT ARE NOW IN YOUR BLOODSTREAM! THEY'RE CAUSING YOU TO SHRINK! BUT DON'T WORRY, FATHER! I'LL RESCUE YOU!
PEW PEW
I WON'T LOSE YOU AGAIN!
SHUT UP AND GET US OUT OF HERE!
Rich guys, right?
And yeah, I know letting those whackjobs get away is bad.
TECHNOLOGICAL
But I have more important things to worry about at the moment.
DOC! HOW IS SHE?!!
I'M SORRY, SCOTT...

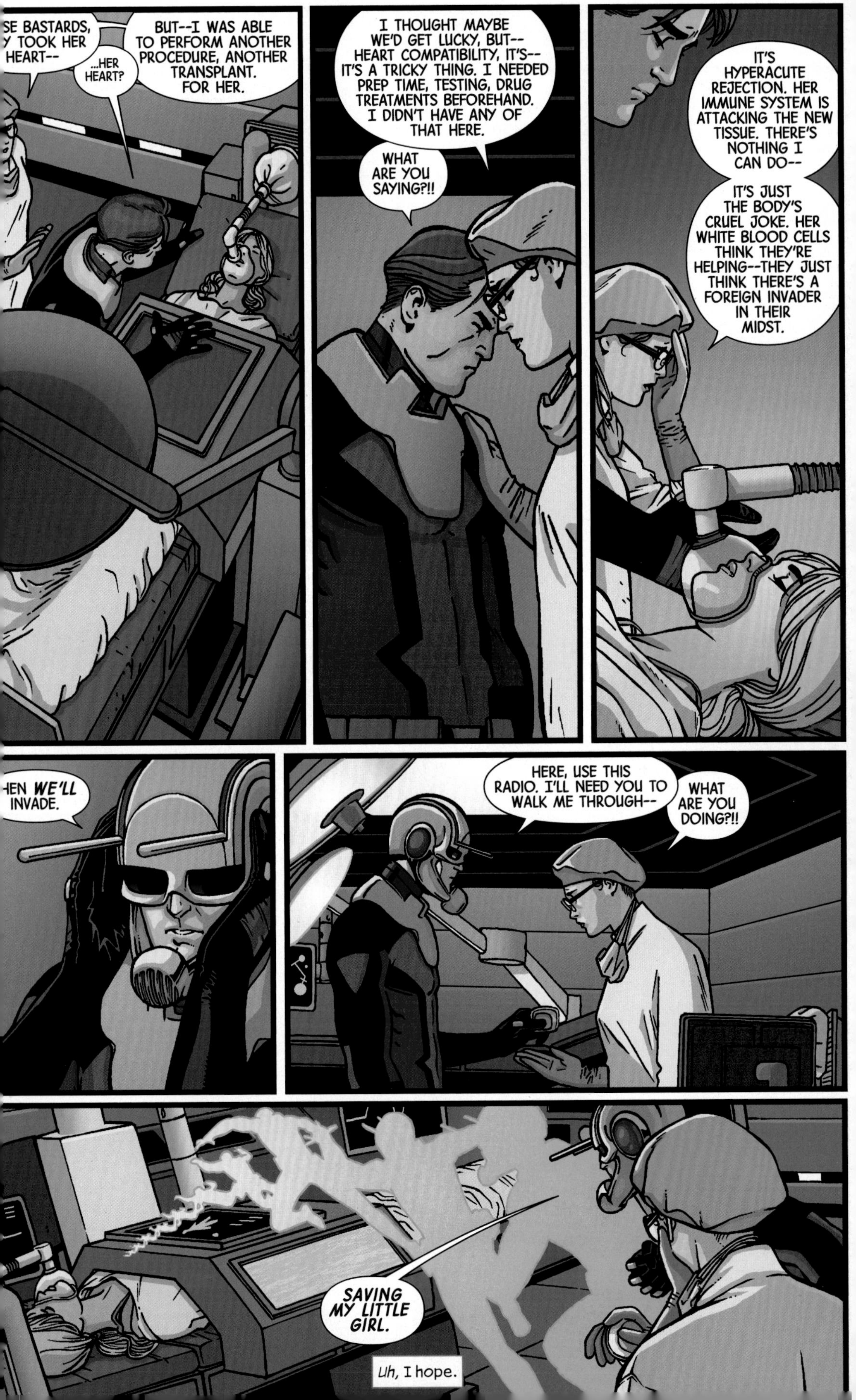
SE BASTARDS,
Y TOOK HER
HEART--
...HER HEART?
BUT--I WAS ABLE TO PERFORM ANOTHER PROCEDURE, ANOTHER TRANSPLANT. FOR HER.
I THOUGHT MAYBE WE'D GET LUCKY, BUT-- HEART COMPATIBILITY, IT'S-- IT'S A TRICKY THING. I NEEDED PREP TIME, TESTING, DRUG TREATMENTS BEFOREHAND. I DIDN'T HAVE ANY OF THAT HERE.
WHAT ARE YOU SAYING?!!
IT'S HYPERACUTE REJECTION. HER IMMUNE SYSTEM IS ATTACKING THE NEW TISSUE. THERE'S NOTHING I CAN DO--
IT'S JUST THE BODY'S CRUEL JOKE. HER WHITE BLOOD CELLS THINK THEY'RE HELPING--THEY JUST THINK THERE'S A FOREIGN INVADER IN THEIR MIDST.
HEN WE'LL INVADE.
HERE, USE THIS RADIO. I'LL NEED YOU TO WALK ME THROUGH--
WHAT ARE YOU DOING?!!
SAVING MY LITTLE GIRL.
Uh, I hope.

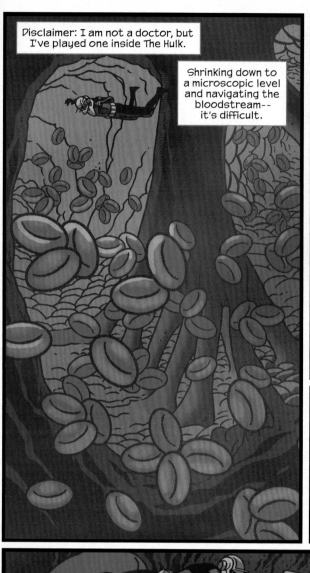

Disclaimer: I am not a doctor, but I've played one inside The Hulk.

Shrinking down to a microscopic level and navigating the bloodstream-- it's difficult.

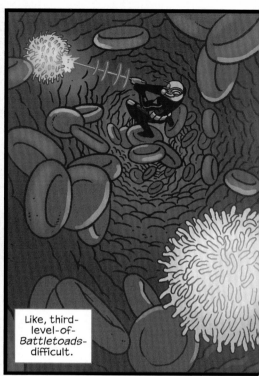

Like, third-level-of-*Battletoads*-difficult.

But it's our only chance here--

And I am not gonna lose Cassie again!

SCOTT, LISTEN TO ME--YOU HAVE TO WORK FASTER!

TARGET THE CLUSTERS OF WHITE BLOOD CELLS! GAMMA THERAPIES CAN REPLENISH THEM LATER--

RIGHT NOW SHE'S RUNNING OUT OF TIME!

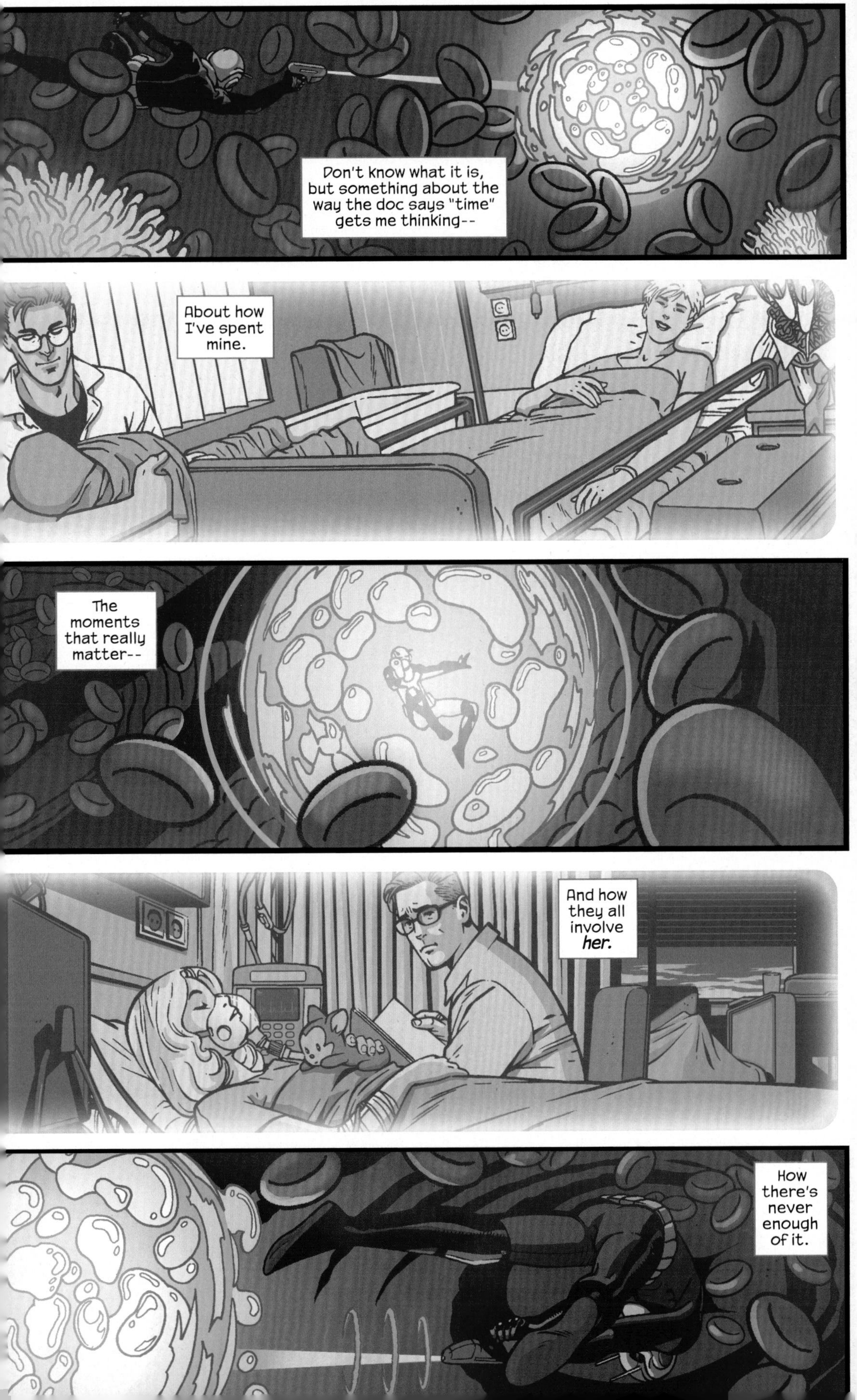
Don't know what it is, but something about the way the doc says "time" gets me thinking--
About how I've spent mine.
The moments that really matter--
And how they all involve *her.*
How there's never enough of it.

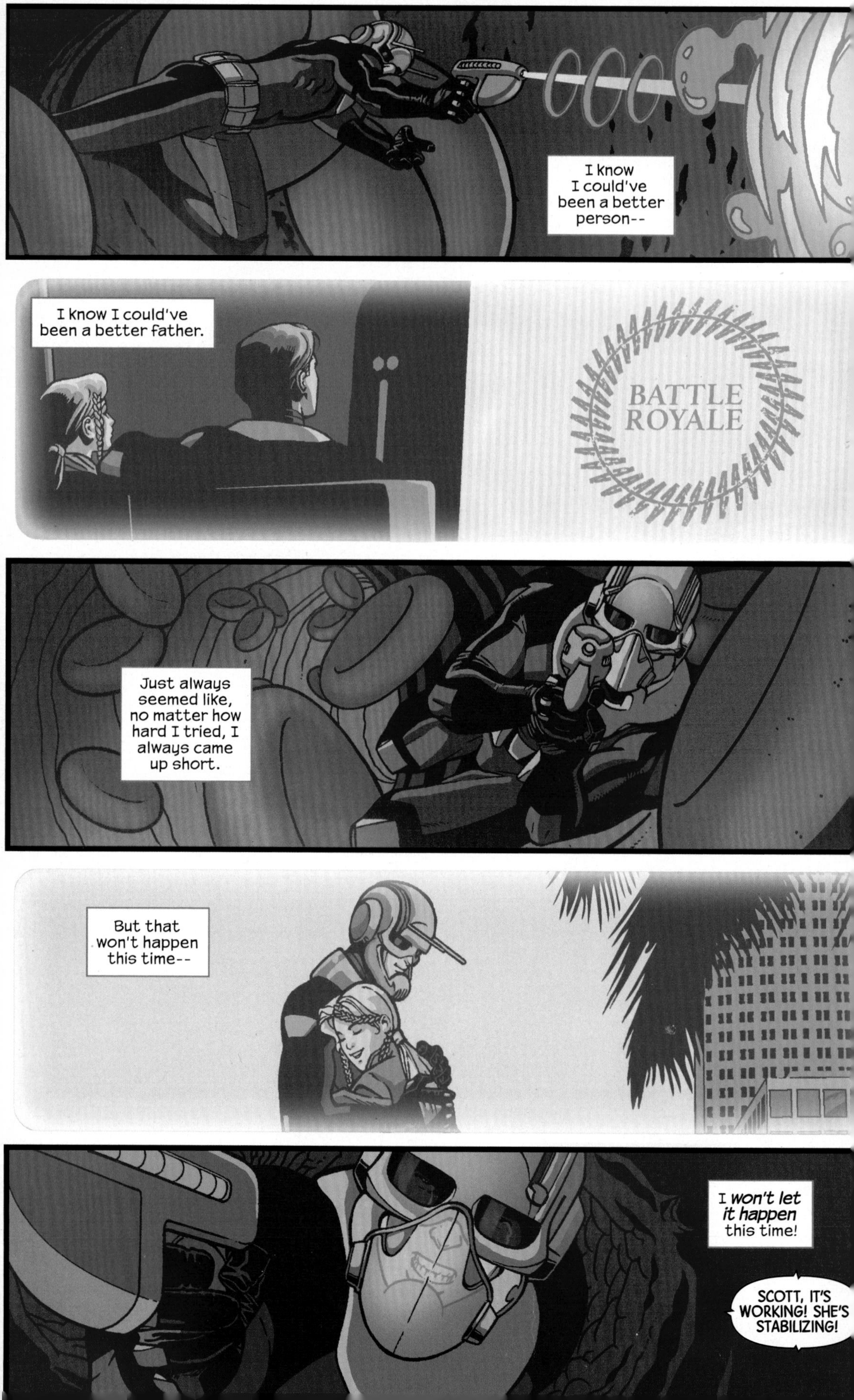
I know I could've been a better person--
I know I could've been a better father.
BATTLE ROYALE
Just always seemed like, no matter how hard I tried, I always came up short.
But that won't happen this time--
I *won't let it happen* this time!
SCOTT, IT'S WORKING! SHE'S STABILIZING!

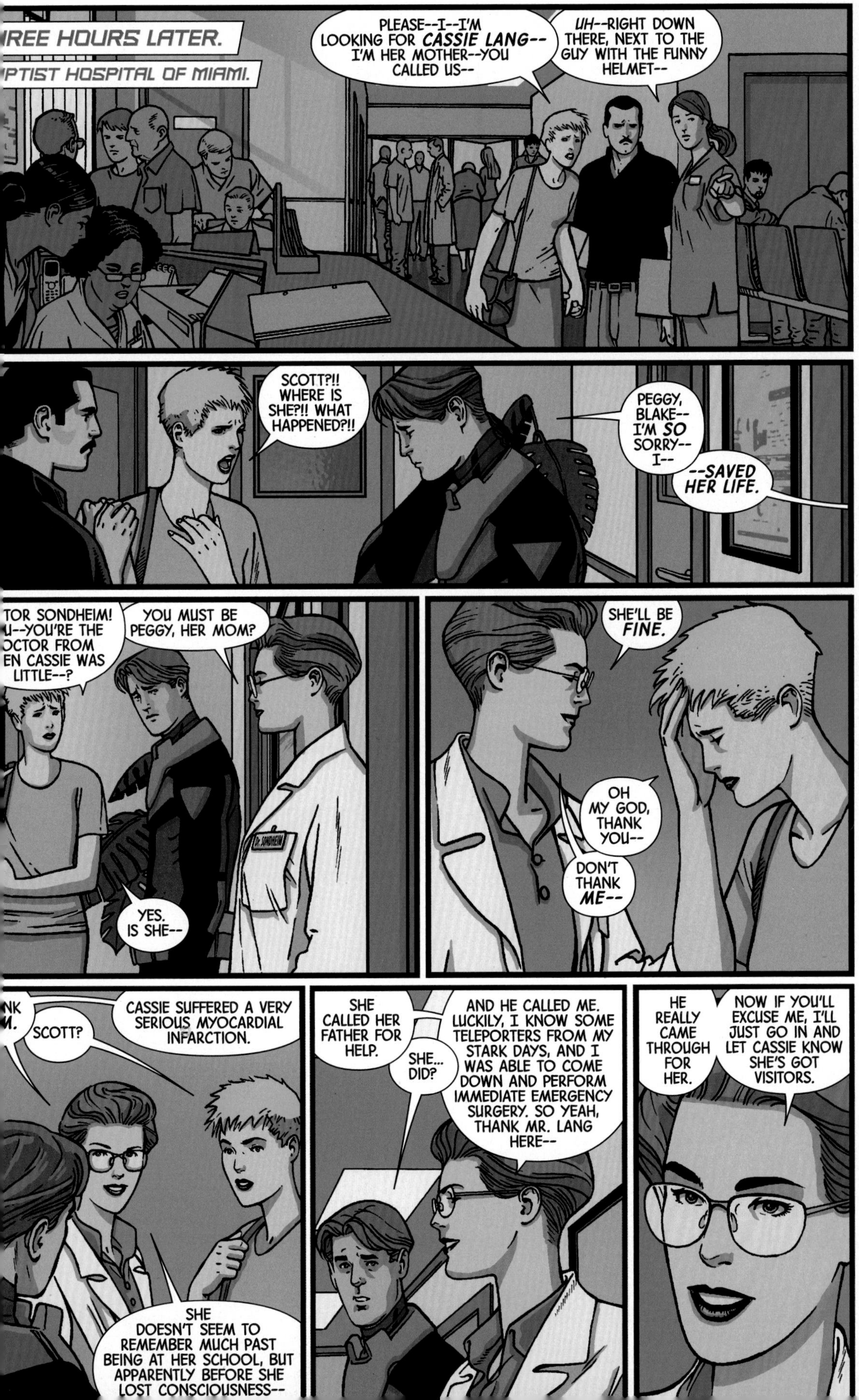

REE HOURS LATER.
PTIST HOSPITAL OF MIAMI.
PLEASE--I--I'M LOOKING FOR CASSIE LANG-- I'M HER MOTHER--YOU CALLED US--
UH--RIGHT DOWN THERE, NEXT TO THE GUY WITH THE FUNNY HELMET--
SCOTT?!! WHERE IS SHE?!! WHAT HAPPENED?!!
PEGGY, BLAKE-- I'M SO SORRY-- I--
--SAVED HER LIFE.
TOR SONDHEIM! U--YOU'RE THE OCTOR FROM EN CASSIE WAS LITTLE--?
YOU MUST BE PEGGY, HER MOM?
YES. IS SHE--
DR. SONDHEIM
SHE'LL BE FINE.
OH MY GOD, THANK YOU--
DON'T THANK ME--
NK M.
SCOTT?
CASSIE SUFFERED A VERY SERIOUS MYOCARDIAL INFARCTION.
SHE DOESN'T SEEM TO REMEMBER MUCH PAST BEING AT HER SCHOOL, BUT APPARENTLY BEFORE SHE LOST CONSCIOUSNESS--
SHE CALLED HER FATHER FOR HELP.
SHE... DID?
AND HE CALLED ME. LUCKILY, I KNOW SOME TELEPORTERS FROM MY STARK DAYS, AND I WAS ABLE TO COME DOWN AND PERFORM IMMEDIATE EMERGENCY SURGERY. SO YEAH, THANK MR. LANG HERE--
HE REALLY CAME THROUGH FOR HER.
NOW IF YOU'LL EXCUSE ME, I'LL JUST GO IN AND LET CASSIE KNOW SHE'S GOT VISITORS.

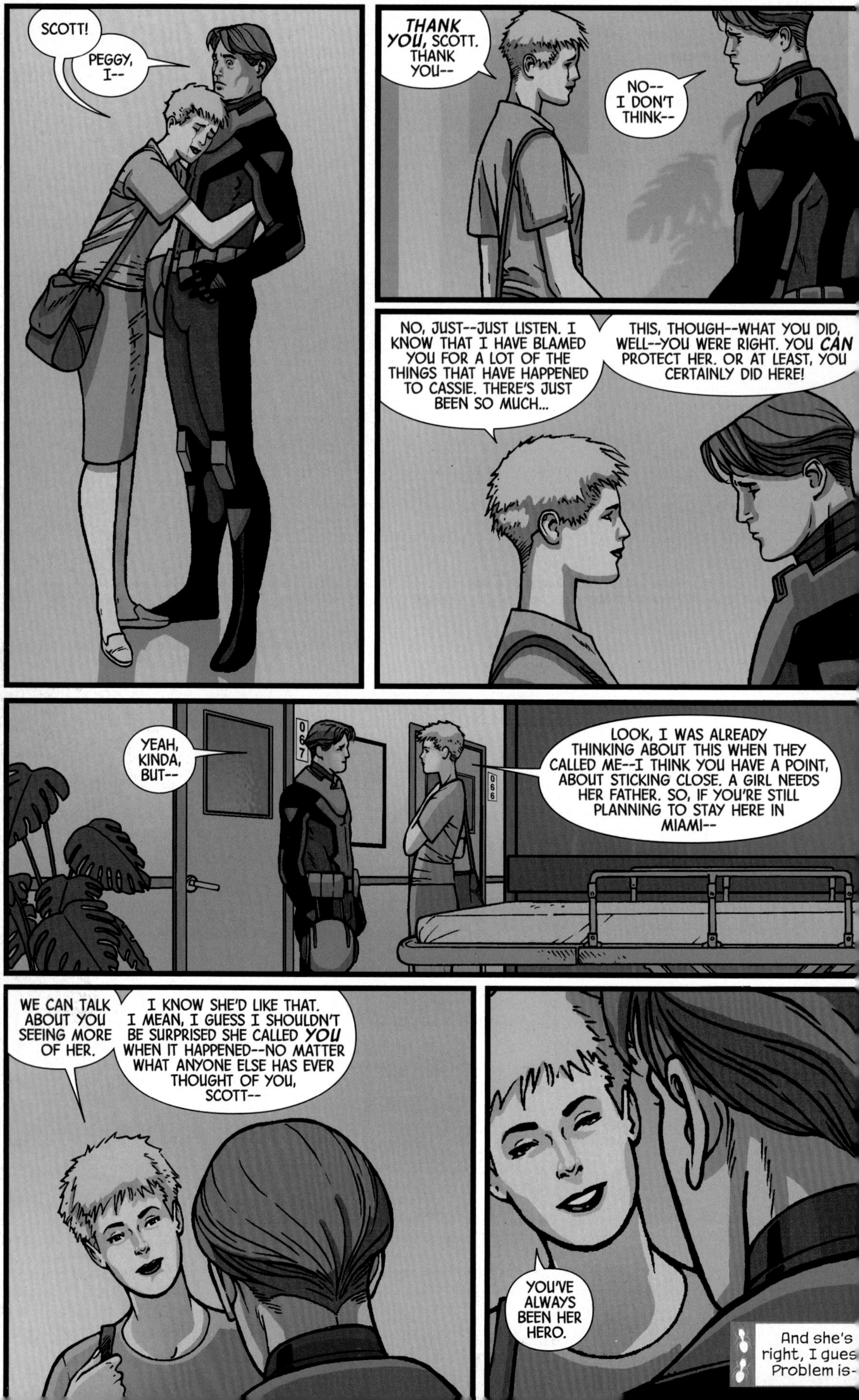
SCOTT!
PEGGY, I--
THANK YOU, SCOTT. THANK YOU--
NO-- I DON'T THINK--
NO, JUST--JUST LISTEN. I KNOW THAT I HAVE BLAMED YOU FOR A LOT OF THE THINGS THAT HAVE HAPPENED TO CASSIE. THERE'S JUST BEEN SO MUCH...
THIS, THOUGH--WHAT YOU DID, WELL--YOU WERE RIGHT. YOU CAN PROTECT HER. OR AT LEAST, YOU CERTAINLY DID HERE!
YEAH, KINDA, BUT--
LOOK, I WAS ALREADY THINKING ABOUT THIS WHEN THEY CALLED ME--I THINK YOU HAVE A POINT, ABOUT STICKING CLOSE. A GIRL NEEDS HER FATHER. SO, IF YOU'RE STILL PLANNING TO STAY HERE IN MIAMI--
WE CAN TALK ABOUT YOU SEEING MORE OF HER.
I KNOW SHE'D LIKE THAT. I MEAN, I GUESS I SHOULDN'T BE SURPRISED SHE CALLED YOU WHEN IT HAPPENED--NO MATTER WHAT ANYONE ELSE HAS EVER THOUGHT OF YOU, SCOTT--
YOU'VE ALWAYS BEEN HER HERO.
And she's right, I gues
Problem is-

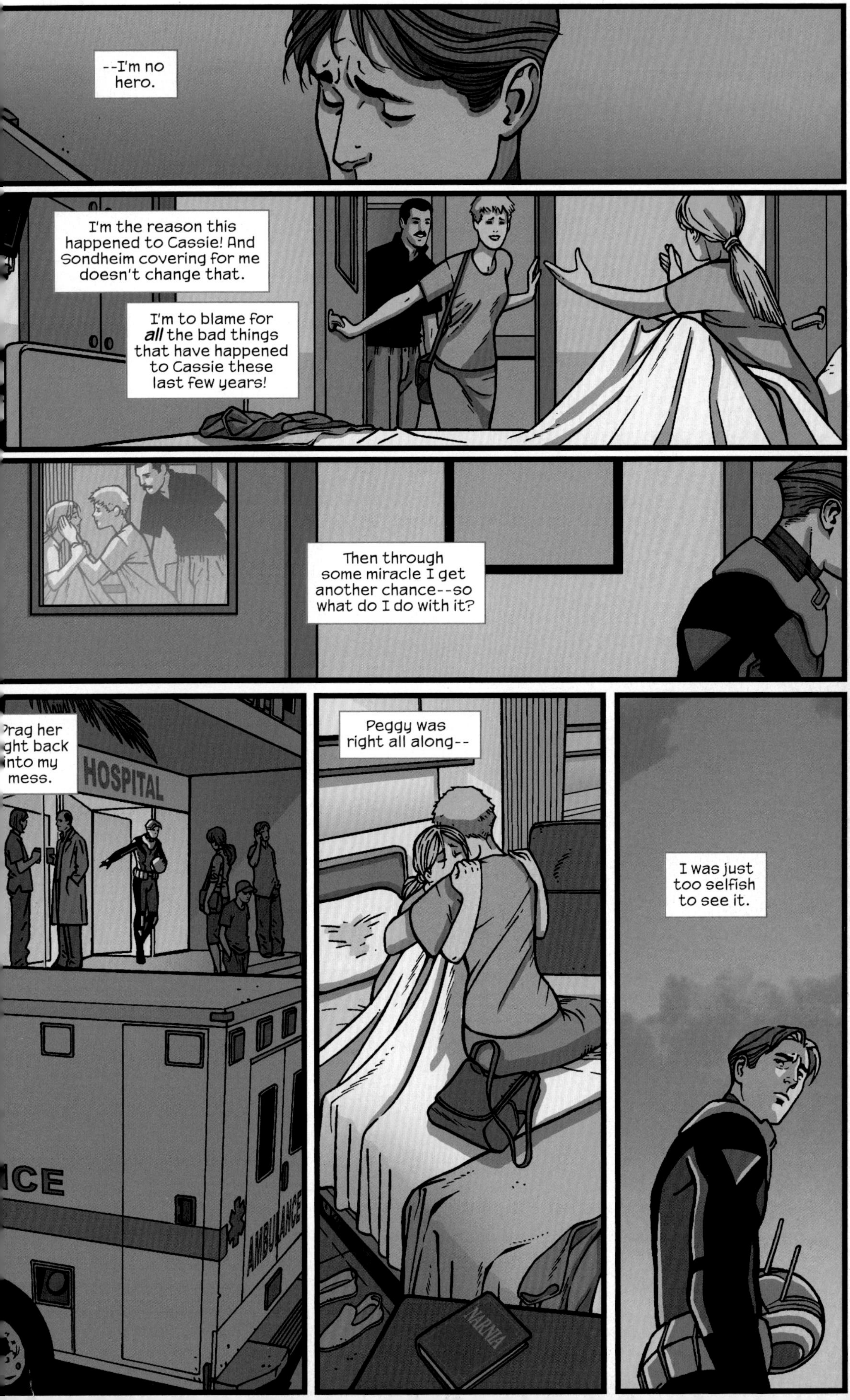
--I'm no hero.
I'm the reason this happened to Cassie! And Sondheim covering for me doesn't change that.
I'm to blame for *all* the bad things that have happened to Cassie these last few years!
Then through some miracle I get another chance--so what do I do with it?
rag her ght back into my mess.
HOSPITAL
ICE
AMBULANCE
Peggy was right all along--
NARNIA
I was just too selfish to see it.

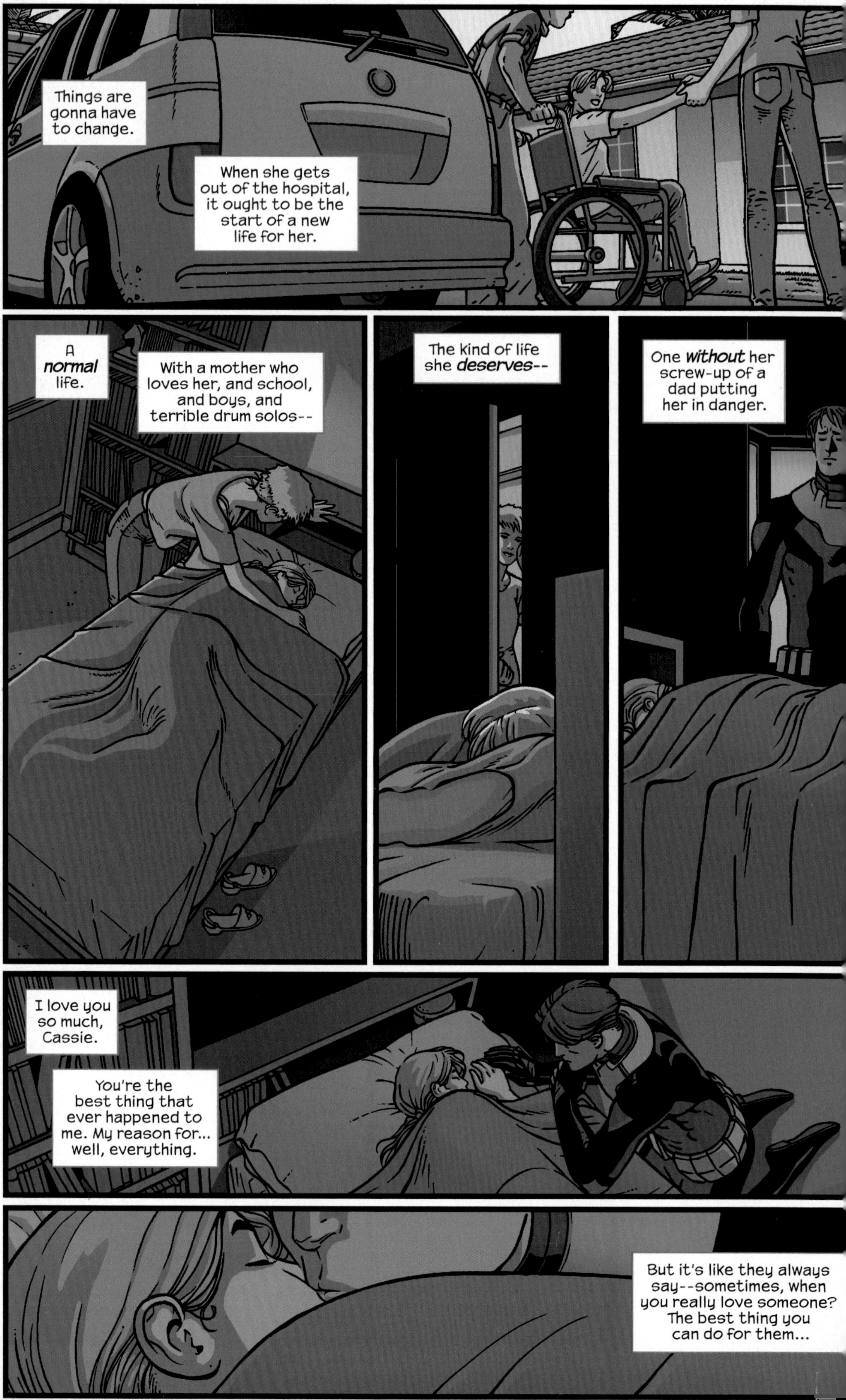
Things are gonna have to change.
When she gets out of the hospital, it ought to be the start of a new life for her.
A *normal* life.
With a mother who loves her, and school, and boys, and terrible drum solos--
The kind of life she *deserves*--
One *without* her screw-up of a dad putting her in danger.
I love you so much, Cassie.
You're the best thing that ever happened to me. My reason for... well, everything.
But it's like they always say--sometimes, when you really love someone? The best thing you can do for them...

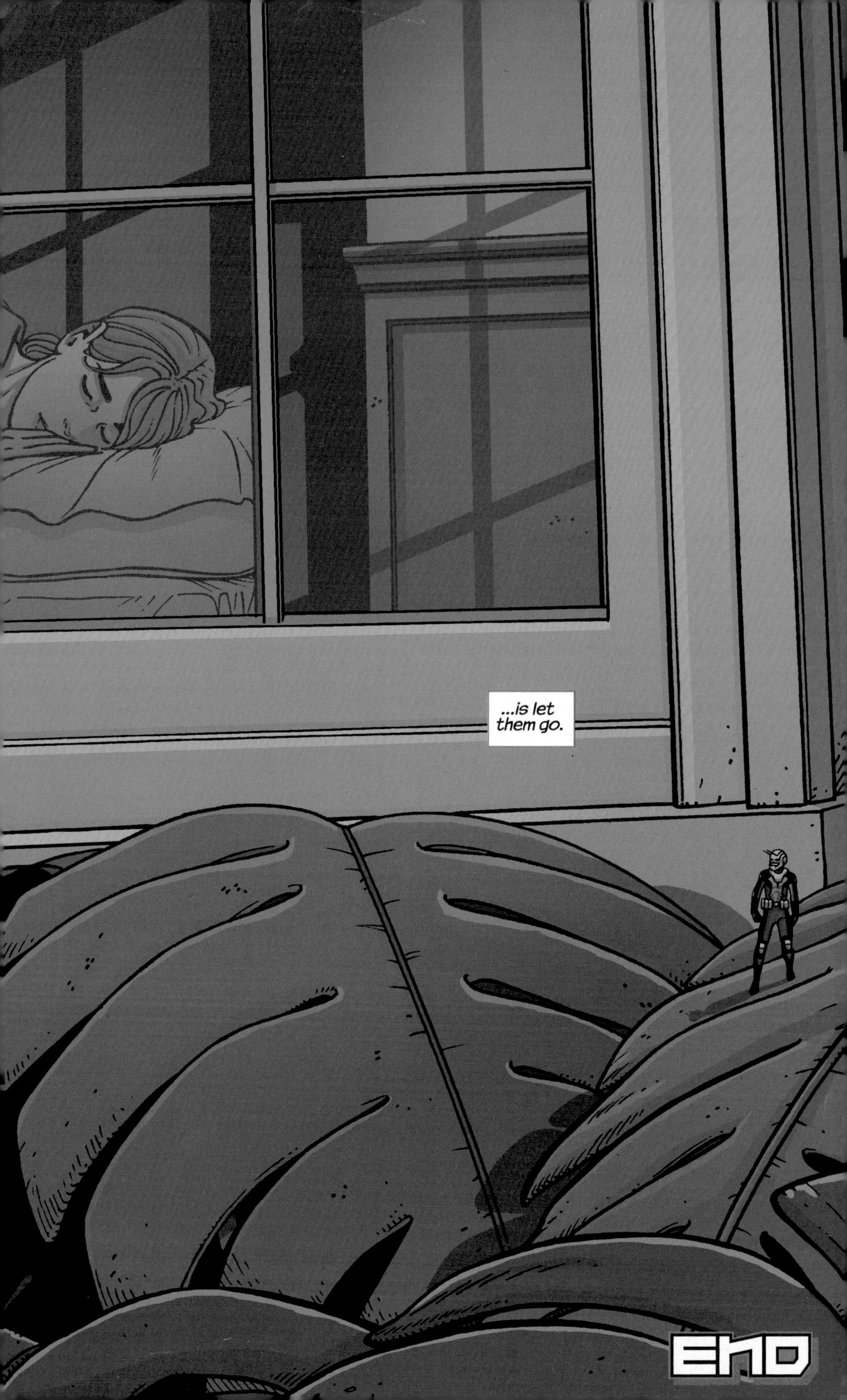
...is let them go.
END

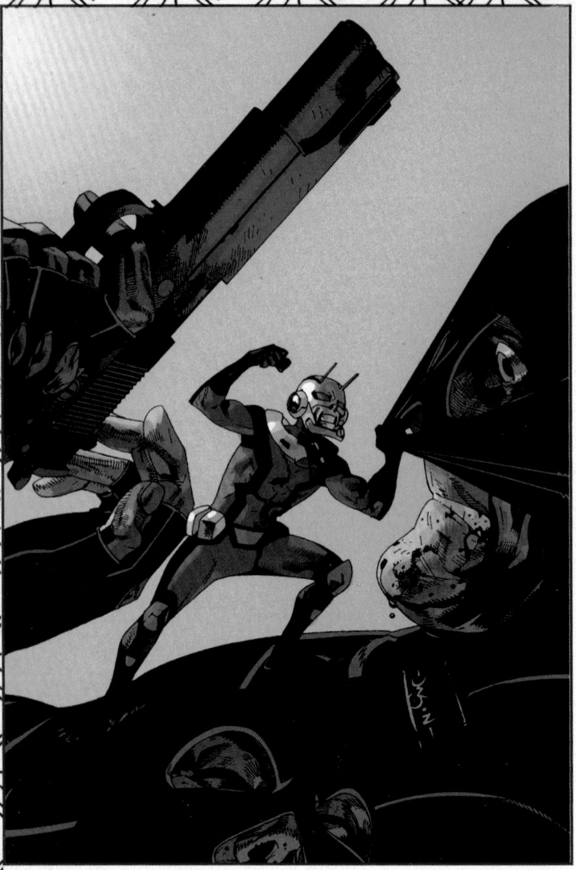

#1 variant by Jason Pearson

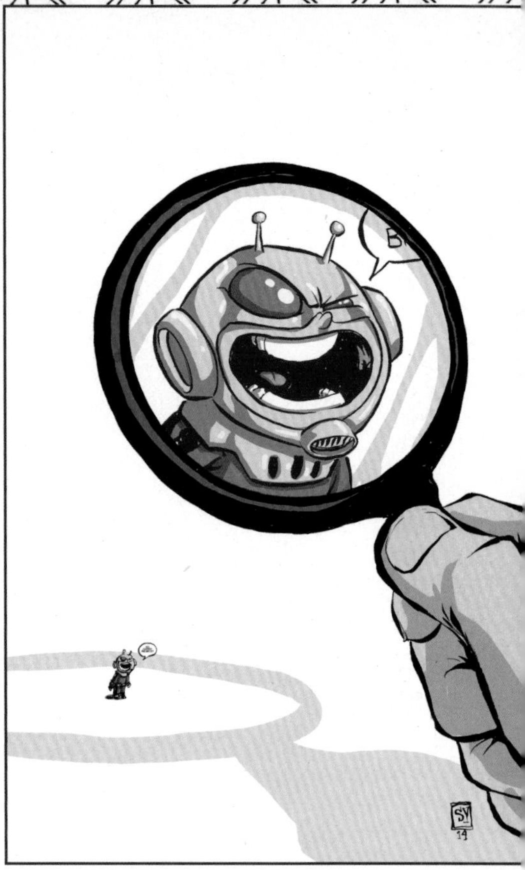

#1 variant by Skottie Young

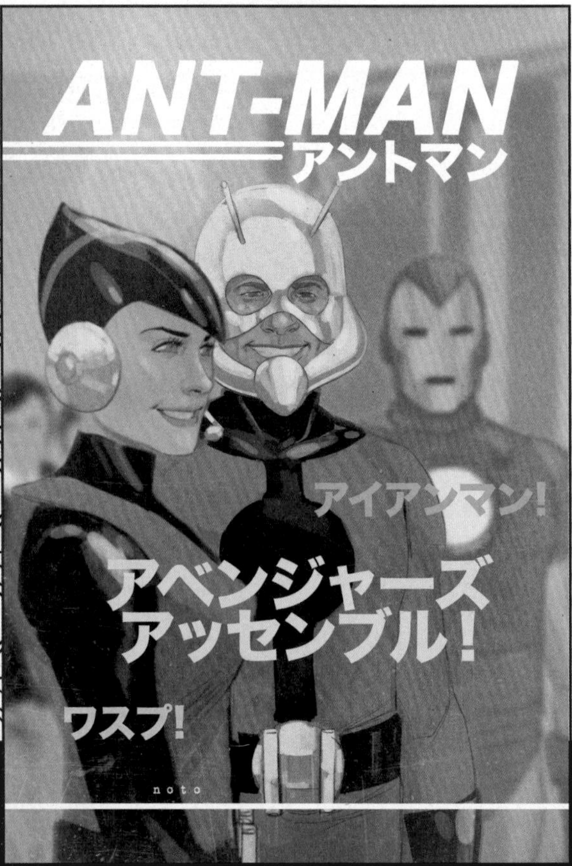
ANT-MAN
アントマン
アイアンマン!
アベンジャーズ
アッセンブル!
ワスプ!
noto

#2 variant by Phil Noto

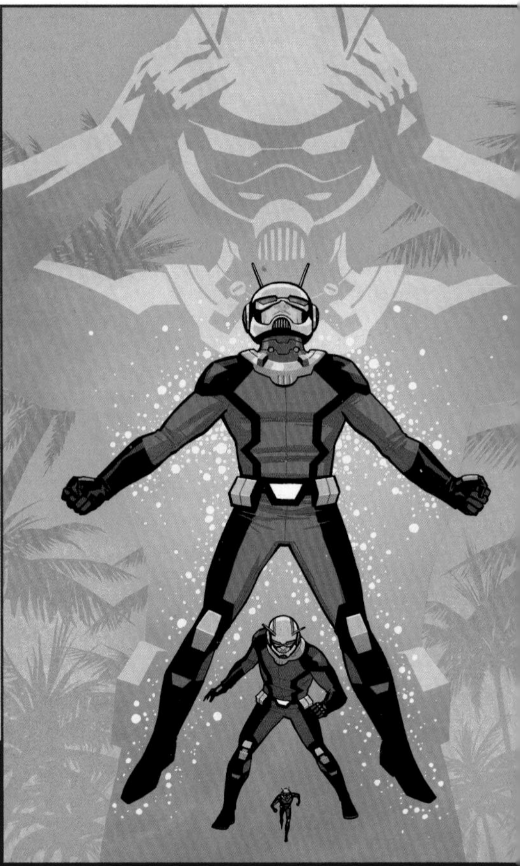

#3 variant by Cliff Chiang